SHRIMAD BHAGAVAD GITA

Shrimad

BHAGAVAD GITA

A Simple, Warm and Human Rendering with brief Comments

PROF. GOPAL MAYEKAR

GYAN PUBLISHING HOUSE

New Delhi-110 002

SHRIMAD BHAGAVAD GITA

A Simple, Warm and Human Rendering with brief Comments

(Religion)

ISBN: 81-212-0800-9

Published in 2003 in India by
Gyan Publishing House
5, Ansari Road
New Delhi-110002
Phones - 23282060, 23261060 Fax: 23285914
E-mail : gyanbook@vsnl. com
Visit our website at : www.gyanbooks.com

Lasertypesetting by: Varsha Graphics, Delhi
Printed by: Chawla Offset Press, Delhi

।। श्रीकृष्णार्पणमस्तु ।।

Dedicated to Lord Krishna

Contents

Preface

The idea of presenting Bhagavad-Gita in an illustrated form on computer disc came up in a friendly but serious discussion and I was prompted to attempt a new kind of rendering of Gita. I was supposed to provide an independent running commentary, short in nature, faithful to the text and explaining the core contents of the Gita to commonplace but curious admirers. I started the work in right earnest and the present book is the outcome of the humble adventure. Taking into account the thousands of Gita-editions already made available by the great spiritual masters, highly revered saints and renowned philosophers this work is like a drop in the ocean. My aim is not to compete with scholarly works on Gita but to present a pragmatic view to those who as beginners are eager to acquaint themselves with this great book with a desire to learn some moral lessons. Since the Gita philosophy is nowadays becoming strange to our own people, it can be safely presumed that this humble trial will also be useful to them, especially to Indian youth who have lost their identity in the present day turmoil.

Original text of the Gita is a part of the epic Mahãbhãrata forming chapters 25 to 42 of Bhishma-parvan and its writer sage Vyãsa has adopted a literary strategy in presenting this great treatise in the midst of a terrible war. Sanjaya, Dhritarashtra's charioteer is a medium through whom the dialogue between Krishna and Arjuna is reported. Sanjaya experiences divinity in Krishna and presents a verbatim report of his utterings. In my rendering, instead of first person I have used third person narration to facilitate better understanding of the text. At selected places, however, first person narration is retained for special emphasis. Wherever possible short comments are added (shown in italic) to explain the thought or to connect the thoughts.The Gita-verses also are grouped topicwise for convinient reading.

Selected explanatory notes are added, some in the beginning and some at the end as annexures to facilitate the readers to have proper perspective for better understanding of the greatness of the divine song.

In my search of right interpretation and logical meaning I was guided by the great works of Dr. Sarvapalli Radhakrishnan, the teacher-philosopher of the twentieth century and saint Dnyaneshwara, the poet-philosopher of the thirteenth century. Lokmanya Tilak and Vivekananda also came to my rescue whenever I was puzzled. They all have become my perennial source in the journey of self discovery.

The book will remain incomplete if I do not mention the service and advice rendered to me by Mr. C. Radhakrishnan who not only corrected the manuscript but suggested valuable improvements to make the book attractive and perfect.

At the last but not the least let me record with gratitude that Prof. Mahesh Vengurlekar was the real inspirer of this book. He was instrumental in preparing the manuscript and its beautiful presentation. Still he is not happy. He wants me to write a book in Marathi so that the journey becomes complete. I have no other choice than to fulfil his wish, sooner or the later.

(10 A)

In the Footsteps of Great Thinkers

"Man must persist in his belief that the incomprehensible is comprehensible otherwise he would cease to explore. The highest happiness of a rational being is to have explored what is explorable and quietly to revere what is unexplorable".

—Goethe

"The Scientists's religious feeling takes the form of a rapturous amazement at the harmony of natural law, which reveals an intelligence of such superiority that compared with it, all the systematic thinking and acting of human beings is an utterly insignificant reflection. This feeling is the guiding principle of his life and work, in so far as he succeeds in keeping himself from the shackles of selfish desire. It is beyond question closely akin to that which has possessed that religious geniuses of all ages."

—Albert Einstein
"The world as I see it"

The Teacher of the Gita is therefore not only the God in man who unveils himself in the world of knowledge, but the God in man who moves our whole world of action, by and for whom all our humanity exists and struggles and labours, towards whom all life travels and progresses. He is the secret Master of works and sacrifice and the Friend of the human peoples.

—Shri Aurobindo

"This Country from its early beginnings has looked upon the human being as a spark of Spirit, an amsha or fragment of God. To realise the divine destiny in him is his task. It has therefore worshipped the monk meditating in the cave and preferred him to the prince living in luxury in a palace or a military hero or an industrial magnate."

—Dr. Sarvepalli Radhakrishnan

Inspired by such guiding principles
Let us Sing and Study
The celestial song called Bhagavadgita for self discovery !

(11 A)

Says the Unmanifest . . .

Behold the blue, ever expanding sky
Millions and millions stars shining within
Galaxies whirling with unknown speed,
Solar systems in countless number
With planets on their destined path.

Among them, this your tiny planet
Earth you call, with mortal creatures
Towering there, this embodied soul
Known as man with mind and brain.

This cosmic process that moves ahead
From matter to life, from life to mind
From mind to brain from brain to spirit
Know me the reality that supports and sustains
Creation that evolves in cycles divine
I am the Brahman, the supreme spirit
Immense, unending mystery they say.

I am Brahma, Vishnu and Shiva
To create, to preserve, to dissolve this all
Functions threefold, the sages divide
Limitless as I am, your words imperfect
Will of mine only stands behind
I am the Ground of the Brahmã to the ant.

In many splendoured world I shine everywhere
Expanse of my glory very difficult to grasp
Forms of mine of uncommon nature
I present to the man to meditate upon
The beauty, the glory, the power you see
Sprung from the fraction of my splendour divine.

I am the beginning, the middle and the end
Known as Brahmã, Vishnu and Mahesh

I am the radiant sun of the brights
I am the moon of the stars of night
The fire in things and ocean among waters
I am the meru among peaks of mountains
Things unmoved, there Himãlaya, the great
I am the Gangã among rivers flowing
I am the mighty banyan among trees
I am the Mãrgashirsha, the month so bright
I am the spring of flowers in seasons

I am Ananta, the holiest serpent
I am the lion, the king of the beasts
I am the eagle among birds that fly
I am the crocodile among beings in water

Of all the alphabets I am the 'अ'
Om that I am in the language you speak
Among the compounds I am copulative

Among the Vedas, I am sãma the musical
Among the musical I am sãma the great
Gãyatri I am among meters poetic
I am Vyãsa, I am Krishna, and Arjuna that I am!

Shrimad Bhagvad Gita

The Gitã is a part of the Indian epic called Mahãbhãrat which consists of about one lac verses conferring on it the honour of the world's longest poem. Mahãbhãrat has a heterogeneous character with so many narratives, skilfully woven round the central story of the descendants of king Bharata and of ancient India. It is also full of philosophical, religious, and ethical discourses, strewn intermittently, to throw discerning lights, on various human problems, posed to men of wisdom from time to time. As a culmination of this thinking process the Gita emerges at the most appropriate moment and becomes a lighthouse for entire humanity on account of its universally accepted, Perennial Philosophy.

Bhagvad-Gitã means the song of the divine. Herein speaks the God incarnate to man face to face and heart to heart. The fundamental doctrines revealed earlier in *Vedas Brahmanas* and *Upanishads* and which formed the basic tenets of Indian religion called Hinduism found their way in the holi utterances of Lord Krishna on the battlefield of Kurukshetra in its entirety and most comprehensive manner.

The Gitã is in a dialogue form and king Dhritarãshtra, Sanjay, his charioteer, Arjuna and Lord Krishna are the main speakers. Sanjaya is endowed with psychic power of clairvoyance and clairaudiance obtained through the grace of sage Vyãsa, the author of Mahãbhãrata. In his answers to Dhritarashtra's questions Sanjaya is reporting to his master everything that he sees and hears on the distant battlefield. The conversation between Lord Krishna and Arjuna which contains Gita's main philosophical discussion is reported through the medium of Sanjaya only. Occasionally Sanjaya takes freedom in the midst of his reporting, to add descriptive comments of his own.

The Sanskrit in which Gita is writen has its own simplicity, music and poetic diction, not withstanding its effective use of compressed philosophical terminology developed earlier by the Indian religious tradition.

The Geeta reiterates its faith in no uncertain terms in the universal ethical prinicipals and moral virtues properly fitting them into its own system of Cosmology, having a typical Indian character borrowed from the then available scientific view of the universe, known as Sankhya Darshan.

At the same time one should not forget the transcendental aspect of the prophetic utterances of Lord Krishna. They crossed the barriers of phenomenal world of matter (Prakriti) and individualises consciousness (Jiva) and untiringly speak for the all pervading ultimate called Brahman. Geeta categorically states the limit of discussive reasoning in order to know the Divine power of the Godhead, through intellectual discussions. Geeta's emphasis on direct, immediate and intuitional experience of the divine needs to be properly understood through the ecstatic mystical expressions so profusely spread throughout the Gitã-text while describing the nature and attributes of God.

Many great thinkers of the world have agreed upon the greatncss of the Gitã for its perennial philosophy of enduring value not only for Indians but for all mankind. The Gitã has become a universal Gospel because of its eternal message to everyone irrespective of land, race, language or time. It wonderfully combines scriptural poetry and logical reasoning of high order.

(15 A)

Mysticism : Gita's Ultimate Aim
A Universal Phenomenon of Blissful State of God-realisation

There always remain a mystery about the origin and the nature of the universe. Physical Sciences have advanced theories after confirming the well-ordered progressing nature of the world which, in Dr. S. Radhakrishnan's words "has grown from the state of mere materiality to one of life, from life to animal consciousness from animal conciousness to human intelligence. It has to grow from the level of human intelligence to that of spirituality. Cosmic evolution has not come to stop with the advent of intelligence. The further evolution will not be in the physical make up of the man, it will be in his psychical nature. The purpose of religion is to help this world of divided consciousness with its discords, dualities to a life of harmony, of freedom, of love."

The personal encounter with the Supreme Reality is what is called mysticism, the name derived from its mystic character since it is beyond verification by any empirical means. Dr. R. D. Ranade, the great scholar of philosophy defined it as : 'Mysticism denotes that attitude of mind which involves a direct, immediate, firsthand, intuitive apprehension of God.' The greatest of the mystic saints Dnyaneshvar in his Dnyaneshvari, Amritanubhav and other writings gives vivid description of this state in most unsurpassable manner. It is an extraordinary experience of strange and wondrous nature wherby the soul penetrating beyond this mundane world realises the origin of the origin within himself in the divine light of the Supreme Being. Time and space lose its hold on him and he enjoys the life eternal. 'Tatwam asi', that thou art. The real which is the inmost of all things is the essence of self. By capturing the essence of one's self he captures the Reality which is the innermost cause of entire universe. To achieve this one has to conquer his personal nature and bring utmost purity to his life by adopting highest ethical standards with total humility even to the smallest creatures of this world. Dnyaneshvara says, "Keeping aside one's greatnes and forgetting one's learning one who bows down to the world the Lord is always in his company." Ignorance of our own self is the cause of our sorrows and our pride in our limited strength of perception, intellect and feelings create the barriers that separate us from the divine. He is beyond seeing, knowing or defining since he is the seer, knower or definer. "Vidnyataram are ken vijaniyat" How shall you know the knower who knows everything?

The aim of life as per Hindu philosophy is the communion with the Supreme, which in other words means vision of God. It is the state of absolute freedom, 'Paramukti' which can not be realised through logical investigations or scientific analysis. Katha Upanishad declares, "nayamatma pravachanen labhyo, na medhaya, na bahuna shruten." This self can not be attained by instruction, not by intellect nor through much hearing.

Intuition is considered to be essential factor for gaining certain immediate and direct contact with the Supreme. That is Aparokshanubhuti. This relationship is not of dualism, i.e., Dnyata-Dnyeya (Knower - knowable) Drishta-Drishya (seer-to be seen) and Karta-Karma (Doer-Doing) type which depends on something external. It is the total surrendering of the self to Godhead. Dnyaneshvara says, "without differentiating oneself from me one who knows, that he is one with me, is said to be real surrendering unto me." Thus illumined and inspired the seer realises the difference between the Infinitude and finite and declares in unequivocal terms, the impossibility of capturing this divine light into literary descriptions or logical concepts. The sense of mystery prevails and the total experience remains ineffable. Dr. Ranade calls it silent enjoyment of God.

The mystic experience through some unknown faculty called intuition is a universal phenomenon. Throughout the cenuries all the major religions of the world have produced many great men who have through their revelations enlightened the world about that immanent principle which pervades the universe at all times. Such mystics always speak the same truth though in different languages. In fact this spiritual unity has helped the world to unite, irrespective of diversity in human behaviour and thought

Late Dr. R.D. Ranade in his book 'Mysticism in Maharashtra' has cited several examples of the mystics of the western world, both from Christianity and Islam and their contribution to mystical literature is highlighted. Alongwith Jesus Christ Moses, Isaiah, Jeremiah and others had, according to Dr. Ranade, direct mystical experience of God. Jesus Christ himself was one of the greatest mystics that ever lived. Saint Paul was also a great mystic. Plautinus, a non christian from Greece has to his credit famous volumes on philosophy of Mysticism. Saint Augustine, Dionysius de Areopagite, female Saints Hilderguard and Saint Gertrude, and Saint Francis of Assisi, Angela of Faligno, Thomas Aquinas, Dante are some of the important mystics from the Christian world. From Germany Meister Eckhart, Tauler, and Suso are important names of enlightened mystics. Ruysbroeck of Flanders is also noteworthy mystic. English tradition of mystics starts from Richard Rolle and includes Lady Julian of Norwich. Catherine of Siena and Catherine of Genoa are two Italian ladies who reached sainthood through their genuine mystical experiences. Among the Spanish mystics Ignatius Loyola, Saint Teresa,

Saint John of Cross are famous. From Germany Jacob Boehme, the saint from shoemaker caste is wellknown for his intelligence. France produced Francis de Sales and Madame Guyon. John Smith of Cambridge, a Jew mystic Banyan, George Fox, Willium Law, William Blake, John Keble and English famous poets Wordsworth, Browning, Tennyson, Carlyle and Emerson are some of the English names cited by Dr. Ranade. While citing mystics from Islam religion Dr. Ranade has mentioned Al Gazali (12th Century) Sadi, Jalaluddin Rumi, (13 Century) Hafiz, (14th Century) and Jami (15th Century) for their contribution to the school of mysticism. Dr. Ranade has done lot of studies giving such a long list of European and Islamic mystics hihglighting the features of their mystical literature.

In India there is a rich tradition of great mystics who have enriched the culture of this great country. Since Upanishadic times the history is replete with ecstatic writings of great seers who through their wisdom and knowledge have contributed to the spiritual progress of mankind. In fact they have provided beacon light to the faltering world at regular intervals in history. Idea of religion in India is all-comprehensive and beyond any kind of dogmas, ritual and orthodoxy. This is very much proved by the fact that all sects and creeds, all castes and religions and all regions and languages have produced series of great saints from Kannyakumari to Himalayas who always remained above narrow sectarianism.

Comparison between Western mystics and the mystics of Maharashtra studiously recorded by Dr. Ranade deserves all praise for his genuine approach to prove the universal character of the mystic experience. His efforts to give a short survey of Indian mystics from different regions and languages is a great contribution to the history of religion and philosophy of India. Dr. Ranade has compared Dnyaneshvara with Plauntinus, Eckhart and Augustin; and has brought out the similarities found in them. Women saints Muktabai, Janabai and Kanhopatra of Maharashtra are compared with Julian of Norwich, Catherine of Siena and St. Teresa. He finds resemblance between low cast Chokhamela and a cobbler saint Boehma of Germany, Saint Tukaram has his counterparts in Suso, Banyan, Dionysius de Areopagite and saint Ramdas has his counterparts in Pythogorus, lgnatius Loyola and Ruysbroeck. The similarities observed in mystical experiences and their poetic expressions of these mystics as cited by Dr. Ranade amply proves the universality of this extraordinary phenomenon. Oriental and Western mystics have exhibited astounding parallels in their transcendental experiences ultimately proving the veracity of its ineffable character.

The divine character of mysticism as glorified in Bhagavadgita shows two distinct characteristics. One is moral awakening and the second is duty-consciousness. The medieval mystic saints of india had the urge of uplifting common men to divine level through love and devotion to God without venturing into intellectual discussion of philosophical nature. The medieval India saw Vaishnava and Shaiva cults of devotion flourishing. Emergence of great devotional treasure of 'Shrimad Bhagavata' and 'Narada' and 'Shandilya Bhaktisutras' established and spread the schools of devotion throughtout india. Parallel to this devotional movement, there arose the philosophical schools of Shri Shankaracharya, Shri Ramanujacharya, Shri Madhvacharya and Shri Vallabhacharya who, barring Shankaracharya who insisted upon renunciation, Sannyas, as the essential precondition for self realization, has a tremendous influence on Indian mind which resulted into flourishing of different devotional cults that gave rise to great many saintly personalities all over India. Shri Ramanujacharya was instrumental for the emergence of Tulasidas, Kabir and Nabhaji in Hindi belt. Shri Madhvacharya was instrumental for the rise of Chaitanya Prabhu of Bengal who has also inherited the rich devotional tradition from his predecessors Chandidas and Vidyapati. Under the influence of Shri Vallabhacharya Gujrat produced great mystic saints like Mirabai, Narasi Mehata, Surdas etc.

In the Tamil Province of South India there was a rich tradition of Vaishnava and Shaiva cults which had produced great Shaiva saints like Nirudnya Sambandhanar, Appar, Manikkvachagar, Namalwar, Nathmuni, etc. Under the influence of Vaishnava cult Kannad province of south India also produced a long tradition of enlightened saints like Nijagunashivayogi, Akhandeshwar, Sarpabhushan, Kanakdas, Purandardas, Jagannathdas,Vijaydas, etc. Basava, a historically known saintly figure for his progressive social reforms in the 13th Century, is one amongst highly revered saint from south India. Vemana from Telagu region needs a special mention for his phychological exposition of mysticism through his vast literature.

In Maharashtra under the spritual leadership of Dnyaneshvara a great tradition of exalted saints flourished in the thirteenth Century and has remained unbroken till modern times. The history has seen alongwith Nivritti, Dnyaneshvara, Sopana, Muktabai of the same saintly parents and their great contempararies like Changdeva, Namdeva Janabai, Chokhamela, Sanvata-mali, Gora Kumbhar, Visobakhechar', Narahari Sonar, Sena Nhavi etc., a miraculous emergence of saintly personalities from all casts and creeds. Muslim saint Shaikh Mohammad has a place of honour in the higher rank of Marathi saints. The unbroken chain of Marathi mystic saints in the latter part of medieval period include the great names of Ekanath (15th Century) Tukaram and Ramadas (17th Century) who through their vast literature have enriched the school of Mysticism. Kanhopatra, Bahinabai, Venabai are some of the lady saints who deserve special mention for their women emancipation efforts in the past.

In addition to their ethical teachings these saints have created great literature in languages of the common people to educate and bind them together. Their greatness had a solid foundation of spiritual tradition of India. Recognizing the importance of reasoning and also knowing its limitations, these saints surrendered themselves to God for realizing the true nature of human mind and the universe around them. They remained fully absorbed in gaining the most exemplary and rare experience of self-realisation. In their pursuit of absolute freedom from this mundane world they remained very much steadfast in their faith and love to God. With emotions purified and will undeterred they achieved the state of God realisation, i.e., Self-realisation. They all, irrespective of their different regions and times, religious and social status and languages perceived the Ultimate Truth in the same light and colour and spoke about it in the same voice.

The mystic experience was the main source that lifted even the ordinary men to the status of Godhood. It is but logical to think about the uniformity visible in all the mystical experiences, irrespective of space and time, and the underlying current thereof leads to universality. It will be very enlightening to study the unifying force of such mystic experiences which outwardly look different but are intrinsically one and the same. In the context of Indian Saint literature this is very much true. Every province of India and almost every Indian language have proved very fertile in producing a chain of saints of extraordinary merit.

In Maharashtra, there is a galaxy of exalted men who flourished in the medieval age under the great spiritual leadership of Saint Dnyaneshvara. With their own rights they established their identity and found a place of honour in the hearts of the common people of the region. At one end they helped the community to reach high moral standards and at the other end they enriched their life and literature by giving them philosophical ideology of eternal nature. Their philosophical ideas and treatises had the solid foundation of their unique mystical experiences which by their inner strength could surpass the limitations of reason to reach the noblest state of human existence. It would be socially and culturally useful task to undertake the comparative study of the revelations of various Indian Saints and the philosophical ideas expressed in their literature. This will further strengthen the spinal chord of India's unity in diversity. Philosophy, born out of personal revelations has remained a guiding principle for Indian masses throughout the ages. Studying various aspects of mystical experiences of major saints in India, in order to find the unifying principle underlying them and to establish unity of philosophical thoughts on which their teachings are based should be the prime concern of this academic venture. Putting them to the test of rationality will prove its efficacy and though this rare experience is described as ineffable, the critics will have an opportunity to enjoy its sublime character revealed through the words of men of extraodinary genius. Saint Dnyaneshvara, the best among the mystic philosophers of all times through his Dnyaneshvari and Anubhavamrita has formulated his philosophy of Play of cosmic Consciousness in the most systematic manner by employing to the maximum extent logic and reason which are considered to be the best tools of judging the validity of any philosophy worth the name.

Mysticism on account of which metaphysics is dubbed as unscientific and irrational needs a treatment from a different viewpoint. It is unfortunate that the works of mystics are usually kept at arm's length due to two opposite reasons. Firstly due to sense of awe and a feeling of great respect people who accept it as divine gift do not dare to touch upon it for its rational analysis which is required for its better understanding. Second category of people are the critics who due to the ineffable and intuitive character of mysticism, throw it fully out of the realm of logic and rationality labeling this phenomenon as a case of mental delirium totally to be discarded from the world of intellectual creation. Despite both the oppostie and extreme viewpoints, humanity in general has been benefited by this uniquely available experience of rare possibility. In fact the mystic literature has become the greatest treasure of human race and remained under worship since antiquity.

Saint Dnyaneshvara the mystic philosopher of high order excelled in his supraginius and profound wisdom while capturing the Unfathomable, Incomprehensible and Unthinkable in extremely beautiful imagery and diction. In the light of his brilliant exposition the mystic Saints of India can be critically studied to bring out the uniform nature of Indian metaphysical thoughts with a view to establish logical connection among the mystics of different regions and languages. This comparative study will convince us about the fact that the logical investigations supported by the direct personal experience were the real means adopted by the great souls to arrive at the knowledge of the fundamental principle of which all the Universe is expression. Their writings are full of logical explanations and also experiences of divine nature and give testimony to the Supreme Reality, they experienced in the most exalted state of their mind. They uphold the rational evidence even when they talk of faith. For the universal acceptance of the mystical experiences, full justification and rational support is essential. This kind of comparative study will be very much useful in doing justice in that direction. It will penetrate through its variations to prove the singularity of purpose and the theme. Since mysticism, as a universal phenomena that consists of sacred, strange and wondrous experience of divine nature, is possible with any human being, it is most democratic in nature.

There shall always remain a demarcating line between the spiritual experience and the intellectual forms in which it is presented. Intellectual abstractions drawn from the live experience will have its own limitations and will not be able to tell us about the immensity and mystery of spiritual life fully. The personal encounter with God is a matter of individual experience and remains always beyond description. Images and concepts can not be formed since it is not a object of knowledge. The Ultimate can not be grasped by the non-ultimate. All the mystic saints of the world speak in the same fashion and give testimony to its all-time existence.

The study should also aim at establishing unity of action and thought of different saints of different time and places by showing how they were not restricted or bound by organizational or doctrinal orthodoxy. Their sole aim was to transform the human society by raising work to the level of worship and reaching salvation through service of God in man.

All these great thinkers were against superstitions, antisocial rituals and customs and unwanted authority. They taught the people to rely upon their own conscience and purity of heart. Conscious self discovery was the path chosen by them to ralise divinity in them. Possibility of this experience is proved by so many instances strewn all over the world. World history bears a solid testimony to this truth.

Gita's Message to Common Man—*A Pragmatic Approach*

What shall be the message to be extracted from Gita for common men who are engulfed in worldly affairs? Gita profusely speaks about ecstatic mystical experiences of difficult order. It is not possible for everyone to have self-realisation or God realisation. Therefore the various paths described by the Gita at length dividing its chapters into three main streams of knowledge, action and devotion remain theoretical in nature for most of us. There are very few who can claim to have achieved the state of superconsciousness called Brahmisthiti .

Hundreds of thousands of readers are impressed by the greatness of Gita-philosophy. But they are unable to practise its teachings since they have no capacity to rise above their mundane limits. Various interpretations rendered on Gita by great spiritual masters, no doubt, provide valuable guidance to humanity. But in modern times when science and technology have taken the control of everything, pragmatic approach to Gita-philosophy will provide another dimension to its social relevance. Admitting that the Gita is a gospel, it can also be used for worldly purposes to build up a sound and healthy social order. Outwardly it may look nonspiritual materialistic approach but in reality it would become an applied philosophy, the application of spiritual ideas to pragmatic use.

It may appear as some kind of compromise with the idealistic position that Bhagavad Gita presents. Majority of the people including the author, renderer of this version belong to the category who admiringly accept the greatness of the Gita but are unable to follow its spiritual tenets to its logical conclusions. It is beyond their capacity to practise. It does not mean that Gita's idealistic position is an impossible proposition. Gita - philosophy has been severely tested time and again and great many people have testified to its validity. The pragmatic approach without any compromise with the basic tenets of Bhagavad-Gita will serve the interests of majority of people who always remain outside the domain of spiritualism.

Gita stands as a culminating point in the evolution of spiritual thoughts in India and it has become a perennial source of philosophical ideas thus developed for the benefit of entire humanity. Whatever has been said earlier by Vedas and Upanishads, by Sankhya of sage Kapil and Yoga of sage Patanjali has found its way in Gita in a finer and better way. As a revolt against the heaven - seeking materialism of sacrificial rituals of the vedas the path of knowledge propounded by Sankhya and the path of contemplation propounded by Yoga flourished and the ideology of renunciation had its sway over the Indian mind. In order to arrest this trend of otherwordliness and bring balance of approach Gita stressed the importance of action thoroughly analysing its mechanism which underlines the spirit of renunciation in wider sense. However Gita's theory of action is not easy to follow. The individual needs power from within to imbibe Gita's approach to life according to which ultimate goal should be freedom of the soul, i.e., Mukti or Moksha. But majority of men in todays' world of economic domination created by science and technology do not subscribe to this view. Influenced by worldly affairs leading to worldly pleasures and happiness they prefer to be slaves of clouded vision.

This state of mind is totally different from that of Arjuna whose mental dilemma prompted Lord Krishna to deliver this immortal song of philosophical wisdom. Even Arjuna, at later stage confessed that Gita-philosophy faded away from his memory and he needs revision of the same. Lord Krishna, too, expressed his inability to recall it since it was revealed through the divinely unique mystical state of his mind. The fact remains that Arjuna also had his own limitations in practising Gita in day to day life. For every commentator Gita remained as unsolved riddle though each one attempted his own interpretation born out of his personal encounter with the Ultimate Reality. The mystical experience must have been the same for everyone but interpretations differ due to their diverse intellectual capacities, different educational settings, varied tastes and worldly limitations.

In understanding the supreme ends of life in the prevalent socio-economic scenario all over the world one can avail the guidance from Geeta. Lord declares, "whenever the evil triumphs over the good, hold of righteousness declines, I manifest myself to establish the kingdom of truth". Today's world is full of tragedies mostly facing the problems of decadence through violence, cruelty, unemployment, over-population, exploitation of the nature, destruction of natural resources, environmental degradation, hunger, ignorance, hatred, quarrels, deaths etc. etc.

In what way Gita can come to our rescue in such a turmoil? Keeping its metaphysical and spiritual conclusions aside for the exclusive benefit of the spiritual aspirants who will always be small in number the remaining vast population all over the world can have a plunge into its nectarlike thoughts about life and all that is related to life to correct man-made ills of modern century. In his pursuit of happiness the modern man remains discontented in today's world of consumerist culture built upon the philosophy of self - aggrandizement. All the social ills witnessed today are arisen out of mindless pursuits of selfish material gains.

The Bhagvadgita shows us the way to destroy these evils and inspires us to lead a happy and peaceful life. According to scholars Gita laid down the foundation of India's ethics, sociology, polity and arts. Gita's ethical teachings if followed in true spirit has an intrinsic strength to cure all our ills. Certain concepts philosophically developed by the Gita can be applied to our life on behavioural plane.

The fundamental doctrine of unity in all diversity, the same eternal principle manifesting itself in animate and inanimate is a matter of mystical experience and remains out of reach of the majority of people. But its connotation that all are equal gives sufficient strength to unite all. The feeling of all-alike, the sense of empathy will make you feel happy when others are happy and unhappy when others are unhappy. Gita calls him a perfect man when one identifies oneself with others in pleasure and pain alike. In today's world this feeling is totally lost creating barriers among living as well as nonliving beings many times resulting into killings and destruction. Gita's fundamental doctrine of oneness of the universe has been already proved on physical plane by the unified field theory of quantum physics in modern times. The mankind can easily adopt this as an unifying force to curb the divisive tendencies so immensely growing today. "One who sees Me everywhere and sees everything in Me is a man of wisdom" thus says the Gita for sustenance of all. Social tensions arising out of greed and hatred can be instantly defused if such a universal approach based on Gita philosophy of monism is practised in our day to day life sincerely and gracefully.

Another concept developed by Gita is that of Swadharma, one's own rightful duty. According to Gita everybody is born with certain tendency and capacity to perform a particular job in this world. According to these jobs the performers are classified into four groups. Gita explains the concept of Chaturvarnya four - cast - system based on this natural classification. Discarding the rigidity and gradation of the system, which developed in the later age, Gita stresses the importance of doing one's own duty cast upon him by his nature and ability, sincerely and perfectly. The absence of this duty-consciousness is the real cause behind many ills of the present times. Gita's emphasis on doing one's own duty unmistakably and skilfully will serve as a boon to modern world of wayward tendencies. "Let everywhere shine the sun of dutyconsciousness so that everyone's desires are fulfilled". Thus prayed the great saints. If this is followed religiously by everyone, world would be freed from poverty. Every one has different tendencies and capacities and accordingly his duties are differentiated. Gita has spoken this highest truth for the benefit of mankind. But due to human failures we fail in recognising our duty and go on performing something else unbecoming of us. One has to do his own rightful duty then he is free from all sins.

The threefold modes called Triguna is a unique concept that Bhagavad Gita has unfolded in details. Devoting one full chapter for it. Sattva rajas and tamas, the three material forces known as gunas are the constituent elements of Prakriti, the creative power of Brahman which by permutation and combination creates this universe of physical and psychological variety. Every individual is also made of these three gunas in different proportion with one guna predominating. Sattva makes him pure and shining, rajas makes him passionate and active and tamas makes him ignorant and sluggish. For self - realisation the aspirant has to cross over the barriers or influences of these three gunas. However this guna-transcendence is a very difficult task, rarely possible for selected few. The transformation from tamas to rajas and rajas to sattva however can be achieved by the individual by adhering to right conduct. The transcendence is difficult but transformation is possible. Therefore every one should try to reach the pure state of sattva thereby spreading happiness and knowledge everywhere because sattva guna develops great virtues like duty - consciousness, modesty, tenderness, contentment, faith, tolerance, compassion, reasoning etc. whereas rajoguna increasing develops vices like hatred, enmity, jealousy, pride, arrogance, greed etc. The tamoguna increasing develops into disharmony, fear, miserliness, ignorance, foolishness, cheating and faithlessness etc. Gita pleads for sattvaguna increasing which ultimately leads the person to higher realms.

Consciously or unconsciously man embarks upon his life-journey through the channels of pleasure and pain, gain and loss, victory and defeat and many other pairs of opposites. They are inescapable. It is natural for everyone to run after happiness and to avoid sorrow. When one's ambitions desiring enjoyment and power are not fulfilled he becomes pessimist and leads a life of frustration. Gita advises us to renounce all selfish desires and work making all life a sacrifice offered with true devotion to God. But for ordinary men it is quite impossible to work without desiring fruits. It is the motivating force behind their actions and whatever advances the mankind has achieved in physical and psychological fields is partly due to this motivating factor. The actions, only when they become self-centred, conservative and for trivial selfish gains, they bring catastrophe.

Therefore Gita's emphasis on raising a sattva - dominated character with controlled passionate actions of rajoguna and laziness of tamoguna is adequate enough to guide men of worldly passions to lead a life of virtues which is so essential in modern times of deteriorated conditions. Man should learn the act of balancing all dualities by acquiring equanimity of mind that will give him strength to accept pleasure and pain, gain and loss and victory and defeat as an integral part of human life. The four categories of devotees recognised by Lord Krishna in 7th chapter also includes devotees in sorrows, and devotees desiring comforts along with devotees who are seekers of knowledge and those who have reached the highest wisdom. Barring a few who are knowledge - seekers and who are enlightened ones the world-weary and happiness-seekers are in overwhelming numbers in this world. This overwhelming numbers need attention and Gita has accepted them with open arms provided they are in the worship of god in their limited capacity.

The mind is considered to be the eleventh organ that functions in between ten organs of knowing and doing on one side and the intellect to the other. It receives the impressions from the senses and carries them to the intellect that distinguishes the sense-objects and classifies them. Gita says, "Feelings of heat and cold, pleasure and pain, are caused by the contact of the senses with their objects. They come and they go never lasting long". Not knowing this men get attached to pleasure and hanker after it unmindfull of its consequences. Starting point in the process of selfrealisation therefore is the control of the mind which is exceedingly difficult exercise in life. Gita suggests many methods to achieve it but the simplest one suggested is to do one's own duty sincerely and effectively without falling prey to rage and lust. Spiritual discipline therefore starts with purification of mind which otherwise is also very essential to lead a life of peace and happiness. With good deeds and thoughts the mind gets purified. Today's socio-economic and socio-political life has become abundantly corrupt due to overwhelming impact of greed and anger. Purified society can only be built by purified actions and thoughts of the purified souls. Rebirth or no rebirth one should try to contribute in building a healthy society.

Bhagavadgita's ethics is universal in nature and needs to be applied to any situation in life. Mahatma Gandhi wrote about Gita so early as 1925, "When disappointment stares me in the face and all alone I find a verse here and verse there and I immediately begin to smile in the midst of overwhelming tragedies - and my life has been full of external tragedies and if they have left no visible, no indelible scar on me, I owe it all to the teachings of the Bhagvadgita". Throughout the centuries the Bhagvad Gita has guided the humanity individually and collectively in the times of upheavals. Today's world all over and especially in India, the very land of its creation, the socio-economic and socio-political life has become full of misdeeds and corrupt practices due to all round corruption everywhere irrespective of unprecedented material progress achieved by the ever flourishing science and technology. The most tragic part of our corrupt life is that the abnormality of corruption has been converted into normality and people accept it as ideal living. Right and wrong, moral and immoral, proper and improper all these terms have lost their meanings and the acquisition of limitless selfish gains and benefits has become the only aim in life for most of the people especially for those so called leaders who have illegally and immorally earned money, name and prestige in the society. Earlier they enjoyed respectability till they were convicted for their wrong deeds but now a days even after conviction they enjoy social status and power. As described by the Gita in fourth chapter the present time the men of demoniac character are ruining the mankind. So as promised by Lord Krishna the God has to manifest in a new incarnation to kill these devils and establish the rule of righteousness. Nobody knows when that day will dawn. Till then we have the nectarlike teachings of Bhagvadgita to save us from self-destruction. The ethical principles enumerated here before if brought in practice by every individual the downfall can be arrested. Realisation or no realisation, rebirth or no rebirth, salvation or no - salvation our efforts should be to purify the disturbed social ethos by applying these principles in our day to day life irrespective of its great philosophy of spiritual and metaphysical discipline of extraordinary height.

Mahãbhãrata—The Great Epic

Some books have tremendous enduring value and power that inspire and uplift the entire humanity. Mahãbhãrata will certainly top such great works by its grandeur and splendour. Expanded from its original twenty four thousand verses to one hundred thousand verses, it has become a ocean of tales of heroic men and women consisting of all varieties of divine, humane and demoniac nature, thus conferring on it the distinction of being an encyclopedia of human characters. It has taken a form of a holistic literature as it churns out lofty ideals of human code from social and ethical problems that it squarely handles in hundreds of human situations. Vyãsa's genius could easily do this wonder.

In essence it is a story of the descendants of the king Bharata that form the history of ancient India meaningfully called Bharata. It is full of artistically presented stories of epic character. Multicoloured personalities taking their shapes from multidimensional situations in Mahãbhãrata have influenced the national character of Indian people, more subtly and powerfully than the actual heroes and events produced in its history. Characters of Krishna, Vidura, Dharma, Arjuna, Karna, Bhima, Bhishma, Drona, Kunti, Gãndhari, Draupadi etc. carry special significance to Indian mind, learned and illiterate alike. So is the case with Rãmãyan with its characters of Rãma, Sitã, Laxman, Bharat, Hanumãn etc. Their trials, tragedies and triumphs have provided this ancient land a guiding light in its long history of peace and turmoil. However this great epic has a potential to transcend national barriers to touch the core of human heart, irrespective of land, race, religion or language. Crossing the regional boundaries, it has now become the treasure of the world, which is so full of vitality of life.

Mahãbhãrata claims to be the encyclopedia of ancient Indian culture as it preserves historical, geographical, legendary, political, theological, philosophical, social, economical, religious and spiritual heritage of this ancient land. Its teachings of *Dharma,* the righteousness above everything else, reigns supreme over all its complexities of life.

At the place called Vishãla Badari on the bank of Bhagirathi river in the Himalayas the great sage Vyãsa worked continuously for three years after the great Bhãrata war was over and completed this ocean like epic called Mahabharata.

While dealing with eternal human problems of universal nature Mahãbhãrata miraculously touched upon Gitã, the greatest Indian scripture rightly called a "celestial song of India". Along with Rãmayan and Mahãbhãrata Gitã also is India's noblest heritage. Though with pride we say so its is our humble attempt to present this immortal divine thought to common people educated as well as moderately educated who can not grasp the scholarly works of spiritual masters and intelligent thinkers who have produced volumes of commentaries on Bhagavad-Gitã throughout the ages.

(36 A)

The Epic Story in the Background

Satyavati's first son Vyãsa was born when she was a virgin. Subsequently she married to Shantanu, the king of Kuru race of Hastinãpura. Shantanu had Gangã as his first wife who had left him on breaking a certain promise leaving behind her eighth son Devavrata who later became famous as Bhishma. In order to fulfil his father's desire to marry Satyavati called by another name Matsyagandha, Bhishma had taken a serious vow not to accept kingdom or get himself married to fulfil Satyavati's condition that only her sons would claim the throne of Hastinãpura.

Satyavati got two sons. Chitrãngada and Vichitravìrya. Chitrangada died in the battle and Vichitravìrya died of sickness. Vichitravirya had two wives by name Ambikã and Ambãlikã but he died issueless. In order to continue the race Satyavati requested her first son Vyãsa to beget progeny from Ambikã and Ambãlikã. It was considered legitimate to have progeny from husband's brother if the husband died without an issue. This custom was then known as 'Niyoga'. Vyãsa begot Dhritarashtra and Pandu respectively on Ambikã and Ambãlikã. Dhritarãshtra was born blind and Pandu was born pale.

Dhritarãshtra being born blind the younger brother Pandu became the king of Hastinãpura. Having committed an offence Pandu had to resort to the forest. His wives Kunti and Mãdri also accompanied him. There he practised penance. From Kunti and Mãdri, he got five sons who became famous as five Pãndavas. Dharma, Bhima, and Arjuna from Kunti and Nakula and Sahadeva from Madri. Pandu died when they were still living in the forest. The sages looked after the Pãndavas in their childhood.

When Yudhishtira attained the age of sixteen the sages brought them all to Hastinãpura and handed them over to their grandsire Bhishma for future care.

After Pandu's death, Dhritarãshtra had succeeded to the throne of Hastinapura. He arranged for Pãndava's education along with his own hundred sons. In addition to mastering Vedas and other arts they became expert in military science but at the same time they acquired great virtues. The great military genius Drona was their common teacher.

The young Pandavas' glory and fame made Duryodhana and other Kauravas so jealous that they started injuring them in various ways. Duryodhana's plan to burn the Pãndavas and their mother Kunti alive by inviting them to stay in a palace specially built out of inflammable material failed as the Pãndavas got the news before hand. They escaped but Duryodhana considered them dead.

Heroically facing hardships and dangers, the Pãndavas lived in the forest disguised as Brãhmins. When one day they heard neighbouring king Drupad announcing the marriage of his daughter Draupadi to a man who would lift a heavy bow and hit the eye of the rotating fish. Out of the skilled aspirants who tried and failed only Arjuna could perform the difficult feat. When informed Kunti unknowingly asked her sons to share the award won by Arjuna. Honouring the mother's words Draupadi became the wife of five Pandavas.

On their return to Hastinãpura Bhishma advised Dhritarashtra to offer half of the kingdom to Pãndavas. Yudhishtira received his share but of a barren land which was soon converted into prosperous place with fine city of Indaprastha built by the Pãndavas toiling day and night.

Duryodana's jealousy had no limits. He was obsessed

with the idea of wining the Pãndavas. Knowing Yudhishtira's weakness for gambling, he planned a game of dice and invited Yudhishtira for a game. As a true Kshatriya king Yudhishtira accepted the challenge and attended the play. Falling pray to Shakuni's deceitful tactics he lost the entire kingdom with all his wealth. Finally he staked his brothers, Draupadi and himself and lost everything. Thus enslaved, the Pãndavas received the most humiliating treatment when Draupadi was dragged to the royal court by Dushasan catching hold of her hair and her clothes stripped off in the most indecent way in front of the royal gathering. Lord Krishna with his divine intervention protected Draupadi from this ugly scene. However the bad omens that followed made Dhitarashtra to realize the danger ahead and he freed Yudhishtira and others. Totally dejected Yudhishtira went back to his kingdom.

Duryodhana enraged at his father's untimely intervention compelled him to permit second game of dice and invited Yudhishtira to come back and play again. Yudhishtira obeying the Kshatriya's code of conduct again played the game and lost only to accept twelve year's exile to the forest with the thirteenth year living incognito.

While suffering manifold miseries of forest life in exile the Pãndavas practised hard austerities and enriched their life and personality through good and pious deeds.

After completing all the thirteen years silently suffering but blaming no one except their own fate the Pãndavas returned back and demanded his share of parental heritage along with his own kingdom that Duryodhana had usurped in their absence. Duryodhana refused to give anything, even the space equal to the tip of the pin. Elders like Bhishma, Vidura, etc., negotiated but their advice fell on deaf ears. Duryodhana, wickedly adamant closed all doors including Krishna's peaceful mediation. Thus no alternative was left except war. Neighbouring kings were dragged into two warring groups. When Krishna's help was sought by both he offered the option; he himself alone or the services of his kinsmen, Vrishnis. He declared that he would not fight in the battle. Duryodhana asked for the army of the Vrishnis and Arjuna happily chose Krishna to accompany him as his charioteer. A day was fixed. The war was to be fought on the battle field of Kurukshetra, a Holy land of their ancestral touch.

Here, on this battleground arose the occasion that gave birth to Divine Gospel called *Gitã,* a nectar flow coming from the lotuslips of Lord Krishna, the God incarnate!

Adhyaya 1

Arjun Vishad Yoga—*Yoga of Arjuna's Despondency*

The first Adhyaya opens up with a scene on the battlefield of Kurukshetra. The epic narrative mood of Mahãbhãrata continues, giving vivid description of army alignments on the battlefield with lively dialogues coming in between. The Gitã bears a distinctive look because of its unique setting. It is not a treatise written in a peaceful atmosphere nor it is a discourse presented to seekers of spiritual knowledge. Unlike Upanishads it is not a revelation, not even prophetic utterances disclosed to close disciples.

Neither a forest nor a hermitage is its birthplace. It is born on tense battle field to solve an immediate problem of a warrior, nay, of every householder so to say, caught in a similar dilemma in similar situation. What to do and what not to do? Well known Shakespearean heroes like Hamlet and Caroilanus and many others faced such dilemmas and were destroyed for want of a good teacher.

Arjuna is a warrior by birth and profession and the first Adhyãya wherein he appears as one of the generals of Pãndava army surprisingly presents him exactly in the opposite mood. The circumstances of the moment give unexpected turn to his brave character.

The first Adhyãya strikes a great blow to Arjuna's established image of a valiant, ever successful and well - experienced warrior of an extraordinary calibre. Here he is seen bewildered and confused, brooding over the disastrous consequences of the war. The compassion that envelops him is the outcome of his suddenly felt love for his blood relations and friends standing in front of him with a resolve to fight or die. Strangely enough he is seen justifying his pensive mood and strongly condemning the war he has to face.

Verses 1 to 11

'Tell me Sanjaya, what did my sons and the sons of Pandu do on the holy land of Kurukshetra?' *This was the opening question of king Dhritarashtra. In reply Sanjaya describes how Duryodhana, seeing a well-organised Pãndava army went to Drona, his teacher and expressed his apprehension. His citing the names of leading warriors on either side brings to fore the gravity of the war. Both the armies had a large number of neighbouring kings joining them in this war, Remember, the whole of India was involved in this great Mahãbhãrata war.*

Verses 11 to 19 verses

Duryodhana anxiously told Drona to guard his commander-in-chief from enemy's deceitful tactics - But Bhishma, a true warrior, sensing Duryodhana's mental agony blew his powerful conch-shell-horn in order to raise his failing courage and to boost up the morale of his army but in reply the chieftains from Pãndava army blew their conch shell horns so forcefully that their noise resounded through heaven and earth and pierced the hearts of the Kauravas.

Verses 20 to 31

In a true epic style the charged atmosphere of the battlefield was picturesquely narrated in the opening verses thus creating a sense of awe in our mind preparing us for the most fearful civil war. Resounding trumpets brought down a queer silence every where and all of a sudden something strange and unexpected happened and Arjuna*, the main hero of the war, looked something different.*

Arjuna in a heroic style requests Krishna to bring his chariot to no man's land between the armies to facilitate him to see the warriors he must fight with. Krishna accordingly drove the chariot to the desired place confronting Bhishma, Drona and other rulers of Kaurava's army and exclaimed — "O prince, behold the assembled Kurus!' Whereupon at the very first look, Arjuna sees and recognises fathers and grandfathers, teachers, uncles, sons, brothers, grandsons, fathers in -law, dear friends and many other familiar faces. Forgetting his bravery Arjuna is immediately filled with deep compassion. He is unable to bear a thought that his own kinsmen are involved in the battle".

Arjuna might have fought several battles before but this time it is his direct and immediate realisation about the evil effects of a war especially when four generations in succession are facing each other with a resolve to kill or to be killed.

His heart melted and as a result he finds his limbs weakening, mouth parching, with hair upright, body trembling, skin seems burning and greatest of the surprise! His powerful bow (Gandiva) slipping from his hand. He complained of his mind whirling round and round "I can stand no longer! "He exclaimed to Krishna, "I see evil omens ahead, I doubt whether by killing of kinsmen, I shall have any holy gain".

Verses 32 to 39

Arjuna's mood of revulsion due to his kind-hearted compassion for his own near and dear ones, no doubt, invites sympathy from us. Since every one of us is basically a pacifist, very much against war killings in normal condition, we feel like agreeing with Arjuna when he starts justifying his compassion on emotional ground. His realisation that he is about to kill those whom he loves better than life itself was his honest reaction. Emotionally feeling attached to his beloved ones, he is reluctant to accept victory, empire or their enjoyment, even the throne of the three worlds much less the earthly lordship by killing his own kinsmen. Boastingly he calls the Kauravas, his brothers fools, foul - hearted and blinded with greed and therefore eager to ruin family bonds and comradeship. But calling himself clear-sighted Arjuna foresees the destruction of royal families with a chain of terrible evils to follow. *Krishna is quietly listening to* Arjuna*'s emotionally charged arguments and allows him to ventilate his feelings, he himself not uttering a single word.*

Verses 40 to 45

Arjuna continues saying, "O Krishna! Once families are destroyed, the ritualistic religions break, vices taking over the hold, women folk gets defiled resulting into corruption of the caste. Not only the victimised kinsmen but their destroyers also are condemned to hell. The ancestors, not getting their rightful offerings, fall dishonoured. The ancient and sacred family tradition, thus destroyed, hell forever is the only reward to such sinners. *Arjuna is thus appealing in the name of ancient religion and innocent victims of the family facing destruction.*

Verses 46 to 47

A stunning picture of horrifying effects of family destruction, naturally results into Arjuna strongly condemning the war by calling it the most hateful murder of his brothers. He is now so much convinced about the sinful character of the war, that he declares, " Let the evil children of Dhritrãshtra attack me with their weapons, I shall not retaliate. Let them kill me, that will be better !" Having spoken thus, Arjuna throws aside his arrows and his bow in the midst of the battlefield, with his heart full of sorrow, he sits down in the chariot.

One has to understand clearly the significance of the war setting and emergence of compassion in Arjun's heart. Such a contrast raises several questions in our mind. Had Arjuna any right to disturb the war situation? Was it Arjuna*'s* wisdom *or delusion when he condemned the war? His common place argument has certain human strength but is it possible to eliminate wars altogether?*

Arjuna's basic problem outwardly appears to be a philosophical one. Neither he wanted to be a "killer" nor his opposing men to be killed. To him death means total and permanent destruction and he would not like to be the cause for such sinful act.

Arising out of the first dilemma he raises the second one of ethical nature. "Is killing legitimate? Can violence be a good thing in life? How to decide what is good and what is bad? Right or wrong on what basis ? In addition Arjuna was facing men of his own blood ties. Is it fair to kill your own loving people? And for what gain? Just for the greed of power? To fight for the right cause and to punish injustice was Arjun's sacred duty caste upon him as a warrior. But he prefers sacrificing his own interests, whatsoever, for the sake of protecting his family, religion and to uphold righteousness. Lord Krishna is just looking at him, quietly listening, with a inner resolve to take the opportunity to enlighten the world under the pretext of solving Arjuna's immediate problem raised in the first ***Adhyãya*** *called "****ArjunavishãdYoga****", i.e. Arjuna's despondency.*

Adhyaya 2

Sãnkhya Yoga—*Yoga of Knowledge*

Introduction

The first **Adhyãya** *was a reflection of Arjuna's simplicity of heart and god-fearing pious character and searching mind. As a troubled humanist he is in search of something higher than mere victory and killing. How painfully and honestly Arjuna justifies his mood of revulsion and plays a role of a pacifist is also seen in the opening part of the second* **Adhyãya**. *He is prepared to throw away the warrior's conventions that do not recognise the respectability of the elderly persons like Bhishma and Drona. Arjuna's magnanimity reaches its height when he declares his preference to begging than to killing them.*

Rest of the second **Adhyãya** *is solely devoted to Lord Krishna's reply to Arjuna's objections. The Gitã's real teaching starts now onwards and Lord Krishna initiates some of the very fundamental and lofty doctrines of India's perennial philosophy so well established and developed throughout the ages.*

The **Atman**, *the indwelling Supreme Divinity, called* **Brahman** *has an eternal existence and the body is simply a passing phase. Man's every action is to be judged in this absolute sense. Human Being possesses a double nature, a bodily existence and an Eternal Self, the Spirit, the Soul. The first is transitory. Immortality of the soul and the mortality of the body and nonbinding character of one's natural duty called* **Swadharma** *are the basic postulates established in this* **Adhyãya** .

Verses 1 to 9

Lord Krishna was not happy with Arjuna's depressed mood. His untimely compassion evoked a sharp reaction from the Lord. Calling it unmanly, disgraceful, unworthy of a man of enlightenment, Lord Krishna said, "Oh foe-consumer, shake off this cowardice and arise, such petty weakness and impurities of heart are unbecoming of a warrior like you!" Lord Krishna's direct reference to Arjuna losing heaven and fame due to his cowardice did not appeal him much. For him these things were not greater than the respectful superiors like Bhishma, the grand father and Drona, the veteran teacher who were worthy of veneration. Any wealth or pleasure would be cursed with blood guilt if earned by killing elderly persons. "Better to live by begging than to commit such a sin!"

Although Arjuna said this, his resolution dwindled and he started suspecting his own position, "What is better: we defeating Kauravas or they defeating us" He asks desperately:

"I am confused about my duty, I wish to know what is good for me. I am your disciple. Please show me the right path. Till then neither the supreme and the unchallenged world's kingdom nor the throne of heavenly gods will be able to remove my sense - killing sorrow. I will not fight!" Saying this Arjuna became silent.

Verses 10 to 25

Lord Krishna begins his reply by striking at the very root of Arjuna's dilemma over the act of killing. The dweller in the body, the ***Ãtman*** *is the sole reality and the body is merely a passing phase, simply an appearance. Life and death are the stages attached to the body alone. The dweller* ***(dehìn/ sharìrin)*** *in the body, i.e., the* ***Ãtman*** *has no birth, no death.*

Though outwardly people seem to die, there never was a time when they including Lord Krishna, Arjuna and the kings at the war did not exist in the past nor they shall cease to be in future. Lord Krishna emphasises on the immortality of the soul, the ***Ãtman***. The immortal soul dwelling in the body passes through the stages of childhood, youth and old age, likewise at the death he merely passes in to another kind of body. The soul merely changes bodies after bodies in a manner similar to a person discarding his old clothes and donning new ones.

At the very outset Lord Krishna has thus lifted the discourse to such a philosophical height where superior intellect and objective analysis reign supreme over Arjuna's emotional and subjective thinking. A spiritual framework is provided in the beginning itself and in the later ***Adhyãyas*** *these fundamental doctrines are fully exposed in minutest details with logical explanations.*

Lord Krishna wants Arjuna to imbibe discriminatory wisdom whereby he can distinguish between permanent and transient. "The truly wise mourn neither for the living nor for the dead, therefore your sorrow is for nothing, "Thus advising Arjuna Lord Krishna starts defining the transient and ephemeral nature of this phenomenal world.

"Feelings of heat and cold, pleasure and pain are caused by the contact of the senses with their objects. They come and they go, never lasting long. You must bear with them". *Existence of the world is nothing but experiencing the pairs of opposites (**Dvandva**) that keep on changing every moment. Reality stands beyond this.*

Pointing out the ever-changing and destructible nature of both the phenomenal world of matter and individualised consciousness Lord Krishna draws our attention to the real, permanent and infinite principle that pervades the entire universe. Whatever the man experiences and reacts through his body, mind and intellect is of transient nature and therefore finite but that Reality which pervades all things, animate and inanimate is indestructible and no one has power to destroy it or change it. *The same Eternal Principle,* ***Brahman*** *when dwells in the body is called* ***Ãtman*** *which is birthless, deathless and changeless, whereas the bodies it possesses are said to be perishable.*

The ***Ãtman*** is incapable of slaying or being slain. It is neither born nor can it die. "It is immutable, illimitable and imperishable!" Declares the Lord. Arjuna's anxiety about committing a sin of killing becomes meaningless since the "Soul can not be cut to pieces by any weapon, can not be burnt by fire, can not be wetted by water and can not be dried by wind". *In modem terms it can be said to be extending beyond all dimensions of time and space. Thus it being beyond the comprehension of time and space limited senses, these senses can not perceive it at all. Hence described as* ***Avyakta,*** *without concrete manifestation. It is also beyond one's mental capacity to grasp,* ***Achintya.*** *It is also changeless,* ***Avyaya,*** *as it has no manifested form or shape or period of existence that are the characteristics normally capable of being changed.*

Here the implied meaning is very important. The ***Ãtman,*** *the Self, being the Knower, the Seer or Doer in the body, a sense - mind - intellect combination which function under Its power is incapable of external observation or experimentation. It is not an outside object with name and form so that weapons, fire, water, wind and similar instruments, can experiment on it to know its nature.*

Immortality and various other descriptions of ***Ãtman*** *forming this section of the second* ***Adhyãya,*** *become the core of Gita's perennial philosophy and with its power of logic and rationality it dispels Arjuna's delusion arising out of mundane thoughts.*

Verses 26 to 31

After teaching the highest of the metaphysical truth ever spoken, Lord Krishna comes down to worldly plane to remove Arjuna's doubts that led to his despondency. If according to Arjuna's own conception, this ***Ãtman*** is subject to constant birth and death even then he should not mourn since all beings who are born had to die and rebirth is certain for the dead. So it is unwise to grieve for what is unavoidable. *Lord Krishna has skilfully touched upon the great truth propounded by **sãnkhya** philosophy.* "None knows where we come from and where we would go to, but in the middle for a brief spell, interim between birth and death, we become manifest in our bodies. Death is merely a preordained passage of the soul from the limited body into limitless Unmanifest. Once this truth is realised, there remains no cause for any grief."

Lord Krishna, then praises the wondrous experience of those who have realised the ***Ãtman*** in its true nature. But there are many ignorant ones who are told about it and still do not understand a word about it. The Lord wanted Arjuna to be one amongst the enlightened souls who have realised the eternal nature of the dweller in the body so that he has no reason to mourn for anyone's death.

The question then arises what one should do in his bodily existence? The Lord now brings the discourse to practical level without breaking its link with the metaphysical foundation so wisely laid down so far. It was also necessary to dispel the doubt whether all types of killings were permitted under the pretext of the immortality of the Soul.

Verses 32 to 38

The Lord glorifies the warrior's profession. The battle opens a door to heaven and therefore Arjuna should feel happy to get such a rare opportunity. He was expected to maintain his reputation as a formidable warrior whereas if he turns aside from his lawful war-duty he would be disloyal to his innate nature, would lose his fame and would be called a sinner. The arguments came down to a very human level when the Lord talks about Arjuna's colleagues misunderstanding his reluctance to fight, as arising out of fear and to a man of self-respect "that is surely worse than death. Your admirers will despise you and your enemies will slander your courage. What would be harder to bear than to hear such words of infamy and insults". In such touching, emotional words Lord exhorts Arjuna to rise and fight. After enumerating negative effects of Arjuna's inaction the Lord, then starts painting a bright picture of his getting earthly pleasures if he emerges victorious and he would attain the heaven if he dies a hero's death in the battle.

Thus urging Arjuna to rise and fight Lord Krishna strikes a vital chord by telling him the secret of nonbinding actions. Action by itself is not good or bad, neither sinful nor meritorious. The mental attitude that puts opposites like victory and defeat, gain and loss, pleasure and pain and so forth on the same plane makes one's actions non binding and therefore Arjuna was encouraged to do ***Kshatriya's*** prescribed duty while being non-attached to results thereof. In such mental equipoise when war is fought as a part of lawful duty, it is not a sin.

Verses 39 to 46

Arjuna was urged to perform his ***'Swadharma'*** *with a mind illuminated by the knowledge of the Eternal Reality. It was not merely doing a duty for duty's sake. It was really a duty for God's sake. The unitive knowledge of the Divine Reality through self realisation can be attained by practising* ***DnyãnYoga****, here refers to as* ***Sãnkhya*** *Buddhi the path of knowledge by observing metaphysical discipline of discrimination between real and apparent. Thus the* *metaphysical discipline was the focal point of the earlier part of the second* ***Adhyãya*** *referred to as* ***Sãnkhya****, by the Lord.*

But this discriminatory knowledge can lead to renouncing all actions including that of a ***Kshatriya,*** *the warrior. Arjuna too, had to some extent suggested the same by his reluctance. Lord Krishna now begins explaining the method of* ***KarmaYoga****, here referred to as* ***Yoga****-Buddhi the path of action. Every action born out of desire has a binding effect that remains in the form of* ***Vãsanas****, the subtle impressions of one's past experiences and actions. These effects have to be carried by the doer in this life or subsequent ones for atonement. Affected ones are those who perform actions with attachment to fruits thereof, and not those who consider the actions their sacred duty, cast on them by their innate nature called* ***Swadharma****. They perform it as their offerings to God, and thus keep no* ***Vãsanas*** *behind.*

One's little efforts in acquiring this attitude of non attached action is never wasted and it has no contrary results. "Even a little practice of this ***Yoga*** can save you from the terrible wheel of rebirth and death". Arjuna is thus reassured by the Lord to make a humble beginning.

But then what are the means to reach that state of mind? The Lord discloses the secret by telling the importance of discriminatory intellect that makes one's will concentrated upon Divine ideal. The will of the person lacking the power of discrimination, and as a result lacking concentration, is confused. Such irresolute mind wanders in all directions, being attached to material pleasures. *Most of the people fall in this category.* Their confused minds drove them towards the letter of scriptures. And overlooking the inner truth they desire earthly happiness and heavenly rewards. Involving themselves in elaborate rituals they grow deeply attached to pleasure and power. As a result they are caught in the cycle of rebirth and death.

***Vedas** are sacred scriptures of Hindus and Lord Krishna refers to their ritualistic portion that invariably comes under the influence of three **Gunas**, sattwa, rajas and tamas, which are three natural but material forces. Living and non-living beings have their own characteristics born of the **Gunas** combining in a vast variety of ways. Matter and mind get their differentiating tendencies and traits due to **Guna**-influence. These forces keep a human being chained to pairs of opposites like pleasure and pain, gain and loss, heat and cold, etc.*

Arjuna is persuaded not to become involved in the play of these ***Gunas***. To become free from the pairs of opposites, his mind has to be absorbed in ***Ãtman*** without caring even for his personal livelihood. Unlike the well in the flooded country the ***Vedas*** become useless to a person who is enlightened by the unitive knowledge of ***Brahman***. *What is important is selfless detached action. **Vedic** rituals and sacrifices when performed for purification of mind and for the well-being of the common people also become selfless activity that leads to spiritual freedom.*

Verses 47 to 53

Lord Krishna summarises the KarmaYoga in a very beautiful couplet. "You have the right to work, but for work's sake only. You have no right whatsoever to the fruits of work. Desire for the fruits must never be your motive. Never get attached to laziness either."

*These well-known principles stand as four cornerstones of **KarmaYoga**. The result of any act does not solely depend on its doer, but also on various other known-unknown factors. Therefore one's actions should be free from the anxiety about the fruits. To achieve this goal, every action needs to be* *performed fixing one's heart on the Supreme Reality. By renouncing attachment to fruits one becomes indifferent to success and failure and as a result becomes calm and peaceful. That evenness or steadfastness of mind is called* "Yoga," *That is the state of unity with **Ãtman**.*

Work done with anxiety about results is inferior to work done without such anxiety. Surrendering oneself to Supreme Lord is rewarded by achieving equanimity of mind. Selfish ones who run after fruits of their actions are miserable. Lord Krishna asks Arjuna to devote fully to gain unitive experience of Brahman to enable him to detach himself from the bondage of good and evil. Skill of doing work without attachment keeping mind fully absorbed in ***Ãtman*** is ***Yoga***. He who maintains the mental equilibrium can easily renounce the fruits of actions. He is bound to reach enlightenment and braking the cycle of birth and death becomes a perfect human being.

Arjuna's intellect was clouded by delusion and Lord Krishna wanted to clear it so as to make him indifferent to fruits of his actions. Arjuna's arguments were indicative of his intellect being bewildered by conflicting interpretations of the scriptures. Lord tells him to make his confused mind steady and undistracted and poise it in the contemplation of the ***Ãtman***. That was the sure way to self realisation.

Verses 54 to 63

Lord Krishna impressed upon Arjuna's mind the necessity of acquiring mental equanimity to enable him to overcome his grief and delusion. Arjuna had wilfully and with full confidence accepted the discipleship of the Lord. His receptive mind was so much alive to the inspiring thoughts that breaking his silence he asked the Lord very basic and intelligent question:

"Krishna, How can one identify a man who is firmly established and absorbed in the ***Ãtman***, the Divine self and therefore whose intellect has become steady ? In what manner does the illuminated soul speak? How does he sit? How does he walk ?

Arjuna's eagerness to see the perfect human being, the personified wisdom in the surrounding world is clearly reflected in these short questions. It is noteworthy that the Lord does not prescribe 'dos' and 'don'ts' of human conduct as arbitrary commandments, but brings out beautifully the virtues of the Realised Man who lives amidst us and sets an ideal before others.

Man of steady wisdom;

—Abandons all desires of the mind.

—is blissfully absorbed in the ***Ãtman*** itself.

—Remains unshaken in the adversity and does not hanker after pleasures.

—Is free from attachment, fear and anger.

—His worldly bonds are broken.

—Neither rejoices on good luck nor hates bad luck.

—Withdraws his senses from sense -objects like a tortoise withdrawing his limbs from all sides.

—The abstinent outwardly runs away from the objects of enjoyment by negative restrictions but really carries his desires with him, but in the case of the man of steady wisdom, having once tasted the joy of ***Ãtman***, his desires also disappear.

-Senses are so strong and impetuous that they forcibly drag the mind even of a wise man who is trying to control

them. But the man with the steadfast mind restrains the senses keeping them under full control. Thus recollecting the mind he fixes it on 'Me' the Lord.

Lord Krishna *demonstrated the qualities of the man of steady wis*dom *by stressing indirectly the need of the mind-control. He now draws our attention to the very fundamental pitfalls of human mind. Lord describes the process:*

Thinking about sense-objects develops attachment to sense-objects. From the attachment grows the addiction. Addiction thwarted produces anger. Anger leads to mental confusion which in turn kills the power of memory. Once memory is lost discriminatory intellect is lost and when power of discrimination is lost the man is doomed.

What a realistic picture of our worldly affairs!

Verses 64 to 70

In contrast to the human failures, the man of steady wisdom exhibits extra ordinary qualities while living in the pairs of opposites.

A person who is obedient to ***Ãtman***, walks safely among the objects of lust and hatred. His peace of mind is not disturbed. In this peace all sorrows melt. Once his mind is peaceful his intellect becomes steady.

Whereas one who has no knowledge of the *Ãtman*, can have neither a steady mind nor a steady intellect. Without steadiness there is no peace and where there is no peace, from where can there be happiness?

As the strong wind sweeps away a ship from its course upon the waters a mind engaged in wandering senses drag away the intelligence which is the main instrument of gaining wisdom; But in the case of man with steady wisdom senses get detached from their objects.

Lord Krishna in a famous couplet brings out the contrast between the illuminated soul and the common people.

"The man of restraints is awake in his enlightenment which is a dark night to all other beings, and the beings are awake in sensual fife which is a daylight to them; but to a seer it is a dark night."

Water flows continually into the ocean but the ocean remains undisturbed, likewise when desires are flowing in to the mind of the seer his peace is not disturbed. This is not possible with a passionate one.

Verses 71 to 72

After profusely praising the man of steady wisdom by presenting his shining virtues, Lord Krishna now concludes by glorifying the state of enlightenment in ***Brahman***, called ***Brãhmi sthiti.***

A person who has deserted all his desires of sense gratification and who is passionless and devoid of sense of possession and ego takes the seat of peace in the heart of ***Brahman.***

This is, Lord Krishna reiterates, the state of enlightenment in ***Brahman.*** Once attained there is no chance of becoming a victim of any delusion. Even at the time of death the man thus situated, gets freed and enters into ***Brahman.***

*Since the second **Adhyãya** stresses the importance of knowledge as a precondition to self realisation, it is rightfully called **sãnkhyaYoga**.*

(57 A)

Adhyaya 3

KarmaYõga—*Yoga of Knowledge*

Introduction

The second ***Adhyãya*** *lays down the foundation of* ***DnyãnYoga****, i.e., the metaphysical discipline of discrimination between real and the apparent in a very condensed form leaving the scope of expansion to future* ***Adhyãyas****. This basic knowledge was essential to dispel* ***Arjuna's*** *delusion that arose out of his ignorance about the self and his false notion of calling a just war unjust. The Lord also assured him that this knowledge results into making one's intellect steady that enables him to reach self- realisation. To gain this self-knowledge one needs to have utmost purity of heart that exclusively depends on desireless and non-attached actions performed by the individual. Prompted by* ***Arjuna's*** *pointed question Lord Krishna, now commences teaching how the path of non-attached* ***Karma*** *leads to self realisation.*

Verses 1 to 9

Arjuna wanted to know why he should indulge in any action at all and particularly action involving terrible deeds of killings when Lord himself considers steady wisdom superior to any kind of actions. Frankly admitting his confusion in understanding the real meaning of knowledge and action he requests the Lord to tell him one definite way of attaining the highest good.

The Lord explains that he propounded two different paths; one of knowledge for the contemplative and the other of selfless action for the active. *Both lead to the same goal, though one is speedy as a bird and the other is slow like an ant. Their adoption depends on one's degree of ability. To say that to act or not to act depends on one's will is meaningless.* Freedom from action, the ***Naishkarmya*** is never achieved by abstaining from action. Nobody can reach perfection by merely ceasing to act. Similarly in bodily existence it is impossible to rest from activity even for a moment because ***Guna***-dominated natural forces forming the tendencies would force him to act against his will.

Verses 10 to 16

Brahma - the creator created all beings he appointed each one to his duty following which they were to prosper. ***Yadnya*** *in its true spirit is pulling together of everybody's efforts and resources for collective well being.* But he who desires every thing for his own enjoyment is a thief.

Here Lord Krishna emphasises the importance of socially committed duties and their complementary nature and derides those sinful ones who leaving their God-appointed duty become the slaves of the senses and live for their own greed.

The Lord describes the universal cycle of sacrifice in the form of collective efforts. Pleased with this sacrifice the heaven sends down rainfall, that in turn make the food that ultimately sustains the living beings. The sacrifice results from actions and actions spring from the ***Brahman,*** the Ultimate Reality. This is how the All-pervading Reality is present in every dutiful action.

Lord Krishna elevated every duty - bound activity to divine level, condemning the man who does not play his role in this divinely moving cycle of selfless activity. His lustful, sense - oriented living is evil and life of such a human being is good for nothing.

Verses 17 to 25

The Lord admiringly praises the man who has found delight, contentment and tranquillity in his ***Atman*** only and therefore has no obligation to perform any duty. He has nothing to gain in this world neither by performing action nor by refraining from it he has no self interest whatsoever.

Arjuna is advised to do his duty always without attachment since such a human being having no anxiety for fruits reaches the ultimate truth. The Lord glorifies this thought by citing the examples of great men like king ***Janaka*** who reached perfection simply because they did their duty in a non-attached way.

Arjuna might think that the action is to be performed because it is inevitable and also purposeless. Hence the Lord adds special significance to such selfless actions. He plants a very high motive to these actions. They set others on the path of duty by following such grand examples. Because whatever a great man does ordinary people imitate it calling it a ***Dharma,*** a right action. The Lord quotes his own example by saying that as the Supreme Godhead, he is neither bound by any duty nor he has to acquire anything, still he ceaselessly works. If he stops working that would lead to confusion, universal disorder and destruction of the creatures. It is therefore the duty of the wise not to create bewilderment in the minds of the ignorant who are hungry for actions but to encourage them to do their holy and divinely useful work by imitating his examples.

Verses 27 to 35

The question arises how to distinguish between the work done by the illuminated soul and that of the ignorant people. The Lord starts analysing the mechanics of action and also deals with its metaphysical aspects.

All actions really are performed by the ***Gunas***, well known three modes of natural forces functioning in the material world. But the man getting deluded by egoism thinks, "I am the doer". The wise having insight into the operation of the ***Gunas*** and their various functions knows that the relationship between the senses and their objects is merely an interplay of the ***Gunas***. Therefore he remains detached from the action.

But the ignorant under the delusion of the ***Gunas*** of the nature fall in love with the senses and their activities. Such people need guidance. Therefore the Wise should not confuse them by Lord Krishna *sensing this doubt clarifies his standpoint by emphasising:*

"It is better to do your own duty however imperfectly than to assume the duties of another person. Prefer to die doing your own duty. The duty of another will put you into great fear".

Every individual is endowed with certain qualities and is best suited for a particular job. No duty or profession is high or low. Better to follow one's own innate nature to give best results which in turn will keep the cycle of the universe moving in right direction.

Verses 36 to 43

Arjuna *got puzzled over the powerful nature of human tendencies and therefore he asked the Lord a very poignant question.*

"O ***Krishna***, what is it that compels a man to do evil even against his own will as if forced by someone?"

The Lord explains drawing the realistic picture of human pitfalls. The rajo ***Guna***, the tendency indicative of passion, restlessness and aggressive activity produces rage and lust. They are the most ravenous and deadly enemies. They envelop the wisdom, the knowledge of ***Atman*** as the smoke smothers fire, as dust covers a mirror and the womb hides the embryo. The wise treats this lust as his persistent foe that envelopes his wisdom and which is almost like an implacable fire that destroys the judgement Senses, mind and intellect, are its working place where they mislead the self by hiding knowledge.

So the Lord cautions Arjuna to kill this evil by controlling the senses first because they destroy spiritual as well as material knowledge. *In the end the Lord explains the hierarchical order of the instruments of knowledge so that* ***Arjuna*** *may select the right one.*

"The senses are higher than the sense-objects. The mind is higher than the senses. The intellect is higher than the mind but 'that' ***(Atman)*** is higher than the intellect."

So Arjuna has to realise ***Atman***, which is above the intellect. Controlling the mind through spiritual discrimination ***Arjuna*** has to kill the strong enemy that appears in the form of lust.

Adhyaya 4

Dnyãn Karma Sanyãsa Yõga—*Yoga of Renunciation Through Knowledge*

Introduction

Nobody can avoid ***Karma***. Even after one's steady intellect remains non-attached he has to work. Knowledge frees your intellect from lust but not from your duty. Therefore the illuminated soul is obliged to work, ceaselessly. It is also necessary for the guidance of the common people. This was the purport of the 3rd ***Adhyãya***. The fourth ***Adhyãya*** further strengthens what has been said about the path of action so far. What mental attitude the seeker of knowledge should adopt while performing various types of activities is the main theme of the fourth ***Adhyãya***.

Verses 1 to 8

Lord Krishna narrates the ancient lineage of the ***KarmaYõga*** that he himself taught to various luminaries in succession but ultimately got lost and forgotten through the ages. ***Arjuna*** finds it hard to believe that ***Krishna*** was the first to teach this ***Yõga*** to ***Vivaswat*** who was born long before him. In reply to ***Arjuna's*** astonishment the Lord proclaims his Over lordship that appears in various incarnations at different times. He brings out the difference between His previous lives and those of ***Arjuna.*** Lord ***Krishna***, being the master of ***Prakriti***, He is not conditioned by ***Maya*** his mysterious power of creation and therefore has the knowledge of all his previous births. Whereas the animate and inanimate beings under the control of ***Maya*** have no such power and knowledge. *Here comes the Gita's most important doctrine that affirms the existence of one or more human incarnations* *of Godhead. These incarnations provide to the worshippers the scope for meditation to get the mercy of the Lord. Lord announces:*

"When virtues decline and the evils flourish, I give myself birth to protect the good and destroy the sinners. In every age I appear for establishing righteousness.

Verses 9 to 12

Worship of the God incarnate is the sure way to realisation. Knowledge of the divine births of the Lord and his wondrous tasks frees the man from rebirth and unites him with God. *How does unmanifest, nonthinkable and changeless* ***Brahman*** *appear in human forms can only be understood through spiritual revelation and the God's task once understood discloses the secret of non-attached work.* Lust, fear, and anger run away from him. Purified by knowledge the man of wisdom takes shelter in the Lord and finally merges into Him.

The Lord declares

"In whatever form men worship Me I accept them as they are and their wish I grant them." Proclaiming this lofty principle the Lord announces the all-embracing approach of his divine will.

"Whatever path men travel is My path. It ultimately leads to Me."

However such farsighted and industrious human beings are very rare. Most of them worship gods and goddesses with desire of worldly success that can be gained quickly in this world.

Verses: 13 to 23

The Lord now explains how the world order is established by him creating four types of duties that correspond to the different kinds of ***Guna*** and ***Karma***. However he cautions to keep in mind that though he is their creator one should recognise him as passive since natural qualities and tendencies a person possesses decide what duty he deserves. Thus he has no hand in establishing this social order. He has no desire for fruits as well hence the actions do not contaminate him. The ancient seers who knew this secret could safely engage in action. Arjuna has just to follow this spirit and act.

If by renouncing actions alone one can attain Liberation then why one should get involved in any action at all? The Lord now tries to explain the true nature of 'action' as well as 'inaction' . . . . That remains the most persistent and perplexing question even to the learned. One should know what kind of work to do, what kind of work to avoid and how to reach a state of calm detachment from the work because the real nature of work is hard to understand. Only the wise person can see inaction in action and action in inaction. Such a wise man is always busy in his works with his mind fixed in Brahman. *What is action and what is inaction is determined by its binding power.* By this definition one who acts without lust or scheming for the fruits of the act the seers call him wise. His actions get burnt in the fire of knowledge and thus they become inaction. He remains satisfied within his self. Outwardly though he acts it is as good as inaction. He remains contended with whatever is given by God. He is not troubled by opposites like pain and pleasure, gain and loss etc. He has no jealousy for anyone. He is not imprisoned by his actions. With all bonds broken and mind established in ***Brahman*** he performs the action in the spirit of ***Yadnya*** and gets his ***Karma*** destroyed in the fire of knowledge.

Verses 24 to 32

Lord ***Krishna*** defines the ***Yadnya*** spirit in which different modes of worship are adopted by human beings of different ability but equate them with ***Brahma Yadnya*** in which ***Brahman*** is the offering, the ***Brahman*** itself is the ritual, sacrificial fire also is Brahman and the offerings are made by the ***Brahman***, the offerer. As everything is the manifestation of ***Brahman*** all actions and things Naturally become ***Brahman***. What is important is ***Brahman*** Consciousness in all matters. *The Lord Krishna uses the **Yadnya** metaphor to describe various practices called, **sadhanas** to reach the absolute.*

Some ***yogis*** address their sacrifice to devas whereas some offer the sacrifice itself into the fire of ***Brahman*** meaning thereby that they offer their self into the fire of ***Brahman.***

Some offer their hearing and other sense organs into the fire of self restraints whereas some others offer their sense objects into the fire of their senses . Some offer the actions and functions of their senses as also of their vital force in the fire of regular practice of self control where in knowledge burns every thing.

In addition there are others whose ways of worship are described thus. Some offer their worldly possessions by performing material sacrifice. Some offer their austerities or their ***Yoga*** practices whereas some others who have controlled their mind and who have observed hardest vows offer their studies and knowledge in their sacrifice. Some offer their physical and mental powers acquired through breath control by ***Raj Yoga*** practice. Some offer their energy into their vital breathing by observing strict fasting. All such types have the true knowledge of sacrifice. Thus who understand the real meanings of sacrificial worship burn their sins in them and eat the nectar like food left in the end and attain immortality and finally reach Eternal ***Brahman.***

*Thus universalising the **Yadnya** concept the Lord brings into its fold the message that the sacrifice is not only necessary* *for personal salvation but also for the universal well being. Universal cycle constantly moves by the spirit of sacrifice only.* In this world there is no place for him who does not perform some kind of sacrifice. Then what position he has in other world ?

Verses 33 to 42

The Lord concludes by glorifying *Dnyãn Yadnya,* the sacrifice of knowledge where one's intelligence is brought as the offering that gets purified in the fire of unitive knowledge burning out ignorance and where the residue emerges as pure wisdom. Compared to this, ritualistic sacrifice with material offerings stands too inferior. Lord proclaims. In the sacrifice of knowledge all types of actions culminate into enlightenment.

"Remember oh! Dear ***Arjuna,*** the enlightened souls will instruct you this knowledge of the identity of ***Atman*** with the Absolute ***Brahman*** if you totally surrender to them, question them and serve them as a disciple". In these words the Lord assures ***Arjuna*** and showers praise on the unique character of this divine knowledge". This knowledge will tear out all the delusions and will make you to realize that the entire creation is present in your own ***Atman*** and in the Brhman as well." "With the vessel of this knowledge you will be able to cross all your sins even if you happen to be the worst of the sinners." In this fire of knowledge all your ***Karmas*** will be burnt to ashes.

There is nothing more sacred than divine knowledge. Once an individual becomes perfect by practising spiritual discipline he attains this divine knowledge internally within his own heart.

The Lord explains one more requisite for attaining this supreme knowledge. Man of faith absorbed in devotion, equipoised by the sense control obtains it and at once attains supreme peace.

Whereas the ignorant, the faithless and the non believer meets his destruction. In this world as well as in the next world there is no place for such doubting characters. Happiness is not for them.

The Lord finally tells Arjuna the specific effects of the divine knowledge and practice of non attached action. By the knowledge his doubts are torn to pieces and by the practice of ***Yõga*** he renounces all actions. Such a man of self-realisation can not be bound by any actions. ***Arjuna,*** therefore is advised to take the sword of knowledge and slice the doubts born out of his ignorance and engulfing his mind. Establishing himself in the ***Yõga*** of non attached action he should get up (and fight the war.)

Adhyaya-5
Karma Sannyãsa Yõga—*Yoga of Renunciation*

3rd & 4th ***Adhyãyas*** *were dedicated to explain why actions are to be performed and what should be the attitude while performing them. These two* ***Adhyãyas*** *laid down the basic postulates of the path of a action called* ***KarmaYõga****. Selfless and detached actions performed as the will of God, in the spirit of worship are not only free from any bondage but are capable of liberation. But all this lastly end into the knowledge of God. The 2nd* ***Adhyãya*** *had already stressed the need of discriminatory knowledge essential to know the nature of the Self and the surrounding world. At the end of 4th* ***Adhyaya*** *again the lord reiterated the greatness of this divine knowledge as the culminating point where all actions get burnt into it.*

Arjuna *was puzzled and wanted to know why the Lord is praising both the knowledge that lead to renunciation as well as the path of non attached action. The 5th* ***Adhyaya*** *clarifies the deeper meanings of sannayas and the action that leads to the state of inaction. This* ***adhyaya*** *gives beautiful description of the enlightened soul of high calibre.*

Verses 1 to 3

Arjuna *appears convinced about the superiority of selfless action over the egocentric one and that of God-centred knowledge over object-centred one.* Still he asks a categorical question to know which of the two, whether ***KarmaYõga*** or Renunciation of action in favour of knowledge was better.

Lord *Krishna* without hesitation promptly replies that both the paths lead to highest good but to work selflessly

is better than renouncing action after enlightenment. It does not mean that the path of knowledge is inferior. *Even from the point of view of a new student of spirituality, a metaphysical discipline is hard intellectual exercise and is almost beyond his reach. For them the path of detached action is simple and easy to follow. It too leads to liberation.*

Outwardly these two paths appear to be different but in principle they are one and the same. With logical disposition the Lord proves the unity of the two. Firstly he gives the definition of the constant sanyasi.

He is said to be always in renunciation who does not hate nor does he desire. He is beyond all opposites, and is easily freed from bondage. *What is important is total dissolution of one's 'I ness and 'my' ness'.*

Verses 4 to 6

Only an ignorant one thinks that *sãnkhya* and *Yoga* are different paths. But the wise knows that faithful adoption of one fetches the fruits of both. In the end they meet at the same place. The path of renunciation of actions in favour of knowledge is difficult to attain without following the *Yõga* of detached action. *The renunciation is knowledge - based but with detached actions becomes fruitful and **KarmaYõga** is action - based but with the light of knowledge gets illuminated. This is how they merge and fuse into each other.*

Verses 7 to 10

The mental equipoise is the base of action-oriented ***Yõga***. It makes the heart pure, senses obedient, mind stable; all of which result in realising that his ***Atman*** is the ***Atman*** in all creatures. Such enlightened soul though doing action, does not get tainted by it. While moving about in the material world seeing, hearing, touching, smelling, eating, moving, sleeping, breathing, speaking, excreting, grasping, even eye opening and closing, the illuminated soul absorbed in ***Brahman,*** knowing reality realises that he is not doing any of these things but the senses do all such activities resting on their objects. Remaining untouched like a water drop on the lotus leaf he is not tainted by any sin since all his actions are surrendered into ***Brahman.*** When personal ego is detached from actions the senses do not commit any evil and thus such actions have no binding effect on him.

Verses 11 to 13

The Lord elucidates further the nature of the detached attitude. Men of selfless detached action work only with the body, mind, intellect and the sense organs treating them as instruments but without his self involved in it in order to purify his soul. Abandoning the fruits of actions the man fixed in ***Brahman*** finds enduring peace. Whereas the man with unsteady mind, motivated by desire gets attached to fruits and is placed in bondage. Renouncing his actions mentally, mastering his nature, the dweller in the body stays happily in the city of nine gates not doing any thing nor involving others in action.

Verses 14 to 17

Lord shifts the argument to metaphysical reasoning when he proclaims:-

"Godhead produced neither the doer nor the deed nor the union of deeds and fruits. They are activated by their own nature. The Supreme Lord present every where is neither concerned with any body's sin nor merits. Knowledge is covered by ignorance and hence the creatures get deluded". *Apparent diversity in the universe appears real and the Real remains clouded under this delusion of ignorance.*

But those wise whose ignorance is destroyed by divine knowledge, to them shines the splendour of the supreme, their knowledge illuminating like the sun. Their intellect and heart absorbed in the Supreme, making It their sole objective, fully devoted to It they reach that state from where they have no return. Their sins get purified by their knowledge.

Verses 18 to 21

The Lord records one significant factor in this process of self realization. The United state of being one with ***Brahman*** *is achieved in this life here on this earth itself.* ***Karmayõgi*** *becomes* ***Brahmasanstha.*** *The Lord is pleased to glorify his characteristics as he did in case of a man of steady wisdom, i.e., a* ***sthitapradnya*** *in second* ***Adhyaya.***

Such persons of wisdom would see everything as manifestation of ***Brahman*** and separate individualistic identity would disappear for them. Learned and gentle ***Brahmin***, a cow, an elephant, a dog, a dog-eaters all are equal to them. Their minds becoming equipoised, they have conquered this world here itself. ***Brahman,*** the Supreme Reality is blameless and equal in all manifestations; hence they are fully abiding in ***Brahman.***

He is neither happy by getting the pleasant nor unhappy by getting the unpleasant. His intellect becoming stable without having any delusion the knower of ***Brahman*** is absorbed in Brahman.

He remains unattached to external touch of sense objects and enjoys bliss inherent in the self. Having engaged in the ***Yõga*** of ***Brahman*** he attains eternal bliss.

Verses 22 to 28

Pleasures arising out of sense contacts with their objects really generate sorrows. They come and they go. The wise has no interest in them. Here on this earth before leaving the body, one whose perseverance easily master lust begotten and anger-produced impulses finds ***Brahman.*** He is a happy man. His joy, his peace, his visions all are born inwardly. Such a ***Yogi*** becoming ***Brahman*** attains supreme bliss. All impurities diminished, all doubts erased, mind fully controlled and engrossed in the welfare of all beings, the holy sages attain the supreme state of union with ***Brahman.*** Self-controlled, freed from desires and anger, realising the self, the men of austerity always remain close to the state of ***Brahman.***

Keeping off external sense contacts, concentrating his gaze at the root of the eyebrows, equalising inhaling and exhaling breathing within the nostrils, commanding the senses, mind and intellect, getting rid of desire, fear and anger, a sage who is sincerely concerned about his liberation, is really a free soul.

Verses 29

Realisation of *Brahman* the Godhead is the highest goal in life. Means may differ. Lord *Krishna* finally draws the major conclusion:

"Knowing me to be the ultimate enjoyer of all the sacrifices and austerities, the Supreme Lord of all the worlds and the friend of all creatures, that sage obtains peace."

Every soul is as great as the Supreme Lord. Because it is conditioned by various worldly factors it is under control of material nature, i.e., ***Prakriti****. The Lord is the master of everything including this nature. It follows therefore that man's prime duty is to surrender his total existence at his feet to become free from material control.*

(73 A)

Adhyaya 6

Ãtmasanyama Yõga—*Yoga of Meditation*

Introduction

Although only knowledge and nothing else is required to attain liberation, the enlightened man should take up action for the good of the people and with a skill of not allowing these actions to create bondage. They are to be carried out without attachment, acquiring the power of mental equipoise. This is how ***KarmaYõga*** is defined by the Lord and was proved to be superior to the path of renunciation. In the third Adhyaya a mention was made about lust, anger and fear that overpower the senses, mind and intellect of the man and destroy his spiritual as well as material wisdom. Therefore Arjuna was first advised to bring total control over his senses. Now the question arises how to control the senses. The discipline to be practised to reach the state of absorption in ***Brahman*** is the main theme of the sixth ***Adhyaya***.

Verses : 1 to 6

Merely discarding actions is not renunciation. One who does not burn sacrificial fire and does not perform any and ***yoga*** performance a rituals is not a man avowed to renunciation. Real renunciation what has been called Sannayasa is really ***yoga*** lie in discarding the desire for the fruit of action and not the action. Without renouncing future dreams nobody can become ***yogi***. This is how the path of action and path of renunciation get amalgamated. *Lord's preference to the path of detached action is because of its positive side.* The path of action has two distinct stages. The first is the climbing state described as ***ãruruksha***, one who has just begun to climb and the second is, finally reaching the top, described as ***Yõgãrudha***, one who has attained union with ***Brahman***. In the first which is the preparatory stage ***Karma*** or action becomes the means and at the second when ***Yõga*** is perfectly achieved than tranquillity becomes the means.

Yõgarudha, the person elevated in ***Yoga***, is he who renounces all motivated desires and is engaged neither in sense objects nor in fruit bearing action.

Reaching this stage is possible with every one provided he tries to elevate himself by his own efforts and does not engage in degrading his self. Self only is his friend and self alone is his enemy. One who has conquered his lower self by his higher self becomes his own friend and one who can not control his lower self and therefore unable to reach his higher self, his self only remains his enemy.

Here the Lord is emphasising the importance of self-help based on self-freedom. In spiritual journey one has to make his own efforts. By capturing one's self what rewards one gets? The Lord explains.

Verses 7 to 9

Once the mind is conquered and tranquillity is attained his higher self is always absorbed in unitive knowledge a trance and he remains undisturbed in heat or cold, in pain or pleasure, in honour or dishonour.

Earth, stone and gold become all alike to the self - realised ***Yogi***. His self is satisfied through spiritual and inferential knowledge. He remains undisturbed by the external changes due to his conquering the senses. He is said to be one with ***Brahman.***

He treats, friends, comrades and foes, neutrals and mediators, envious and loving, pious and wicked with equal mind. He is considered great.

Verses 10 to 14

The Lord now explains the technique to be adopted to attain this mental state of equanimity.

To shut outside contacts he should stay alone in a solitary place. Exercising full control over his mind, freeing himself from all desires and possessions he should constantly concentrate his will in to ***Atman***. Establishing his seat firmly on place of purity, neither too high nor too low, first covering with ***Kusha*** grass, then with skin then laying a cloth over them, he should sit there fixing his mind on a single point, holding his thoughts and the senses under control and practice this exercise of meditation to purify his self. And he must hold his body, head and neck still and erect fixing his gaze at the tip of his nose not letting the eyes to see elsewhere. Being tranquil in mind, fearless, observing celibacy, holding the mind in check all his thoughts focused on Me, the Lord, he should sit making him alone his final aim.

Verses 15 to 19

After describing the posture and mental attitude, the Lord then enumerates the resulting effects of this ***Yoga*** *practice.* The mediator ***Yogi*** who has conquered his mind, by regularly practising this ***Yõga***, reaches the crowning peace inherently present in me.

The power of mental concentration can be misused in troubling others, therefore the Lord stresses the need of fixing it on God.

This ***Yõga*** is not for him who either eats too much or does excessive fasting, who either sleeps too much or remains wakeful beyond limits. Moderation in eating, recreating, acting, sleeping and walking makes the, ***Yoga*** discipline comfortable by destroying all pains.

Yogi is said to have achieved union with ***Brahman*** when the mind coming under control, and freed from all worldly pleasures, stands absorbed in ***Atman*** alone. "The flame of a lamp does not waver in windless place". The Lord uses this simile to describe a ***Yogi*** who has held his mind in check and who is practising meditation on ***Atman***.

Verses 20 to 23

*The Lord gives the vivid description of the blissful state of **Samadhi**, a trance.*

The mind brought under control by ***Yõga*** practice loses its restless nature and becomes calm. In this state, ***Yõgi*** seeing his Self by the Self experiences the joy of the Self. He enjoys infinite transcendental happiness to be realised and which is beyond the grasp of the senses by the intellect. Staying in this blissful state he remains unmoved. The inmost truth is realised by him. From this position he is not shaken even by the greatest of sorrows. The word ***Yoga*** is to be known as breaking the contacts with sorrows and it is to be practised with firm resolution and without getting disheartened.

Verses 24 to 29

*How to attain this blissful state of **Samadhi** is equally important and the Lord in short explains some aspects of intensive concentration of the mind.*

One should renounce all desires arising out of selfish motives and control all the senses from all sides by using mental force. Then step by step, with the aid of steady intellect and mind fixed in ***Atman*** he should attain tranquillity and need not think of any thing else. The fickle and unsteady mind may wander to whatever direction but he should curb it and bring it back in submission to ***Atman*** only. ***Yõgi*** whose mind is utterly quiet with his passions subdued, sinless as he is, united with ***Brahman*** reaches the highest Bliss. Being freed from evil, always meditating on ***Atman*** the ***Yõgi*** easily attains the highest delight that is produced from the contact with ***Brahman.*** ***Yõgi*** who reaches the state of Brahman -

consciousness and gaining equal vision sees his self present in all beings and all beings present in his Self.

Verses 30 to 32

*Next the Lord brings new awareness to **Arjuna** when he proclaims.*

"For him who sees me every where and every thing in Me, I am nearer lost to him nor he is ever lost to me. ***Yogi*** who is established in me and worships me who is present in all creations remains always in me whatever his present might be".

Of all the ***Yõgis*** he is the perfect one who considers all things alike seeing them as his own self irrespective of his being in happiness or sorrow.

Verses 33 to 36

***Arjuna** raises his doubts about the enduring continuity of the **Yoga** of equal vision because of the restless character of the mind.*

"In this ***Yõga*** of equanimity of mind explained to me by you oh ! ***Madhusudan***, I am unable to see its enduring position due to mind's restlessness. This mind Oh! Krishna ! is not only restless but very strong, turbulent and stubborn and unlike wind, very difficult to tame".

The Lord in reply agrees and says that the mind no doubt is restless and is very difficult to control but by regular practice and dispassionate attitude it can be mastered. For a man having no control over his self, to master this ***Yõga*** is certainly very difficult but he who has control over his self, can easily master it by putting hard efforts and using right means.

Verses 37 to 47

Arjuna raises another doubt and wants to know from the Lord what happens to well-meaning person who earnestly attempts with faith but fails due to insufficient efforts and absence of self-control. His mind runs away from the practice of ***Yõga*** and he fails to attain perfection. What is his future?

Arjuna equates him to scattered cloud and asks further, whether fallen from the path of ***Brahman*** such a confused man misses both the spiritual as well as worldly success. Does he get destroyed like a torn cloud? ***Arjuna*** requests the Lord to remove his doubt altogether since no one else is capable of tearing this doubt.

In all endeavours failure is a grate deterrent factor. The Lord explains with assurance.

"Oh ***Arjuna*** ! Such a man is never lost either in this world or the next. Oh dear, he who embarks upon the auspicious work never ends in peril."

A man fallen from the practice of ***Yõga*** reaches the world of blessed ones and stays there for many long years and thereafter is reborn in the home of pure and rich parents or it is possible that he may be born in a family of intelligent ***yõgis***. But such a birth in this world is very rare. There he gets back his intelligence and expertise earned in his previous body and from there he again strives harder to attain perfection. His previous practice automatically drags him to progress. Acquiring basic knowledge, even a man of inquisitive quest taking primary steps progresses further than the performers of ***Vedic*** rituals. But the ***Yõgi*** getting cleansed of his impurities struggling very hard and advancing gradually to perfection through many births ultimately reaches the supreme goal.

Lord ***Krishna*** now advises Arjuna to become a ***yogi*** of his special choice. He proclaims.

"***Yõgi***, the man meditating on Brahman is greater than the ascetics who mortify their bodies, is still greater than the learned. He is also greater than those who do motivated works. Therefore ***Arjuna*** should become a ***Yõgi***.

But even among all the ***Yõgis*** the Lord considers him the best who fully united with Him; worships him in faith with his heart completely merged into him.

(79 A)

Adhyaya 7

Dnyãn-Vidnyãna Yõga - *Yoga of Knowledge and Experience*

Introduction

*Sixth **Adhyãya** dealt with the practice of meditation as an effective way to bring sense - mind - intellect combination under control to kill lust and anger, two powerful enemies which obstruct discriminative knowledge and self - realisation. In the seventh **Adhyaya** the Lord finds it necessary to throw discerning light on the nature of Absolute **Brahman.** He is preparing **Arjuna** to receive full knowledge required to realise It, keeping direct spiritual experience in the centre. The Lord also describes many other ways that lead to self - realisation. In addition to knowing the pure nature of the **Atman**, the Lord wants **Arjuna** to know **Brahman** in its totality including Its manifestations that collectively make the universe.*

Verses 1 to 7

The Lord urges ***Arjuna*** to listen how with the mind intent on Him, making Him his only shelter and practising ***Yõga*** he would be able to know Him fully without any doubt. The Lord promises him teaching of direct knowledge of unitive experience as well as all knowledge about the manifested universe knowing which nothing else in this world remains to be known.

"Among thousands of men perhaps one endeavours for perfection, out of those who try and achieve perfection hardly anyone realises me in my true nature."

Thus pointing out the most difficult nature of spiritual journey, the Lord proceeds to educate Arjuna about the essential nature of the Absolute. Here - onwards emerges the clearly defined Indian view of human body and the soul.

Earth, water, fire, air, ether, mind, intellect and ego, appearing differentiated in this eight fold form is my nature called ***Prakriti***. This is my lower nature called ***Aparã Prakriti***. Also know, behind this and distinct from it, there is my higher nature called ***Parã Prakriti*** which appears as 'living beings as the ***'Jiva'*** on whom the whole world depends for its sustenance'.

Here the individual existence is clearly divided into two integrated parts, the world of matter, appearing as body and the differentiated consciousness appearing as soul. Thus every individual has two aspects, body and soul, ***Sharir*** *and* ***Atma****, the field and the knower of the field.*

"Know this ***Prakriti*** as the womb of all creation. I am the origin and also the dissolution of this entire world. There is nothing superior to me. All things are held by me as the gems are strung on a thread".

Verses 8 to 12

There is nothing in this world different or separate from the Absolute **Brahman.** *Supreme Lord can be known by his different energies and qualities which are so essential to make the object that particular object. Active principle existing in the objects is representative fraction of the Absolute. Lord* **Krishna** *quotes few of his opulence.*

"I am the taste of water, I am the light of the moon and the sun, I am the syllable Om in ***Vedas***, sound in the sky, and manliness in men".

I am the holy fragrance of the earth, splendour in the fire, the life in all creatures, I am the penance of the ascetics. Know me as the eternal seed of entire creation, I am the intelligence of the intelligent, the vigour of the powerful. I am the strength of the strong who are devoid of passion and desire. In creatures I am the desire that does not transgress virtue.

Whatever states of sattwa, (the pure), rajas (the active), and tamas (the lazy) exist they all proceed from me alone. Try to understand this. Yet I am not in them but they are in me."

Verses 13 to 19

The Absolute manifests in everything but still remains beyond all. It means that though the universal diversity is the creation of the Absolute, this diversity does not exist in the Absolute which has no attributes. This is the magical power of the Absolute ***Brahman.***

Thus the Absolute is beyond the phenomenal world. To know It one has to cross the barriers of this illusory world. The Lord starts explaining why the world can not know the Absolute that encompasses everything.

Deluded by these manifestations of three ***gunas*** of ***Prakriti*** the whole world fails to recognise the Absolute which stays beyond them all, supreme and inexhaustible.

Guna-oriented senses create illusions. The Lord describes the formidable nature of the Divine Power when he states.

"How hard indeed to cross this my ***Māyā***, the divine power which is made up of the ***gunas***. Only those who faithfully surrender into me can easily pass beyond this ***Māyā***, and no one else." Those fools involved in bad deeds and who are the worst among men, do not surrender unto me. Their knowledge is destroyed by illusions, and they really belong to demoniac nature.

Those virtuous ones who worship me are classified in four categories. They are: The person in distress, the seeker of knowledge, the seeker of wealth and the man of enlightenment described as ***ãrta, jidnyãsu, arthãrthi*** and ***Dnyãni*** respectively.

Dnyani, the man of enlightened wisdom who is constantly in union with ***Brahman*** and who is solely devoted to me alone is the best among them all. " I am very dear to him and he is dear to Me. says the Lord.

All these devotees really are very noble but the enlightened one, I consider as my very Self, because fully absorbed in ***Yõga*** he establishes himself in Me alone as the highest goal. At the end of many births this man of divine knowledge realising all this as God ***Vãsudeva*** reaches me. Such a great soul is very rare.

Significance of these four categories of devotees needs to be properly understood. God's worship with worldly motives make the worship of inferior nature. So also the seeker of knowledge is still unripe and he is far away from perfection. They are all people with good intentions traversing a good path. But the enlightened soul has nothing to gain; still he offers a selfless service. Certainly he is the best.

Verses 20 to 23

Now one may ask a question. If everywhere there is only one Absolute present why do people worship different types of gods and goddesses and what kind of fruits they get out of that worship? The Lord explains :

Men whose understanding is stolen away by worldly desires and who are controlled by their natural impulses, adopting their own cults and rituals resort to various other deities.

"I make his faith firm in the deity of his choice in whatever form the devotee wishes to worship it with faith. Accepting that faith he cherishes to worship that deity and obtains from it the desired fruits. In fact these benefits are bestowed on him by me alone."

But the fruits these men of little intelligence get are perishable. The worshippers of gods go to gods so also my devotees come to me.

Verses 24 to 30

In this universe there is nothing except the Absolute ***Brahman.*** *So all other deities, their worshippers, their longings, their fruits - all are nothing but the Absolute. Only the worshippers under the delusion of ignorance fall short of their prayers. They do not know that the Absolute Supreme Lord is the real giver.*

The Lord clarifies further:

"The ignorant ones not knowing my real, changeless and supreme nature, think that I, the unmanifest have appeared in personal form."

He is not visible to many since he is covered by his creative power called ***Māya***. This deluded world does not know Him who is birthless and changeless.

The Lord tells ***Arjuna*** how to free oneself from the veil of ***Māya***.

"Oh ***Arjuna,*** I know all the creatures of the past, the present and the future. But no one knows me".

All living beings are born into delusion created by the pairs of opposites that arise from desire and hatred.

But the sinless men of meritorious deeds who are freed from this delusion created by the pair of opposites, worship Him remaining firm in their resolve. They who surrender unto Him striving to get free from old age and death, fully realise ***Brahman***, the Absolute, the nature of ***Atman***, the self and all action.

They continue acquiring knowledge even at the time of death getting enlightened about the supreme power of the God head called ***Adhiyadnya***, the nature of the phenomenal world, the ***Adhibhuta*** and the individual soul, the ***Adhidaiva***.

By mentioning this specific terminology, the Lord introduces the subject matter of the eighth ***Adhyãya***.

Adhyaya 8
Akshara Brahma Yõga—*Yoga of Eternal Brahma*

Introduction

The Lord is continuing his discourse on ***Dnyãn*** *which is direct and immediate intuitive knowledge of the Absolute as well as* ***Vidnyãn*** *which deals with nature of phenomenal world of matter. Metaphysical terms like* Brahman, ***Adhyatma****,* ***Karma****,* ***Adhibhuta,*** ***Adhidaiva*** *and* ***Adhiyadnya*** *are briefly explained giving their concise definitions. Different people conceive the idea of the creator differently. Gita's monastic theory is based on* ***Vedant*** *that propounded one universal principle manifesting in different objects through its divine power. Diversity is a manifestation and Absolute behind it is the origin. 8th* ***Adhyãya*** *clarifies the important aspects of Indian system of cosmology.*

Verses 1 to 4

Arjuna asks Lord ***Krishna*** to explain to him what is meant by ***Brahma*** and ***Adhyatma***. What is ***Karma***? What is said to be ***Adhibhuta*** and ***Adhidaiva***? Who is ***Adhiyadnya*** in this body and how? And how can the self-controlled men know the Lord at the time of death?

The Lord explains these terms by giving brief definitions. He defines ***Brahma*** as that which is indestructible and independent of any cause, existence by itself. *It is the dormant creative force behind all beings and manifestations. It is Absolute, Supreme and Eternal.*

Adhyatma is defined as the constant and natural state of ***Brahman*** *dwelling within the individual being called* ***Atman***.

It is the self that stands behind the senses, mind and intellect of an individual.

Karma is defined as the creative activity that is in constant action of sending forth manifestations from the unmanifest ***Brahman.*** *The divergent universal creation in constant cyclic movement without a doer is what is called* ***Karma****.*

Adhibhuta is the relative world of our experience taking some forms and names ***(Nam Rupa)*** and is always perishable. *Its existence is transitory. It is born out of the combinations of five elements; earth, water, fire, air, and ether, the body made out of them, and the phenomenal world of matter. It is destructible in nature.*

Adhidaiva is in principle ***Brahman*** itself but due to ignorance and as if separated from the Absolute ***Brahman*** gets deluded by the bodily identity and ego consciousness, takes interest in worldly affairs and experiences joy and sorrow. *It is called 'jiva'. As if it is the deity of a body it is called* ***Adhidaiva****.* ***Adhiyadnya*** is that state of oneness in the ***Adhidaiva, Adhibhuta*** and Brahman. *It is achieved only after disappearance of ego-consciousness of the self. Everything in this body is Absolute* ***Brahman.*** *Knowledge of this unity is* ***Adhiyadnya****.*

Verses 5 to 8

Thus explaining the metaphysical terms the Lord answers ***Arjuna's*** last question how are you revealed to the self controlled at the hour of death.

"He who remembering me alone at the time of death discarding his body, quits this world becomes one with my nature". There is no doubt about this.

Because while quitting the body whatever a man remembers due to his life long interests he achieves that state only due to his constant absorption in it.

Therefore ***Arjuna*** is advised to engage in fight, always remembering the Lord. When his mind and intellect are concentrated on the Lord, he is sure to attain him without a shadow of a doubt.

One who constantly contemplates on the Supreme Lord by engaging his mind in the practice of meditation without causing any distraction, certainly reaches the divine.

For one's liberation, the Lord emphasises on the prolonged and non-wavering, constant devotion to him. The last minute - repentance will not do.

Verses 9 to 16

Concentration of mind through devotion and by the power of ***Yõga*** and fixing his life-breath between his eyebrows who follows this attains the divine and supreme personality of the Lord.

The Lord intends to enlighten ***Arjuna*** about that state described as the Imperishable by the learned in ***Vedas***, entered into by the great sages of non attached character and for the attainment of which one practices celibacy.

Leaving his body he who quits this world by closing all the gates of the senses, holding the mind firmly into his heart, fixating the life force between his eyebrows, chanting the sacred syllable ***Om,*** the symbol of ***Brahman,*** concentrating through ***Yõga*** and constantly remembering the Lord, reaches the Supreme goal.

With undistracted mind when a ***Yõgi*** constantly meditating on the Lord always remembers him, The Lord is easily attainable by that ***Yõga***.

These great souls who have the highest perfection after attaining the Lord, do not get the rebirth which is a home of sorrows and is transitory in nature.

The Lord clarifies further that all the world right from the heavenly place of ***Brahma*** the creator, to the worlds of lower plane are subject to rebirth. Only by reaching the Lord one escapes rebirth.

Verses 17 to 22

The Lord now describes the cycle of universal creation with its time duration.

The men who understand that the day of ***Brahma,*** the procreator is of thousand aeons and his night also is of thousand aeons long, they are the knowers of day and night.

At the dawn of the day all the entities come forth into manifestations from the unmanifest and with the arrival of night all are dissolved into the same state known as the unmanifest.

The same swarm of creatures successively coming into being gets, helplessly, dissolved with the fall of night and return back to manifestations with the arrival of the day.

The unmanifest, the source of all creation in this context is known as ***Prakriti***. *The Lord brings out distinct features of Avyakta **Prakriti** and Avyakta* Brahman.

But behind this unmanifest there is another higher unmanifest which is eternal. Existence and which does not get perished even after all creation is destroyed.

It has been called 'imperishable Unmanifest' Avyakta Akshar. It is also called as the supreme destination. Those who reach It never return. That is his highest abode. That Supreme Lord in whom all creatures exist and by whom this universe is pervaded can only be attained through unswerving devotion to him alone.

Verses 22 to 28

*The Lord continues the topic by detailing the paths of return and no return available to **yogis** as per the time of their deaths.* Knowers of ***Brahman*** who quit this world by the path that covers the fire, the light, the day, moon's bright fortnight and six monthly journey of the sun to the North reach the ***Brahman*** the Absolute.

Whereas the ***yõgi*** who quits this world during the time that covers the smoke, the night, moon's dark fortnight and the six monthly journey of the sun to the south availing the lunar light return back to birth in the end.

The path of light and the other of darkness; these are considered to be two eternal paths of this world. He who takes the first does not return back, but who takes second returns back.

Here the Lord symbolically presents the spiritual truth using the opposite states of light and darkness suggesting there- by the power of knowledge and the evil of ignorance that play their parts in one's life in granting liberation or bondage respectively. The Lord then concludes.

Yõgi who understands these two paths never gets deluded. Hence ***Arjuna*** is advised to be always in unitive knowledge of Brahman.

Yõgi knowing all this wisdom goes beyond the fruits of merits earned by studying ***Vedas***, performing ritualistic sacrifices, practising penance and giving alms etc. He reaches the highest abode which is the origin of everything.

Adhayaya 9

Rãjavidyã Rãjaguhya Yõga—*Yoga of Mysticism*

Introduction

The eighth ***Adhyãya*** *ended with a note of glorification of* ***Brahman****-conscious state to be attained through devotional meditation. This state surpasses all pious fruits derived from studying* ***Vedas****, performing sacrifices or austere penance's and giving charity etc. Knowing the Absolute he reaches the highest abode. Path of meditation requires the physical and mental control through the practice of* ***Pãtanjal Yõga****. Concentrating one's mind on syllable* Om, *the symbolic representation of the* ***Brahman,*** *the Absolute, is an essential factor in this exercise. However effective this method be it is very difficult for* common *men to follow it. Getting the knowledge of Imperishable Unmanifest and to attain the state of transcendental bliss remains beyond* common *man's reach. Understanding this difficulty the Lord opens up a royal path easily to be practised by anybody irrespective of his mental, intellectual and physical power. This is the path of devotion wherein the Absolute Formless* ***Brahman*** *appears in the manifested form and becomes the object of personal love. The theme of the ninth* ***Adhyaya*** *is* ***Saguna bhakti****, the devotion of the God manifesting in human form.*

Verses 1 to 6

The Lord promises ***Arjuna*** that he would impart to him the most profound of the secrets, the Divine knowledge of God along with the knowledge of Its universal manifestations in physical world. This enlightenment will free him from the evil.

This knowledge is royal and supreme, the king of secrets, the most sacred realised through the direct experience, of righteous nature, easy to be practised and eternal.

But those who do not keep faith in this sacred path fail to attain him and again return back on this path of mortal world.

The supreme Lord has pervaded this entire universe by His unmanifest nature. All creatures exist within him but the Lord does not exist in them. And yet these creatures do not exist in him. Know this as His miraculous power, the divine mystery. He being the very source of creation and though sustains all creatures, he does not exist in them. As the mighty wind wandering every where always stays in the sky, know in the same manner these creatures stay in him.

Godhead being in two opposing forms, one ***nirguna****, having no attributes and the second* ***saguna*** *having attributes these contradictory statements arise. The Lord's mystic power is beyond intellectual understanding. The Lord now turns up to describing the cycle of creation.*

Verses 7 to 10

At the end of the ***kalpa*** of millennium years all these creatures return to his nature called ***Prakriti*** and at the beginning of another ***kalpa,*** he again brings them out.

Activating his divine power called ***Prakriti*** he automatically and repeatedly creates the entire cosmic order which is helpless being under the control of ***Prakriti***.

But these acts do not bind him because he remains indifferent and totally detached from such activities.

Under his supervision this ***Prakriti*** produces moving and non-moving beings and that is why this world spins into creation and dissolution.

Verses 11 to 19

*Even after creating the entire universe how is it that the Absolute **Brahman** remains action less? Every entity is born according to its own **Karma** in previous life and the Godhead has no hand in it. After explaining the cycle of creation, the Lord briefly describes the two categories of people divine and demoniac.*

The ignorant fools insult him who has taken a human form not knowing his status as the Lord of all beings. These people take the shelter of demoniac and monstrous but attractive nature. Vain are their hopes and in vain their activities. Their knowledge in vain. They are lost in madness. But the great souls who possess the divine nature worship him with undivided mind knowing him as the eternal source of all living entities.

Always chanting his glories, striving hard with steadfast vows, offering salutations to him and always following ***Yoga***, they worship him.

Others worship him with the sacrifice of knowledge realising ***Brahman*** everywhere, in one form or many forms or in the universal form.

The Lord starts describing his presence in various things of noble existence. He says "I am the sacrificial rituals, I am the sacrifice. I am the offering made to forefathers. I am the medicinal herbs. I am the ***mantra,*** hymn. I am the purified butter. I am the fire and I am the oblation offered.

I am the father of this world. I am the mother, the sustainer; the grandfather. I am the goal of knowledge, I am the sacred **Om** I am ***Rik, sama*** and ***yajus.***

I am the place where the journey ends, I am the sustainer, the Lord, the witness, the refuge, the friend. I am the beginning and the dissolution, I am the preservation, the resting place and the seed that is imperishable. I offer heat, I send and withdraw rains. I am the nectar, I am the death. I am the real, I am the unreal.

Verses 20 to 28

The Lord presented a brief picture of diversity of forms of the Absolute Godhead and it's relationship with it's creation Now he starts telling the difference between the worship of the Higher and the worship of the lower.

Those well versed in triple vedas, the drinker of ***sõma*** juice and whose sins are purified, worship Him by offering sacrifices and pray for heavenly abode. And attaining the sacred world of heaven there they enjoy godly pleasures.

Having enjoyed pleasures of specious heaven, they return to the mortal world once their merits are exhausted. Thus following the path of rites of ***Vedas*** and motivated by sense enjoyment they obtain the constant cycle of birth and death.

The Lord brings to our attention his important obligation when he proclaims: -

I take care in fulfilling the needs and protecting the possessions of those who become constantly absorbed in me by their worship of undistracted meditation upon me.

Verses 28 to 34

And those devotees who worship the other deities with faith, they too really worship me but in a wrong way. I am the only enjoyer and the Lord of all sacrifices. But they do not understand me in my true transcendental nature and therefore they fall down.

The worshippers of gods go to gods, the worshippers of the forefathers go to the forefathers, worshippers of the spirits go to the spirits and those who worship me, they come to me. In fact all types of worships reach the Supreme God only but because they are ignorant about the Supreme Godhead they miss reaching him. The fruits of worship depends on the level of worship. Even these lower fruits are granted by the Supreme God only.

"The devotee who offers Me with love a leaf, or a flower or a fruit or mere water I accept that offering gifted to me with devotion and pure heart".

The Lord therefore advises Arjuna to offer Him whatever he does, whatever he eats, whatever sacrifice he performs, whatever he gives, whatever austerities he performs. Everything he should offer to God.

Thus he will be freed from the bondage of his actions and their auspicious and inauspicious results. Arjuna has to engage his mind in the spirit of renunciation of actions so that getting liberated he would reach the Lord.

The Lord had referred to easy and happy nature of the devotional worship in the beginning of this ***Adhyaya****. Now he is referring to another great virtue of equanimity of the mind. The Lord says :-*

"In all creatures I am equal I hate nobody so also I love no body. But those who devotedly worship me they are in Me and I am also in them.

Even if a man be a big sinner if he worships me whole heatedly he should be regarded holy because of his right resolution. He at once becomes the great soul and attains eternal peace. "The Lord proclaims" Arjuna, be certain that my devotee-never perishes.

"They may be the men of lower births, may they be women or vaishya or shudra they also reach the highest spiritual realisation if they take refuge in me. Then this will also be true of holy Brahamins, pious devotees, and saintly kings."

Arjuna, therefore is advised to worship the Lord, finding himself in this transient and sorrowful world. Becoming the Lord's devotee, with his heart always merged into him he should bow down to him surrendering his self completely in the service of the Lord so that in the end he would reach him.

Adhayaya 10
Vibhooti Yõga - *Yoga of Divine Glory*

Introduction

The single Absolute brings out of itself the diversity of the universal manifestations. Unmanifest is the cause of the manifest and itself is beginningless, having no cause. It is the source of everything. On account of it everything evolves and functions. The Unmanitest is very difficult to contemplate upon. The 9th ***Adhyãya*** *dealt with various modes of devotion to worship God in his manifest forms. Lord had enumerated certain objects, essences and energies in which the Absolute manifested.* ***Arjuna*** *became curious to know all forms of the Lord's manifestations and accordingly he puts up a question.*

Verses 1 to 7

The Lord begins with expressing his love for Arjuna in whom he finds a receptive mind that gets delighted by his teachings of high order. He is interested in his well-being, so the Lord urges him to listen.

The Lord states that even seers and the ***devas*** are unable to know his root because he is their origin by all means. He declares that he who knows him birth less, having no beginning and the Lord of all worlds does not get deluded and is freed from all sins.

The Lord explains in what way he is the Lord of everything. Intellect, knowledge, doubtlessness, perseverance, truth, control of senses, calmness, joy and sorrow, existence and non-existence, fear and fearlessness, non-violence equanimity of mind, satisfaction, penance, charity, fame and infamy.... These varied states expressed in many natures of living beings are produced by him alone... *Thus all emotional and intellectual qualities and experiences are induced by the Eternal Principle.*

Seven great sages, the ancient four and ***Manus*** belong to his nature and were the products of his mind. From them descended the living beings on this earth.

One who truly knows this opulence and mystic power of him, practising ***Yõga*** with undeterred mind doubtlessly attains union with him.

Verses 8 to 11

"I am the source of everything and all things evolve from me. Knowing this the men of wisdom worship Me with their hearts full of devotion". Proclaiming this the Lord showers praise on such worshippers and narrates what rewards he grants them in return of their devotion.

Their thoughts, their life forces are always absorbed in him. Instructing each other and singing his glory they remain happy and contented.

To such devotees of constant awareness and love towards him, he grants mental steadiness by which they are able to reach him. Out of compassion for them and still remaining in his own nature the Lord dispels their ignorance by Himself lighting the lamp of knowledge in their hearts. The Lord himself strengthens the devotion and the steadfastness of his devotees who are constantly engaged in his worship.

Verses 12 to 18

Filled with divine emotions Arjuna became curious to know more about the glorious aspects of the Lord. He minced no words in showering high praise on the Lord. He uttered:

"You are ***ParaBrahma,*** the Supreme Absolute, ***Param Dham***, the highest abode, utterly holy, a great purifier. You are the self glowing Eternal Lord, the first God, birthless and all pervading."

Arjuna cites the words of sages and the words of ***Narada, Deval, Asit, Vysã*** including the Lord's own words which praised the Lord in the same glory as ***Arjuna*** did. ***Arjuna*** frankly admits that whatever has been taught to him by the Lord he accepts it as the truth. Neither gods nor the demons comprehend his manifested form. Calling him the great Lord the source of all life, master of all creatures, God of gods and the Lord of the world Arjuna declares that the Lord alone knows what he is by his own nature. ***Arjuna*** urges the Lord to speak to him, holding back nothing, his divine opulence by which pervading all these worlds he stays within and beyond them. ***Arjuna*** asks the Lord how he would recognise Him while constantly meditating on him and in what various forms He should be contemplated upon. He pleads to the Lord to narrate all his divine power and his divine manifestations again at length because he would never be fully satisfied listening to his nectar-like words.

Verses 19 to 30

The Lord responds to Arjuna's prayer and agrees to narrate his divine opulence of prominent nature only since his extensions have no limit. The Lord begins:

"Oh ***Arjuna***! I am the ***Atman*** occupying the hearts of all living beings. I am the beginning, the middle and the end of all beings. I am ***Vishnu*** of the ***Adityas***, I am the radiant sun among the luminous, I am ***Marichi*** among the wind Gods and among night stars I am the moon.

Among ***Vedas*** I am ***Sãma Veda,*** I am ***Indra*** among heavenly gods. I am the mind among the senses. Among living beings I am the moving force. I am ***Shankar*** among the ***Rudras*** and the Lord of the wealth among ***Yakshas*** and ***Rakshasas*** I am fire among ***vasus*** and among mountain peaks I am ***Meru***. Among priests know me the chief ***Brihaspati***, among generals I am ***Skanda***. I am ocean among waters.

I am ***Bhrigu*** among great sages, Among spoken words I am the single syllable ***Om,*** Among the sacrifices I am the silent prayer and among the immovables I am the ***Himalayas***.

Among the trees I am the ***Banyan*** tree. Among godly sages I am ***Narad***, among gandharvas, the celestial musicians I am ***Chitraratha*** and I am the sage ***Kapila*** among the perfected souls. Among horses sprung out of the nectar-churning know me ***Uchaishravas*** I am ***Airavat*** among royal elephants. I am the king among men. Among weapons I am the thunderbolt, among cows. I am ***Kamadhenu*** I am the love God ***Madan*** among the creators of life. I am ***Vasuki*** among serpents. I am ***Ananta*** among the snakes. I am ***Varuna*** among all aquatics. Among departed fathers I am ***Aryama***. Among the controllers I am ***Yama,*** the god of death. I am ***Prahlad*** among the demons, Among those who measure I am the time. I am the lion among the beasts and among birds I am ***Vainateya,*** the Garuda.

Verses 31 to 42

Among the purifiers I am the wind. I am ***Rama*** among warriors. Among the fishes I am crocodile. I am ***Ganga*** among rivers.

I am the beginning, the middle and the end of all creation. I am spiritual learning among all leanings. I am the logic among arguments.

Among letters I am "v" among the compounds I am the dual compound. I am the endless time, I am the sustainer with faces to all directions.

I am death that devours all. I am the source of all that to happen. Among feminine I am fame, prosperity, speech, memory, intelligence, steadfastness and patience. I am the great ***Sama*** of all the ***Vedic*** hymns, among the poetic metres I am ***Gãyatri***. I am ***Mãrgashirsha*** among the months and among seasons I am the spring full of flowers. I am the gambling of the deceitful. I am the splendour of the splendid, I am triumph, I am the enterprise and I am virtue of the virtuous.

I am ***Vasudeva*** among ***Vrishnis*** I am ***Dhananjay*** among ***Pandavas;*** I am, ***Vyasa*** among sages; among great thinkers I am ***Ushana*** (the Great ***Shukracharya***, the master of demons).

Among the rulers I am sceptre; among those who seek victory I am morality. Among the secrets I am silence and I am wisdom of the wise.

"Oh ***Arjuna*** I am the seed of all created things Nothing in this world movable or immovable can exist without me".

Lord **Krishna** *while summing up the various aspects of the Absolute Brahman mentions about its divine power by comparing it with the generating seed. The Lord now concludes by taking the discourse to higher plane. He declares.*

"There is no limit to my divine manifestations. What I have said to you is merely an indication of the vast expanse of my opulence.

"Whatever in this world is powerful, beautiful and glorious that you may know to have sprung from a fraction of my splendour.

But what need is there to know all this huge variety, oh ***Arjuna***? Pervading this entire universe by a single fragment of myself I exist sustaining it."

Adhayaya 11

Vishwaroopadarshana Yõga—*Yoga of Universal Form*

Introduction

In the 10th ***Adhyãya***, to satisfy ***Arjuna's*** curiosity the Lord gave a vivid description of his divine aspects by enumerating certain selected examples. From macroscopic to microscopic things, animate as well as inanimate, moving, non-moving as well. ***Arjuna*** saw behind everything the Absolute as the animating force. It penetrates into material, emotional and intellectual qualities of the manifested objects. The formless ***Brahman*** through its magical form of ***Ishwara*** crates everything and remains immanent in it. The formless ***Brahman*** is difficult to comprehend and can not be seen. Extensive manifestations decried by the Lord induced Arjuna to see for himself the cosmic form of ***Ishwara*** who is the creater, the sustainer and the destroyer.

Verse l to 4

Arjuna was delighted by the Lord's grace in showing him the grandeur of his divine manifestations. He expresses his gratitude in befitting words.

"You have taught me this profoundest secret of spiritual matters to do me a kind favour. By these words of yours my delusion has disappeared. Oh Lotus eyed one! I have learnt from you, extensively about the origin and the dissolution of creatures and about your inexhaustible glories.

Oh Great Lord! If you are as you have described yourself to be, then, oh Supreme Person, I wish to see your divine form.

If you think it possible that I can see that form, then, Oh master of ***Yõga***, reveal to me your eternal form.

Verse 5 to 8

Lord Krishna promptly responded to ***Arjuna's*** sincere prayer and he promised to show him his divine forms in hundreds and thousands, various in kinds, various in colour and various in shapes. He tells Arjuna to see the Adityas and the Vasus and the ***Rudras*** and the ***Ashwins*** and ***Maruts***. Showing him first these various classes of celestial beings Lord asks him to see many more wonderful things which no one had ever seen before.

The Lord promises Arjuna that he would see this very day the entire universe with things, animate and inanimate and whatever else he may wish to see, gathered into one place in the body of the Lord.

But it was not possible to see him thus with human eyes, therefore the Lord offers to give ***Arjuna*** divine sight through his ***yõgic*** power.

Verses 9 to 14

Now Arjuna is well equipped to bear the avalanche of God's most dreadful cosmic form. ***Sanjaya*** who was reporting this whole episode to Dhritarashtra was struck with awe when he himself could see that great master of ***Yõga*** revealing to ***Arjuna*** his supreme and divine form. ***Sanjaya*** describes this form having innumerable mouths and eyes, with many marvellous aspects, glittering with divine ornaments, brandishing heavenly weapons, wearing celestial garlands, anointed with scents of heavenly fragrance. All was wondrous, brilliant, limitless and with mouths appearing all over. If thousand suns were to rise in the sky with their brilliance at once shining, that might resemble the effulgence of the Supreme Lord in that universal form.

Sanjay further narrates. Then Arjuna saw the entire universe though other wise divided in many parts was brought together in one place in the body of the God of gods.

Verses 15 to 31

Arjuna was wonderstruck with his hair standing erect. He bowed his head before the Lord in adoration and with folded hands said:

"Oh Lord, I see gods and all creatures in their specified groups present within your body. I see ***Brahma***, the creator sitting on lotus flower, also see all the sages and divine serpents.

I have lost the sense of directions. Oh Lord I am totally bewildered.

There I see sons of ***Dhitarashtra***, along with the hosts of kings and ***Bhishma, Drona, Karma*** along with our own chief warriors gushing into your fearful mouths which look so dreadful due to your grinding teeth. Some are seen trapped under your teeth with their heads crushed to dust.

As the swift gushing streams of the rivers flow into the ocean so do all these warriors of human world burning in flames rush to your mouths.

As the month swiftly enter into the burning flames and get destroyed, so also these people rushing into your month with full speed - meet their destruction.

Swallowing all these people from all sides by your burning mouths you are licking them. Oh Vishnu ! Filling the entire universe by your effulgence your terrible rays are scorching it.

. Getting Awestruck and frightened Arjuna is puzzled and dazedly asks the Lord about the actual mission of this devastating experience.

"Oh Lord of Lords, I bow down to you Have mercy on me and tell me who you are so forceful in form. I wish to know your original nature because I do not know your functions.

I am seeing your endless form with many arms, many bellies, many mouths and many eyes but Oh ! Lord of the universe, Oh! Universal form, I see neither your end nor the middle nor the beginning.

I am seeing your glowing form which otherwise is difficult to see. I see you wearing a crown, holding a club and a disc. You are blazing like a fiery sun in a immeasurable way.

You are known as the Imperishable Supreme. You are the Ultimate resting Abode of this universe. You are inexhaustible. You are the protector of eternal religion. For me you are the eternal Supreme Lord.

I see you without any beginning, middle and end. You possess unlimited power. You have innumerable arms. The sun and the moon are your eyes. I see you with blazing fire coming out of your month. Your radiance is heating up the entire universe.

By you alone is pervaded the sky and the earth including all space in between and all the directions. Oh! Great soul, seeing your awful and terrible form all the three worlds tremble.

There the groups of demigods are entering in you. Some of them greatly frightened are offering you prayers with folded hands. Uttering 'peace' the hosts of great sages and the perfected beings are singing your praise with hymns of adoration.

The ***Rudras,*** the ***Adityas,*** the ***Vasus,*** the ***Ashwins,*** the ***Maruts,*** the ***Gandharvas,*** the ***Yakshas*** the ***Asuras*** and the ***Siddhas*** are all beholding you in wonder.

Seeing your great form with mouths, eyes arms, legs, bellies and terrifying teeth in manifold numbers all the worlds are frightened including myself.

Seeing you reaching the sky with your glowing colours, your mouth widely opened, big eyes shining, my inner soul is trembling and oh ***Vishnu,*** I have lost my courage and peace,

Oh God of gods, oh shelter of the world, seeing your mouths looking fierce due to your terrible teeth and resembling with the fire flames of death.

Verse 32 to 34

The Lord replies ***Arjuna's*** question pointing to his all devouring nature.

"I am the time, the supreme destroyer of the worlds and growing so big I have come to destroy all people even if you are not there (to fight) all the soldiers of opposing sides will not remain. (As they will be slain)

Arjuna is thus motivated by the Lord to rise and fight to win the war. By conquering the enemies he should enjoy the prosperous kingdom. ***Arjuna*** should become a mere cause because his enemies are already slain by the Lord (in his design)

"You should kill, ***Drõna,*** and ***Bhishma*** and ***Jayadratha*** and Kana and other great warriors who have already been killed by me. Do not worry. Just fight. You will conquer your enemies in the battle."

Verse 35 to 51

Sanjaya then reports to ***Dhritarashtra*** how ***Arjuna*** after hearing the words of Lord ***Krishna,*** folding his hands bowed down to the Lord with his body trembling. With great fear he again spoke to ***Krishna*** in a choking voice. His heart was full of devotion.

The Cosmic revelation brought complete transformation in Arjuna. He started showering words of praise on his master.

"Oh, Master of the sense, It is in fitness of things that the world gets delighted in singing your praise and becomes attached to you. At your sight, however the demons flee to all directions in terror. But the hosts of perfected souls offer salutations to you."

And why should not they offer these salutations to you who is greater than the ***Brahma,*** the original creator? Oh endless one, Lord of gods, ultimate abode of the world, you are eternal, you are exists and what are what exist not and what transcends them.

You are the first God, you are the ancient ***Purusha,*** you are the ultimate refuge of this cosmos. You are the known, you are all that is knowable, You are the highest goal, Oh of infinite forms, this Universe is pervaded by you.

You are the wind, you are the death, you are the fire, you are the water, you are the moon and you are ***Prajapatti*** the great grandfather. Unto you my thousand salutations. Again and again I salute you.

I bow down to you from the front from behind and from all sides, oh All!

Oh! of boundless power, you are of limitless glory. You cover all therefore you are everything.

Carelessly I addressed you as "Oh ***Keshav***, Oh ***Yadav,*** Oh friend" considering you my comrade. Not knowing your greatness I might have done this out of foolishness or love.

I have disregarded you many times jesting in relaxation, while lying down or sitting or while eating, at times alone or in company of others. Please forgive me for all these offences oh, immeasurable one!

For, you are the father of this moving and unmoving world. You alone are worthy of worship. You are the great master. No one is equal to you. Who can then surpass you in three worlds? Oh Lord of infinite power'

Therefore bowing down my body I offer my salutations to you who is the Lord of my worship, to seek your mercy. Oh God, forgive me as father forgives his son, a friend forgives his friend and a lover forgives his beloved.

I am delighted seeing that universal form which no one had ever seen before. But still my mind is fearful and disturbed. Therefore have mercy on me, and reveal to me your earlier form Oh Lord of gods. Oh abode of the world.

I wish to see you with crown, holding mace and a disc in your hands. Therefore please appear in your earlier four-armed form, Oh thousand armed one ! Pleased with Arjuna's prayer, the Lord responded positively and said to Arjuna.

"Oh Arjuna, taking mercy on you and using my internal ***Yoga*** power I showed you my highest form which is illustrious, universal, limitless and primal. No one had seen-this before.

Neither by the ***Vedas***, nor by sacrifices nor by charities nor by studies nor by ceremonies nor by austerities nor to any person other than you in this world I am to be seen in this form, Oh Greatest of the Kurus!"

"Do not get frightened nor you should be confused by seeing this my terrible form. Discarding fear, with comfortable mind, see again that known form of mine."

Sanjay reports how Krishna again appeared in his pleasing form. He narrates:-

Saying thus to ***Arjuna,*** Lord Krishna again showed him his own form. The great soul, once again assumed his mild form to bring solace to Arjuna who was in fearful state.

Sanjay records Arjuna's mental relief after seeing the pleasing form of Lord Krishna. Arjuna reacts.

Oh ***Janardan***, seeing your mild human form, I am fully settled and have come back to awakened state.

Verse 52 to 55

The Lord while summing up, brings out the special significance of his cosmic form and tells the secret by which one is able to see it. Lord says:

"This form that you experienced is very difficult to see. Even the gods remain thirsty to see this form. It is very difficult to see Me in that form in which you saw Me. Through ***Vedas***, penance even charity or sacrifices it is not possible."

"Dear Arjuna, by single-minded and intense devotion alone that form of mine can be fully known and seen and entered into. He who is engaged in my work, makes me his goal, is devoted to me, is free from attachment and feeling no hatred to any creatures reaches me".

(108 A)

Adhayaya 12

Bhakti Yõga—*Yoga of Devotion*

Introduction

*The Lord referred to His unmanitest as well as manifest forms but **Arjuna** being always in the company of his human form expressed his preference to manifested and therefore pleasing and mild form. In seventh **Adhyãya** incomprehensible, unmanifest and changeless form of the Absolute was referred to as the supreme and the best. In ninth **Adhyãya** worship through devotion of the manifested form was glorified and **Arjuna** was advised to carry out actions in the spirit of worship and as offering to God. Then in tenth **Adhyãya** the Lord presented some of his splendid and powerful aspects and in eleventh **Adhyaya** he revealed his cosmic form.*

Now Arjuna wants to know which one of these two - unmanifest and manifest - one should adopt for his devotional worship.

Verse 1 to 7

Instead of asking a direct question to know the superiority of the one Arjuna raises a humble query.

"There are some devotees who steadfastly attached to your human form worship you and some worship your imperishable unmanifest form. Out of these two which one is the most perfect in the knowledge of ***Yoga***? (Who is in perfect union with God?)"

The Lord gives a prompt and decisive reply in favour of those whose minds are fixed upon him who appears in manifest form and who are always engaged in his worship with absolute faith and devotion. These devotees are considered to be the most perfect in ***Yõga***.

Those others who worship the imperishable, unmanifest which is indefinable, omnipresent, incomprehensible, changeless, immovable and constant, by controlling their senses, by being equally disposed to all and joyfully engaged in the wellbeing of all creatures, come to me alone.

But with their minds attached to the unmanifest they face immense troubles because it is painfully difficult for the embodied beings to achieve the goal of the unmanifest.

In contrast to this troublesome and difficult path, the Lord glorifies the easy and joyful way of worship of the manifest form.

"Surrendering their activities into me and meditating upon Me with undivided faith those who worship me, fully attached, with their thoughts in me, 1 become their saviour from the ocean of this mortal world without any loss of time".

Therefore the Lord advises Arjuna to fix his mind in Him and place his intelligence in him so that he would doubtlessly stay in him always thereafter.

Verse 8-15

The Lord now starts explaining the ways and means that help the devotee to intensify his devotion to God.

If ***Arjuna*** finds it difficult to steady his mind in the Lord, then he should desire to get him through the practice of ***Yõga*** of concentration.

If he lacks the strength to practice then he should devote himself in the service of the Lord because by working for the sake of the Lord he would reach perfection.

If however he is unable to work this way also, then he should surrender himself to the divine power of the Lord and controlling himself he should renounce the fruits of his entire actions.

Thus enumerating the possibilities in descending order of easiness, the Lord mentions the reason explaining the comparative greatness of different methods. He says : (Discriminating) knowledge is better than mere practice (of mechanical study). Better than knowledge however is meditation and the renunciation of the fruits of action is better than meditation. After the renunciation one attains peace.

The Lord thus made it very dear that one has to pass through various stages to make himself worthy of the last perfect stage of blissful union with God. The Lord describes the virtues of such a devotee of rare variety:

"Dear to me is that devotee who hates no creature and is friendly and compassionate to all. He is free from the sense of ego and possession. To him pleasure and pain are equal. He is tolerant, ever-contented, self-controlled, steadfast in resolve and his mind and intellect always surrendered to me.

Verse 16-20

"Dear to me is that devotee who neither annoys the world nor gets annoyed by it. He is free from joy, anger fear and anxiety.

Dear to me is that devotee who has no expectation, who is chaste, attentive, indifferent and sorrow free. He does not initiate any selfish action.

"Dear to me is that devotee who neither gets pleased nor becomes, hateful who neither laments nor desires, who has forsaken both auspicious and inauspicious.

Dear to me is that devotee who is alike to friend and foe, alike in honour and dishonour. He remains the same in heat and cold, in pleasure and pain and he is always free from any attachment.

He who considers blame and praise as equal, who observes silence and who remains satisfied with whatever he gets, who is not bound to any single home such a devoted person of steady intellect is dear to me.

Finally the Lord uses the superlative to express his love for his devotee. "But those devotees treating me as their highest goal with full faith follow this pious and nectar like teaching of mine are extremely dear to me".

Adhyaya 13
Kshetra-Kshetradnya Vibhag Yoga—
Yoga of Field and its Knower

The unitised knowledge of the Absolute Brahman and the knowledge of the phenomenal world of matter and individualised consciousness were referred to as ***Dnyan-vidnyan*** *in the 9th* ***Adhyaya****. Discussion about the perishable and imperishable* ***ksharaksharvichar*** *remains incomplete without the knowledge of the human body and the indwelling self called* ***Atman****. All the manifested objects are born out of* ***Prakriti*** *which is a divine power of the Absolute and it remains as an immanent principle in all the created beings. But how the* ***Gunas*** *of the* ***Prakriti*** *expand forming this universe and in what stages, was not explained. The 13th* ***Adhyaya*** *picks up that thread and discusses the theory of the field (kshetra) and the knower of the field (kshetradnya).*

The 13th ***Adhyaya*** *takes a sudden turn and plunges into serious discussion about the nature of the body and its knower. The Lord directly enters into discussion.*

Verses 1 to 4

"This body is called the field, Kshetra and one who knows it is called Kshetradnya."

The body passes through birth, growth and death. Many events take place in it. As if a man sows seeds of actions in this body and after some time or immediately, reaps the crop so it is rightly called the field. However the immanent principle in the body just witnesses all happenings taking place there, remaining unattached. It sees and knows everything hence it is called the knower of the field. The lord brings to Arjuna's attention two aspects of man's personality, his dual character, and proceeds explaining further :

The Lord tells Arjuna to the frim as the knower of all fields and the knowledge of the field and its knower is the real knowledge for him.

The knower of the field in every body is nothing but the all pervading Supreme Absolute Brahman appearing as different individualised souls not getting divided but remaining one and the same.

"What is the field, its nature, the changes that take place in it ? From where it has come and what is the nature of its knower and what are his powers?" These are some important aspects which the Lord wishes to explain in brief.

All this is sung earlier by the sages in many hymns and aphorisms explaining the nature of ***Brahman*** in a well-reasoned and decisive manner.

The Lord thus, giving its rich tradition and lineage starts describing the nature of the field, the body. First, the ***Avyakta,*** the unmanifest called ***Prakriti*** stands behind all visible and invisible features as their unseen cause forming into three ***Gunas*** sattwa, rajas and tamas.

Verses 5 to 6

First unmanifest, ***Prakriti***, (2nd Mahat, (Intellect).

Five great elements; earth, water, fire, air and ether.

Ego, intelligence

Ten sense organs and mind

(Five organs of knowing; eyes, ears, nose, tongue and skin Five organs of actions and organs of reproduction.)

Five objects of the senses: sight, smell, hearing, taste and touch

In addition to these twenty four principles the Lord adds some mental events or states since they are also the objects of knowledge. In fact they are the integral part of Life.

(6) Desire and hatred, happiness and sorrow

(7) ***Sanghãt***: *The totality means coordinating and organising ability of the body.*

(8) ***Chetanã****, animating principle brings movement in the body called life force*

(9) ***Dhriti,*** the fortitude, resolution.

The sum of all these elements along with their changes and interactions make the field. It is prone to changes. *It is born, it grows, stays, produces, decays and at last dies. This field is non permanent.*

However the Kshetradnya, the Knower of the field is totally different, permanent in nature. Knowledge of this knower is the same as that of ***Brahman.*** This knowledge does not merely signify knowing by intellect. In spiritual field what is important is the influence of this spiritual knowledge upon the bodily and mental behaviour of the knower. This influence is a reflection of steady wisdom attained by him- Dawning of this unitive knowledge of ***Atma*** in the seeker of knowledge is indicated by the virtues of greatness appearing in him. Twenty virtues of ethical nature, enumerated in stanzas one to eleven, when are distinctly visible in the behaviour of the knower, are indicative of transcendental knowledge gained by him. The Lord makes the mention of these virtues which speak for themselves.

Verses 7 to 11

(1) ***Amãnitva*** - though deserving he is shy of any respect or honour.

(2) ***Adambhitva*** - Absence of sense of self glorification.

(3) ***Ahimsa*** - Nonviolence; body, mind and speech harming no one.

(4) ***Kshanti*** - Forgiveness as also tolerance.

(5) ***Arjavam*** - Non crooked, righteous, simple.

(6) ***Achãryopasanam*** - Devotional service to the master.

(7) ***Shoucham*** - Purity of body, mind and intellect.

(8) ***Sthairyam*** - Steadiness, Loyalty to principles.

(9) ***Atmavinigraha*** - Self restraint.

(10) ***Indriyeshu Vairagyam*** - Non-attached to sense organs and the pleasures of their objects.

(11) ***Anahamkaram*** - Absence of ego, Absence of 'I'ness that separates oneself from others, feeling identity with everything.

(12) ***Janma - mrutyu - jarã - vyãdhi Dukkha*** - dõshanudarshanam : Correct understanding of the significance of the birth, death, old age, disease and pain.

(13) ***Anãkti*** - feeling of detachment.

(14) ***Anabhishwangah Putradarã Gruhãdishu***: Absence of attachment towards one's son, wife, home etc.

(15) ***Nityam Cha Samchittatwam Istãnistopapattishu*** : Evenness of mind towards pleasant and unpleasant events.

(16) ***Mayi Cha Ananay yogen Bhaktir Avyabhichãrini***- Exclusive devotion to the Lord, constant and non - deviant

(17) ***Vivikta Desha Sevitvam*** : Liking for a solitary place

(18) ***Araijansamsadi*** - Distaste for the company of worldly men.

(19) ***Adhyãtma Dnyannityatvam*** : Constant dedication to the spiritual knowledge of the self.

(20) ***Tattva Dnyãnãrth Darshanam*** : Perception of the goal of knowledge of inner truth.

All this is said to be true knowledge and whatever is other than this is gross ignorance.

Verses 12 to 20

Now the Lord directs his attention to the third aspect called ***Dnyeyam,*** *the object of the said knowledge; the 'Knowable'.*

By knowing what is worthy to be known, the knower gains immortality. That is Supreme Absolute - ***Para Brahma***- which has no beginning and which it is said, transcends existence and non - existence.

*It is non- existence because it is not limited in extent or period. It is beyond time and space, It is existent because its presence is manifested in everything in the universe. The Lord now describes the ineffable character of this **Para Brahma** using opposing terminology to establish its transcendental nature. Its omnipresence, omniscience and omnipotence is vividly brought out :-*

'Its hands and feet are every where. Its eyes, heads and faces are in all sides. Its ears are in all directions. Encompassing all, It stays in this world.

It illuminates the senses to life yet itself devoid of senses. It is detached yet sustains all. It has no attributes yet experiences all attributes.

It is outside as well as inside of creatures. It is inanimate as well a animate. It is so subtle that. It can not be grasped. It is far and also near.

It is one undivided yet stands split up into objects and creatures. It is to be known as the sustainer of beings, their dissolve and their creator.

It is the Light of Lights and said to be beyond darkness. It is knowledge, the object of knowledge and to be known by knowledge itself. It dwells in every one's heart.

With utmost economy of words the Lord so far described the nature of the field, the knowledge and that which must be known. The Lord's devotee who understands this becomes fit to reach His state.

The Lord dosing this topic of the Field and the Knower of the field now turns to their equivalents called ***Prakriti*** and ***Purusha.*** Like ***Sankhya*** philosophers Gita does not consider them separate principles. According to Gita ***Prakriti*** is the lower nature and the Purusha is higher nature of the Supreme Godhead.

It is a mystery when the original ***Prakriti*** is born of the Absolute. The ***Purusha,*** the individual soul, the higher ***Prakriti***, dwelling in the body, the lower ***Prakriti*** is also beginningless. Absolute itself is called Purishottam.

The Lord commences detailing important features of both:

Prakriti and Purasha are to be known as beginnings. It is also to be under stood that the qualities (***Gunas***) and the changing forms (Vikar) are produced from ***Prakriti***.

Prakriti is said to be the cause of the doer, his actions and his instruments. ***Purusha*** is said to be the cause of experiencing pleasure and pain. *The affected body and instruments of the senses are evolved from nature and their functions are also controlled by nature. And the pleasures and pains are experienced, by the* ***Purusha*** *when he identifies himself with the nature, called* ***Prakriti****.*

Verses 21 to 34

The ***purusha*** dwelling in the ***Prakriti*** and getting identified with it enjoys the ***Gunas*** produced from ***Prakriti***. This attachment with these ***Gunas*** decides to what good or bad wombs ***purusha*** would take his birth.

The Lord brings to our attention the greatness of the Purusha who gets involved in the play of ***Gunas*** *produced from* ***Prakriti*** *and forgets his real nature. The Lord speaks about the greatness of the Self that rises to its highest stratum once liberated from the clutches of* ***Prakriti****. The same Purush otherwise is a Parampurusha, the supreme self.*

That great God staying in this body is also known as the Witness, He is one who sanctions, sustains and enjoys. He is said to be the Highest God, the Supreme Self.

One who knows this ***Purusha*** and ***Prakriti*** along with the ***Gunas*** will have no rebirth. The Lord explains various

Some perceive the ***Atman*** within their own ***Atman*** by self-meditation. Some realise it through discriminatory knowledge Sankhya Yoga and some get the vision of the ***Atman*** by following the path of detached action.

But there are others, who not knowing these paths, worship God by listening from others. They who thus listen with utmost faith, also surpass the death.

The Lord now brings out the underlying unity of the universe and stresses the need of knowing this eternal that liberates the self.

All moving and non moving entities have come into existence as combination of the Field and the Knower of the field. Therefore he who sees the Suprerme Lord equally present in all beings and not getting destroyed even after their destruction, that man really sees. And thus seeing the Lord equally present everywhere he does not harm his own Self, He achieves the Supreme Goal.

One who sees that all action is being carried out by ***Prakriti*** and the Self is action less that man really sees. And when he sees that all the differentiated entities have their common ground in that ***Brahman*** and this all expanse also has the same origin, he then attains ***Brahman.***

Because this eternal Supreme Self has no beginning and has no attributes although it dwells in the body. It neither acts nor gets affected.

As the sky does not get tainted due to its subtle nature although it is spread all over, the ***Atman*** also, though situated all over in the body is not tainted.

As the single Sun illuminates this entire universe this Knower of the field illuminates the whole field.

Those who perceive through the eyes of knowledge the difference between the Field and its Knower and know how the beings get liberated from their ***Prakriti*** they reach the highest.

(119 A)

Adhyaya 14

Gunatraya Vibhãga Yõga—*Yoga of Three Gunas*

Introduction

The creation of objects, living as well as nonliving, with their functions are the doings of ***Prakriti****, the nature in its creative form, and* ***Brahman*** *standing aloof and action less is a mere Witness. In the same way in human body all actions and reactions are born out of the play of* ***Gunas*** *of* ***Prakriti*** *and the* ***Ãtman*** *is a mere witness also standing aloof and action less. The first is referred to as* ***Kshara*** *and* ***Akshar*** *- the perishable and the non-perishable and the second one is referred to as* ***kshetra and kshetradnya*** *- the field and the knower of the field. Both are in fact one and the same, only knowledge can give this perception.*

The knowledge of God taught in the 9th ***Adhyaya*** *was object of human eye and the knowledge of the Lord's cosmic form disclosed in XI* ***Adhyaya*** *was possible only with divine eyes. In 14th* ***Adhyaya*** *the Lord talks about his source of creation called* ***Prakriti*** *and the* ***Gunas*** *that play part in creating variety of natures of the things and living beings.*

Verses 1 to 20

The Lord tells ***Arjuna*** that he would again impart to him that knowledge of the highest kind knowing which all sages reached perfection from this world. Taking shelter of this knowledge and made like God's nature they are not born at the time of creation and are not hurt at the time of dissolution. The Lord says that ***Prakriti***, known as ***Mahad-Brahma*** is His source from where all entities are born.

Whatever forms are born in all types of wombs, the ***Prakriti*** called ***Mahad Brahma*** is the original source and the Lord is the seed-giving father.

Here the Lord suggests that ***Prakriti*** *is not an independent entity but an integral power of the Supreme. The process of creating objects of different variety is being described detailing the qualities of* ***three Gunas****.*

Three ***Gunas*** namely ***sattva, rajas*** and ***tamas*** are produced from ***Prakriti*** and they bind the changeless indwelling ***Ãtman*** to the body.

Sattva, being pure is illuminating and blameless becomes the cause of binding the Self to happiness and knowledge.

Rajas of passionate nature causes thirst and attachment. It binds the Self to action.

Tamas is delusion created by ignorance. It binds all men to wrong doing, sluggishness and sleep

Sattva creates attachment to happiness, ***rajas*** to actions and ***tamas*** to evil by, shroudding the wisdom.

Occasionally ***sattva*** dominates over ***rajas*** and ***tamas,*** sometimes ***rajas*** rules over ***sattva*** and ***tamas*** and at time tamas prevails over ***sattva*** and ***rajas.***

When the light of knowledge sprouts through all the gates of the body it is the sign of ***sattva*** growing.

When ***rajas*** grows then greed, activity, new ventures, restlessness and intense desires are born.

When ***tamas*** grows darkness, inertia, foolishness and delusion develop.

After describing how human nature changes according to the dominance of a particular ***Guna*** *the Lord explains the condition of the Self after man's death depending upon the* ***Guna*** *influence.*

The man who meets his death during ***sattva*** - predominance goes to pure region of the wise people who have knowledge of the Highest. He Who dies in ***rajas*** dominance, takes the rebirth among those who are obsessed by activity. And he who dies in ***tama***-dominance is reborn in the wombs of the dullards. The Lord sums up saying that the result of the noble action of ***Sattva*** nature is purity, the fruit of ***rajas*** is agony and that of ***tamas*** is ignorance. From ***sattva*** knowledge is born, from ***rajas*** greed and from ***tamas*** bewilderment, delusion and ignorance.

Men of ***sattva*** go rising up, men of ***rajas*** stay in the midplane and men of ***tamas*** busy with horrible deeds, sink to the lower plane.

The Lord glorifies the man who is above these three categories. He says : But one who has an eye of wisdom sees that these three ***Gunas*** are the only doers and none else. He also knows Him who is beyond the ***Gunas*** thus he attains the nature of the Lord.

When the dweller in the body transcends these three ***Gunas*** which are the product of the body then he becomes free from birth, death, old age and pain. He attains immortality. *Arjuna must have remembered the man of steady wisdom described in the 2nd* ***Adhyāya*** *and also the ideal devotee described in 9th and 12th* ***Adhyāyas****. The Lord had glorified their characters earlier.* ***Arjuna*** *now puts up a question to the Lord about him who has transcended three* ***Gunas****. Arjuna asks:*

Verses 21 to 27

"How to know him Who has transcended three ***Gunas***? How does he behave? How does he overcome these three ***Gunas***?

The Lord's answer is on the same lines. He describes: A man is said to have transcended the ***Gunas.***

When he feels no hatred for light, activity and delusion arising (out of ***sattva, raja*** and ***tama*** respectively) and does not long for them in their disappearance. When he sits unconcerned, and remains aloof not getting disturbed by the ***Gunas*** thinking that the ***Gunas*** only are acting.

When he remains at ease treating pleasure and pain alike, Mud, stone and gold are equal to him. Pleasant and unpleasant make him no difference, fame and infamy considered the same. He is so courageous. And when his behaviour remains the same either in honour or dishonour, either with friends or foes, and who has forsaken all fruit bearing activity.

He who renders unfaltering devotional service to the Lord he is said to have transcended the ***Gunas*** and becomes fit to be one with ***Brahman.***

Thus the Lord expresses his appreciation of this state by equating him with Brahman Then he states.

"I am the last resort of ***Brahman,*** the deathless and the unchanging. I am the abode of eternal ***Dharma,*** and I am also the abode of highest bliss".

Adhyaya 15

Purushõttam Yõga—*Yoga of Supreme Spirit*

Introduction

*In order to gain the unitive knowledge of **Bhraman** by direct transcendental experience one has to destroy first the obstacle of his ignorance about the true nature of the surrounding world. The impression that this world is real, the only existence without anything beyond, creates major impediment to self realisation. Therefore it was essential to show the temporary nature of the universe. The transitory nature of the world is depicted through the metaphor of a big banyan tree in 15th **Adhyãya.** This Adhyaya also deals with the highest form of the Supreme Person refereed to as **Purush** which is beyond this perishable universe's imperishable source called **Prakriti.***

*The Lord continues explaining **Dnyanvi Dnyan** and uses the metaphor of a banyan tree so popularly used in **Vedic** literature. From the smallest of the seed a huge sky-high tree is grown likewise from the subtlest of the Absolute **Brahmasn** the tree of this manifested universe is sprouted and grown to Height. The Lord describes:*

Verses 1 to 7

The Ashwattha, the big banyan tree it is said, is eternal with its roots above and branches downward. Its leaves are the hymns of the ***vedas.*** He who knows it is the knower of the ***Vedas***.

The universal cycle is maintained through ***Vedic*** rituals of the sacrifices hence they are compared to leaves that nourish and protect the tree.

Its branches have spread downward and upward getting nourishment from the ***Gunas***. Sense - objects are its twigs and it roots bound by actions are extended downward in the world of mortals. In this world it is not seen in this form. Also is not seen its end nor the beginning nor its foundation.

Cutting this firmly rooted ***Ashwatta*** with the strong axe of non - attachment he should search for that state from where having reached, one never returns. He should do this search saying, "I surrender to that Primal Lord from whom this ancient stream of activity has flown."

The Lord now describes the attitude and efforts required to attain that state. Those who are free from pride and illusion, who have conquered the evils of attachment, whose all desires are vanished, who are in constant devotion of the ***Ātman***, who have escaped from the dualities known as happiness and sorrow and who are free from confusion, attain to that changeless state.

The Lord declares : "from where having reached they never return that is my supreme abode. Neither the Sun nor the Moon nor the fire illuminates it".

Obviously Sun, Moon and Fire being the objects of the worldly nature are unable to illuminate the Absolute. It alone is the source of their lights.

The Lord now turns to another important topic of the individual soul called 'Jiva'. What is its nature? How does it evolve? The Lord answers:

Verses to 7 to 14

"My eternal fragment becomes the individual soul in this world of mortals and then draws five senses and mind which are made of ***Prakriti***.

When the Lord puts on a gross body and when he leaves it he carries them (mind and senses in subtle form) along with him like the wind picking up perfume from a flower.

He presiding over ears, eyes, organs of touch taste and smell and the mind enjoys the sense - objects.

The fools do not see him when he leaves the body or stays in it or enjoys coming in contact with ***Gunas*** but those who have eyes of knowledge can see him.

The ***yõgis*** striving in spiritual discipline see him situated in the self but those who have not realised the self and whose minds are not developed, howsoever they may try, can not see him.

The Lord insists on the eye of knowledge or the detached action because they help the soul for its evolution. The Lord is present in the body, so also he is present in everything. The lord enumerates:

"The light of the Sun that illuminates the whole world, the light of the Moon and that of the Fire know that as Mine.

Entering the Earth I sustain the creatures through my energy and becoming the Moon full of juice I nourish the medicinal herbs and flowers.

Staying in the bodies of creatures becoming digesting fire and getting mixed with inhaling and exhaling breaths I digest four kinds of food.

I am seated in the hearts of all. From me only memory and knowledge are born and because of me only both are destroyed. I am alone the object of ***Vedas***, I am alone their author of ***Vedanta*** and I am alone the knower of ***Vedas***.

After describing all-pervading nature of **Atman** *the Lord discusses the nature of the Supreme Lord called* **Purushottam.** *The distinction made here is philosophically very subtle and hence important one.*

Verses 15 to 20

In this world two kinds of ***purushas*** exist; perishable and imperishable. All living nonliving entities are perishables and the changeless (kutastha -) ***Prakriti*** is imperishable. *Here the **Kutastha purusha** is referred to meaning thereby the imperishable unmanifest principle called **Mul Prakriti**.*

The subtle primal energy in formless nature this ***mula-Prakriti*** that too is called ***akshar.*** The Lord introduces the third ***Purush.*** He says: besides these two ***Purushas*** there is another supreme ***Purusha*** called ***Paramatma,*** who by becoming ***Ishwar*** enters into these three worlds and maintains them.

"Since I am beyond the perishable and higher than the imperishable I am known as ***Purushottam*** in this world and in the ***Vedas***.

Being free from delusion whoever knows me as ***'Purushottam'***, he knowing everything, worships me wholeheartedly.

This is the most secret knowledge I have imparted to you, oh ***Arjuna,*** knowing this the man becomes wise and the purpose of his life is fulfilled."

Adhayaya 16

Daivãsura Sampad—Vibhãga Yoga—
Yoga of Divine and Demoniac Natures

In order to attain unitive knowledge of the Absolute **Brahman** *one must be freed from all kinds of delusions arising out of ignorance. In previous Adhyaya this need was stressed time and again. The 16th* **Adhyãya** *shows the way throwing discerning light on two types of human manifestations,; one of divine and the other of demoniac. Discarding demoniac tendencies one has to cultivate divine ones to become worthy of liberation. What is useful and what is harmful for spiritual development, 16th* **Adhyãya** *is a major guide.*

The Lord brings the discourse from theoretical level to practical level that speaks about human behaviour. After acquiring the discriminatory knowledge in spiritual matter it is very important to get that knowledge reflected in seeker's behaviour so that the dawn of the unitive experience soon comes close to him.

The Lord straightaway begins describing the virtues that form the wealth of the divine. They are twenty six in number, each one having a distinct flavour.

Verses 1 to 4

1. ***Abhayam :*** The first and the foremost is fearlessness The divinely born has no fear of death because he experiences the same ***Ãtman*** everywhere. He has no reason to be afraid of anybody.

2. ***Sattvasamshuddhi*** *: He has purified his existence by burning the tendencies of* ***rajas*** *and* ***tamas.***

3. ***Dnyãn Yõga*** vyavasthit : Making his mind steady he is devoted wholeheartedly to spiritual knowledge and carries his duty with detached mind not expecting any fruit.

4. ***Dãn:*** His charity is to assist the afflicted by all means, using his body mind and speech, irrespective of his position.

5. ***Dama :*** He controls all passions that create hurdles in spiritual development.

6. ***Yadnya*** : Surrendering his ego and desires, he performs duties in the spirit of sacrifice.

7. ***Swadhyãya*** : *He studies spiritual lessons and meditates upon the name of God with intense desire to attain self realisation.*

8. ***Tapa :*** *His penance is to exploit body, mind and senses in the service of the* ***Ãtman*** *and to remain always awakened to the reality.*

9. ***Ãrjavam*** : *His polite and courteous treatment to all beings is due to his simplicity of heart.*

10. ***Ahimsã*** : He is harmless in true sense. He being non violent in nature, works for the happiness of the world using his body, mind and speech in a positive way.

11. ***Satyam*** : He speaks the truth which is pleasant, beneficial and full of good advice.

12. ***Akrõdha*** : *His mind remains free from anger even in serious provocations.*

13. ***Tyãga :*** His egoless nature makes him to renounce all worldly desires and fruits.

14. ***Shãnti :*** *His tranquillity is of highest nature where the knowledge, the known and the knower gets fully merged into eternal peace.*

15. ***Apaishunam*** : *He is not simply unmalicious but he corrects other's mistakes and puts them on right path.*

16. ***Dayã*** : His compassionate heart is so great that not only he feels sorry over other's catastrophe and pain but also feels himself happy when others are happy.

17. ***Alõlupatvam*** : *He is not greedy.*

18. ***Mardavam*** : He is extremely gentle in his behaviour

19. ***Hri :*** *He feels ashamed of his identification with the gross body that puts him into the cycle of birth and death.*

20. ***Achãpalam :*** *His determination is in controlling his mind, the life force and the senses. He remains steadfast in all circumstances.*

21. ***Teja :*** *His strength is spiritual and it is exhibited in his facing boldly all difficulties that obstruct his devotion.*

22. ***Kshamã*** : *He forgives and forgets all about it. He is also learned to great extent*

23. ***Dhriti :*** *He courageously endures all troubles that come in the way of his spiritual progress.*

24. ***Shoucham*** : His purity is from within and without. His outward actions are clean and inward knowledge is pure. Thus he gets purified internally and externally.

25. ***Adrõha :*** He is free from hatred, so much so that he always cares for the wellbeing of all.

26. ***Nãtimanitã :*** He abstains from esteeming himself as deserving honour from others although he really deserves it.

Thus these twenty six virtues go into making a divine nature. In contrast to this sublime picture of a godly man, the Lord draws a dark picture of the men of demoniac qualities.

1. ***Dambha :*** *His hypocrisy makes him to talk about his virtues and goodness though in fact he does not possess them.*

2. ***Darpa :*** *He takes pride in exhibiting his worldly eminence of learning, wealth, status etc.*

3. ***Abhimãn :*** *Out of his arrogance he nourishes vanity*

4. ***Krõdha :*** *Once his desires are thwarted he becomes angry. He is also enraged seeing others prosper.*

5. ***Pãrushya :*** *His behaviour is so insolent as if he vomits fire and breeds cruelty.*

6. ***Adnyãn*** : The basic defect with such a man is his lack of spiritual knowledge. His ignorance about the true nature of things results into wrong judgements. Divine virtues lead to liberation and demoniac qualifies bring bondage. The Lord compliments Arjuna for being born in divine nature.

Verses 6 to 20

Beings in this world are born in two categories; one divine and the other demoniac. The Lord described the first in detail now turns to the other.

The men of demoniac nature know neither the path of activity nor the path of renunciation. In them, there is no purity, no rightful conduct and no truth also.

They say that this world is unrealistic and it has no support. It is godless and exists without any connection. They think that the world's only purpose is enjoyment. Firmly adopting this attitude, these men of small intelligence, with their self lost, perform harmful and horrible deeds to ruin this world.

These persons getting under the sway of hypocrisy, conceit and pride, attached to insatiable lust, adopting wrong approach due to delusion work for impure ends.

Remaining in limitless worries till the end of life; drowned in enjoyment, entangled in the net of hundreds of desires and always attached to lust and anger, they are constantly busy in hoarding the wealth by unlawful means for self - gratification.

"I have gained this today and I shall achieve that desire tomorrow, this wealth is mine and that also will be mine. I have killed this enemy to - day and I shall kill others tomorrow. I am the god, I am the enjoyer. I am successful, I am powerful and happy. I am rich and I am born of high family. Who else is there like me? I shall offer sacrifice, I shall give charity, I shall rejoice". Blinded by ignorance the men of demonic nature boast in this fashion.

Getting confused by many thoughts, entangled in the network of delusions, always attached to sensual pleasure, they fall in the dirty hell.

Self-praising and impudent as they are, getting intoxicated by the wealth and status they offer sacrifice for name sake only with hypocrisy and without observing sacred rules.

Imbued with egoism, power, pride, lust and anger they hate me getting critical about my presence in them as well as others.

These envious and cruel malignant creatures of evil characters are always thrown by me into the wombs of demoniac nature in this material world.

Thus born into demoniac wombs, births after births, these fools fail to reach me and go on sinking into the lowest state.

After describing the demoniac nature in various ways the Lord suggests the remedy for coming out of it. The Lord continues.

Verses 21 to 24

The hell has three gates, lust, anger and greed that lead to the ruin of the Self, therefore, these three should be abandoned.

One who escapes these three gates of darkness, carries

out whatever is for the good of his self and reaches the highest goal at last.

But he who discards the rules of the scriptures and act according to his own impulses neither attains perfection nor happiness nor the supreme goal.

The Lord in the end advises Arjuna to accept scriptures as his true guide to decide what to do and v~ nut to do. By knowing the rules taught by scriptures he has to act in this world.

Adhyaya 17

Shraddhã—Traya—Vibhãga Yoga—
Yoga of Three Kinds of Faith

Introduction

In the 16th Adhyaya are distinctively described the characteristics of the Divine and the Demoniac persons. But in reality barring a few examples, these states are not permanently separate affairs. Journey from the positive to the negative and vice versa is always possible. ***Kãm, Krodha*** *and* ***Lõbha*** *- Lust, anger and greed described as the gates of the hell suggest the boundary line between positive progress and negative one. Any detached action performed either through discriminative knowledge or intense devotion takes oneself away from these gates. Such detached actions are ordained by the scriptures. At the end of 16th* ***Adhyãya Arjuna*** *was advised to accept authority of the scriptural laws. However* ***Arjuna*** *raised a pertinent question regarding faith that plays important role in one's life even if he has no knowledge of the scriptures. The seventeen* ***Adhyãya*** *completes the teaching of Dyãnvidyãn by extensively dealing with the basic question, why do people have so much diversity of nature?"*

Verses 1 to 6

Arjuna generally observed many persons not caring for the dictates of the scriptures in their offering of sacrifice depending on their immense faith alone. He wanted to know what was the nature of such faith. Whether it belongs to ***sattva*** or ***rajas*** or ***tamas***?

The Lord answered that faith of men is of three kinds: ***sattvika, rajasika*** and ***tamasika***, so characterised by their nature.

Everyone's faith is according to his temperament. Each individual is made of his faith only. Whatever his faith is he is exactly the same.

The Lord describes the resulting effects of the ***Gunas***.

Men of ***sattva*** worship gods, men of ***rajas*** worship yakshas and demons and men of ***tamas*** worship spirits and ghosts.

But there is another category of degraded persons. The Lord clarifies:

Those people possessing ego and vanity, motivated by power of lust and attachment carry out horrible penances not prescribed by the scriptures. Out of foolishness they torture the body harming not only the elements grouped in it but also the Lord who dwells in it. Definitely these people are to be known as demons.

The Lord explains the idea of ***Guna*** - dominance by applying it to selective human activities, thus suggesting its full control over creating universal diversity.

Verses 7 to 10

Even the food that everyone likes is of three kinds. In the same way ***Yadnya***, the scarifies, ***tapa,*** the penance and dan the charity have three different kinds each.

Men of ***sattva*** are fond of food that increases life, purity, strength, health, happiness and pleasure. Such foods are juicy, oily, lasting and agreeable.

Foods that are bitter, sour, salty, hot, pungent, dry and burning are liked by men of rajas nature. Such foods cause distress, misery and disease.

Men of ***tamas*** nature seek pleasure in foods that are spoiled being cooked long before, tasteless, rotten, stale, leftover and impure.

Here the stress is on the effects of the food on body, mind, intellect and entire personality of the eater.

Verses 11 to 13

The sacrifice performed according to scriptural directions considering it as a matter of duty and desiring no fruits, is of ***sattva*** nature. And the one performed for outward show, expecting benefits out of it is of ***rajas*** nature.

But the sacrifice performed not following scriptural instructions, without offering food, without singing of hymns, without any gift to the priest and devoid of any faith is of ***tamas*** nature.

Verses 14 to 19

Before classifying ***tapa,*** the penance according to ***Gunas*** the Lord classifies ***Tapa*** of body, mind and speech with clear cut definitions :

Penance of the body consists of reverence to gods, twice born ***Brahmin***s, the masters and the learned and covers the qualities of cleanliness, humility celibacy and harmlessness.

'Penance of speech' consists in speaking words which are harmless, truthful pleasant and helpful and also includes regular chanting of ***Vedas***.

Calmness, softness, silence, self control, purity of thought are considered as penance of the mind.

These three penance's are further classified as per ***Guna*** influence. When these penances physical, mental and vocal... Practised by men with full faith, without expecting any fruits and with mind absorbed in God, it is called ***sãttvik***.

Penance practised out of hypocrisy to gain praise, honour and worship is said to be ***rãjasik.*** It is always unstable and impermanent.

Penance practised out of foolish determination by torturing own self and hoping the destruction of others is said to be ***tãmasik.***

In the same way act of charity is classified :-

Verses 20 to 22

Charity given out of sense of duty, without expecting any returns, to a deserving person at appropriate time and place is regarded as ***sãttvik.***

Charity given reluctantly with the hope of getting advantage in return or desiring results in future is said to be rajasik.

And charity given at the wrong place at an improper time and to unworthy person, showing no respect but humiliation, is regarded as ***tãmsik.***

Verses 23 to 28

While concluding this ***Adhyaya*** the Lord makes a reference to a sacred mantra "Om Tatsat". These words designate the Supreme Reality ***Brahman.*** 'Om' indicates eternal ***Brahman, 'Tat'*** indicates ***sãttvik*** action and ***'Sat'*** means pure action as prescribed by scriptures. Whatever else is ***Asat***-evil which is to be totally discarded. The Lord making this reference wants to glorify the ***sãttvik*** actions. The Lord explains:-

'Om Tat Sat' is considered a symbol that indicates ***Brahman*** in three ways. By uttering these words ***Brahmanas, Vedas*** and ***Yadnya***s were initiated in ancient times.

Therefore ***'Om'*** is always uttered by the worshippers of ***Brahman*** whenever they undertake the activities of ***Yandnya***, ***Dan*** and ***Tap*** as prescribed by the scriptural laws.

By uttering ***'Tat'*** the seekers of liberation desiring no other fruits, undertake the activities of ***Yadnya***, ***Tapa*** and ***Dan.***

Sat is used to denote state of existence and goodness. The word ***'Sat'*** is also used to suggest good work.

'Sat' also indicates steadfastness in ***Yadnya***, ***Tapa*** and ***Dan*** and therefore any act performed for their fulfilment is also referred to as ***'Sat'***

Sacrifice performed, charity given, penance practised and any work done without any faith is called ***'asat'***, the unreal. It is of no use here in this world nor after death.

Adhyaya 18

Mõksha Sannyãsa Yoga—*Yoga of Salvation Through Renunciation*

Introduction

In the 16th ***adhyãy*** *the discussion regarding the true nature of the world of matters and living beings ended. The expanse of the universe and its vast variety was the product of* ***Prakriti*** *acting through unseen material forces known as* ***Gunas*** *making various shapes, forms, qualities and activities by different combinations. The eternal principle immanent in the whole creation is* ***Bramhan*** *which is a generating as well as resting place of everything that manifests for short period of time. The knowledge of the Absolute and the knowledge of true nature of the manifested world is referred to as* ***Dnyãna - ViDnyana****. The discussion on that knowledge concluded in 17th* ***Adhyãya****. Path of knowledge, path of action and path of devotion though outwardly appear different, are in reality one and the same and all lead to liberation called mõksha.*

In the 18th ***Adhyaya Arjuna*** *asks a penetrating question. He wants to know the distinction between* ***Sannyãsa*** *and* ***tyãga*** *since actions are inevitable for all embodied beings. 18th* ***Adhyãya*** *begins with in-depth analysis of various aspects of* ***Karma*** *and then giving classifications of* ***Dnyãn****a,* ***Karma****,* ***Dhriti, Sukha,*** *etc., deals extensively with idea of swa Dharma attached to the innate nature of living beings. This* ***Adhyãya*** *ends with the glorification of supreme devotion which is based on total surrendering to God.*

Arjuna wants to know the real nature of ***'Sannyãsa'*** *and* ***'tyãga'*** *separately since both the terms literally mean "renunciation". He wishes to know the difference between the two.*

When all actions motivated by desires are completely given up the learned calls it ***'Sanayãsa'*** *and when the fruits of actions are given up the wise call it* ***'tyãga'***

The idea of renunciation is viewed differently by different people. The Lord refers to some of them. He explains:

Verses 1 to 6

Some thinkers declare that all kinds of actions should be renounced since they always carry faults with them. Whereas others maintain that the acts of sacrifice charity and penance are not to be given up but they must be practised because sacrifice, charity and penance are the means of purification for the learned people.

Even these actions are to be performed without attachment to their fruits.

Verses 7 to 17

The Lord turns to classification of actions in order to confirm his preference to detached action by condemning the rest.

Prescribed duties are never to be renounced. If they are renounced out of ignorance such renunciation is said to be ***tãmasik.***

Out of fear of bodily harm when a man gives up his duty considering it as sorrow his renunciation is ***rãjasik*** and such renunciation never gets any reward of fruits. But when one performs one's action ordained by scriptures as a matter of duty, renouncing all attachment and fruits his renunciation is said to be ***sãttvik.***

Intelligent renounce whose all doubts are dispelled and whose nature is ***sãttvik,*** does not hate action which is disagreeable and does not like it because it is agreeable.

It is quite impossible for any creature who possesses the body to give up his actions altogether. Therefore he who renounces the fruits of action is called a true renouncer.

Those who have not given up the desires of fruits, get after death, the threefold fruits of bondage, pleasant, unpleasant and mixed. But those who have truly renounced do not get any fruit at all.

The Lord's insistence on giving up one's ego and sense of belonging to become a true sanyasi or tyagi is further strengthened by metaphysical reasoning. The Lord explains:

"Oh ***Arjuna***, according to ***Sãnkhya*** school of thought there exist five causes that bring all actions to fruition. Learn them from me."

First is the place of action, the body, second comes the doer, the ego, the third various instruments like sense organs etc., fourth, different kinds of life movements in body and the fifth one certainly is providence.

Whatever endeavour, right or wrong, a man undertakes through his body, speech and mind it has these five causes.

Any action initially is in a thought form and subsequently culminates into reality taking a concrete form through these five causes.

This being the position, one Who thinks that he himself is the doer, that fool does not really see the truth due to his immature knowledge.

But he who has no sense of ego and whose intelligence is not tainted by any selfish motive even if he kills these men, he is not at all a killer. Thus he is not tied up to the fruit of his action.

Such a doer being pure in heart, free from any selfish motive and treating all living and non living creatures equally shall not be harmful to anybody. So killing anybody for no reason remains out of question. When the Lord says that one is not a killer even after killing men this is not to be misunderstood. Any duty ordained by scriptures or prescribed by law or sanctioned by conscience when performed without any attachment and ego becomes a pure action accomplished by the just quoted five causes. The self remains above everything.

Verses 18 to 28

The Lord now continues his ***Guna*** classification extending it to many more human activities starting with ***Dnyãna.***

The knowledge, the object of knowledge and the knower; these three inspire action (by generating a mental design). The instrument, the act and the doer; these three form the action (executing the mental design).

The ***sãnkhya*** theory of ***Gunas*** proclaims that knowledge, action and doer have three kinds each according to ***Guna*** - difference.

Knowledge by which is seen only one Imperishable Existence in all living and non living entities, staying undivided in divided many, is to be known as ***sãttvik***. Knowledge by which is seen difference and multifarious forms in all creatures is to be known as ***rãjasik.***

Knowledge by which one who is ignorant about the truth is involved in one kind of work thinking it as everything and having no other cause that meagre knowledge is known as ***tãmasik.***

'One - in all', 'difference everywhere' and 'mine everything' are the three attitudes falling under ***sattva, raja*** *and* ***tama*** *respectively.*

The action prescribed by law or innate nature when performed by him who has no desire for fruits, having no attachment, love or hatred is said to be ***sãttvik.***

The action performed egoistically, with strong desire for fruits employing hard efforts is said to be ***rãjasik.***

The action performed under delusion created by ignorance without caring for destruction, violence and other bindings and without judging own strength is said to be ***tãmasik.***

The doer who is free from attachment, not boasting of his deeds, who is full of courage and enthusiasm and who remains undisturbed in the hour of success or failure is said to be ***sãttvik.***

The door who is passionately attached and desirous of fruits of his actions, who is greedy, brutal and impure and who gets quickly influenced by joy and sorrow is said to be ***rãjasik.***

The doer who is mentally imbalance, uncultured, rude, arrogant, cheat, malicious, lazy, dejected and idler is said to be ***tãmasik.***

Verses 29 to 39

The Lord applies this threefold classification to some abstract human qualities like intelligence, determination, etc., and asks Arjuna to listen to their full details being told separately.

That intellect which knows what is activity and what is renunciation what is worthy of doing and what is unworthy, What is to be feared and what is bondage and what is liberation is sattwik. That intellect which fails to understand what is right and what is not, what is just and what is not, what is right action and what is not is ***rãjasik.***

And that intellect which under the spell of darkness of ignorance considers unrighteous to be righteous and sees all things in distorted form is ***tãmsik.***

That determination which remains steadfast due to ***Yõga*** practice and controls the activities of the mind, life breath and the senses is ***sãttvik.***

That determination by which one remains firmly attached to duty, desires and wealth expecting benefits is rajasik.

And that determination by which the fools do not give up sleep, fear, grief, dejection and pride is ***tãmasik.***

This determination is more on mental plane rather than physical one and it can be good, bad or worst according to the work in which it is used. The Lord talks about the nature of happiness which is of three kinds.

That happiness in which one takes delight by constant study and where ends the sorrow, which is like poison first but becomes nectar in the end, and which is born out of calmness of intellect being absorbed in ***Ãtman*** is ***sãttvik.***

That happiness which is born from the contacts of the senses with the sense objects, which is like nectar first but becomes a poison in the end is ***rãjasik.***

And that happiness which from the beginning to the end keeps the self in delusion and which arises from sleep, laziness and folly is ***tãmasik.***

*Intellect joyfully involved in search of **Ãtman** is very important instrument in obtaining **sãttvik** happiness. Intellect is a powerful instrument available to a man. It can dispassionately see the interplay of three **Gunas** and at the same time has the capacity to realise **Ãtman**. Purity and transparency of the intellect being an important power all the different paths leading to God invariably cherish its help in their accomplishment.*

Verses 40 to 44

Among these threefold ***Guna***-classifications the Lord stresses the greatness of ***sãttvik*** nature which ultimately culminates into the state that transcends all ***Gunas***. *The discussion now shifts to fourfold classification of the social structure which is based upon differentiation. The Lord continues explaining what is innate nature, i.e., swaDharma and how the society performs its fourfold functions through swa Dharma.*

Neither in this world nor among gods in heavens, there is any creature who is absolutely free from these three ***Gunas*** that spring from ***Prakriti***.

The duties of ***Brahmins,*** the enlightened seers; ***kshatriyas,*** the warriors; the ***vaishyas,*** the providers and ***shudras,*** the servers are differentiated by their nature born of the ***Gunas***.

Brahmin's duty consists of tranquillity, restraint, austerity, purity, patience, uprightness, knowledge of self, knowledge of universe and faith in God. All these coming out of his nature.

Kshatriya's duty consists of valour, splendour, determination, alertness fearlessness in battle, generosity, leadership, all these coming from his nature.

Vaishya's duty consists of farming, cattle rearing and trade, all these arising out of his nature.

And ***shudra's*** duty consists of the work of service ordained by his nature.

The four caste system in Hinduism is thus born out of ***Guna****-dominated variety of human nature. The Lord has not given any gradation calling one high or the other low, one pure and other impure. No such distinction is made. On the contrary the Lord gives equal importance to all four. To achieve salvation each one has to perform his duty selflessly and offering it as worship to God. One can reach perfection by following his own duty. Nothing else is required.* Thus says the Lord:

Verses 45 to 56

"A man engrossed in doing his work attains perfection. I shall tell you how he gains perfection by doing his duty, please listen."

"A man reaches perfection when he worships God by offering his actions to him from whom all creatures along with their duties are born and by whom everything is pervaded."

This stanza appears to be the key verse of the Lord's teachings. The first line categorically and clearly states the spiritual truth, and the final goal of the man and the means to be adopted are mentioned in the second line.

The Lord further explains why one should stick to his own duty even if it is imperfect or faulty one. Man's own duty born out of his innate nature, i.e., Swa Dharma is better than the duty of others. Duty performed according to one's own innate nature does not invite any sin.

Thus reassuring, the Lord insists on not giving up one's duty though tainted with fault because he says all actions are some way or the other involved in some faults just as fire is covered by smoke.

Therefore by detachment, control of the mind, desirelessness and renunciation of fruits one attains the highest perfection of bondage-free non-action.

According to the Lord all actions have equal merit and fourfold order of social functions is an integral part of every society all over the world. Therefore renouncement of actions is not advised.

Duty whether difficult or disagreeable performed with non-attached mind certainly leads the doer to perfection. Such are the experiences of saints and sages all over the world. The Lord continues explaining how does one attain union with ***Brahman,*** the supreme state of knowledge after achieving the perfect stage of bondage-free non - action, i.e., ***Naishkarmya***.

With his intelligence purified, mind brought under control with determination, giving up objects like sound, etc., of sense pleasures, attachment and hatred setting aside.

Living in seclusion, eating but little, curbing his speech, body and mind always absorbed in meditation, taking the shelter of detachment.

And discarding ego, power, pride, lust, anger and possessions he who is unselfish and tranquil, becomes fit to be one with ***Brahman.***

Once united with ***Brahman*** and his self becoming serene and calm he does not indulge in grief or hope. Being equal to all creatures he attains the highest devotion of the Lord.

Through devotion he knows the Lord as He is in his real nature. Thereafter knowing Him truly he enters into the Lord.

Love him, know him, and then enter into him, this is a step by step evolution of the self in the process of realisation. The Lord wants Arjuna to follow that path.

Verses 57 to 66

Surrendering into him, always doing his activities, he obtains the eternal and changeless place through the grace of the Lord.

Thus explaining the importance of non attached action performed with most devotion, at the end of his prolonged discourse the Lord focuses his attention on his friend-disciple ***Arjuna*** and delivering his final divine message concludes his teaching.

The Lord utters his guiding words: "Mentally repose all your actions into me, and getting absorbed in me, practising the *Yoga* discipline to stabilise the intellect, concentrate all your attention in me.

Once your mind is full of my consciousness you shall overcome all the obstacles by my grace. And if you do not listen to what I say out of egoistic pride your ruin is certain.

If filled with pride you say, "I will not fight", that resolve of yours is in vain. Your nature will compel you to fight.

Due to delusion created by your ignorance whatever you wish to avoid, you will be helplessly doing the same, because, oh ***Arjuna,*** you are bound by your own action born of your nature.

The Supreme Lord resides in the hearts of all creatures and turns them who are ridden on a machine, round and round by his divine power called ***Mãya***."

Therefore surrender yourself to him totally so that through his grace you shall obtain highest peace and eternal abode.

I have taught to you that knowledge which is the secret of all secrets. Pondering over it from all sides do what you wish to do.

Ãtman *is free but the actions are not free. They depend on many factors; the chief motivating force being the* ***Prakriti****. Actions can be purified by pure intellect and pure devotion.* ***Prakriti*** *is the power of the Supreme Lord. Ultimately he is the grand performer. So one has to surrender fully to him. Arjuna is granted full freedom to act.*

At the close of his teaching the Lord told ***Arjuna*** to take his own decision and again started persuading him to follow his words.

"Listen once again to my last words that consist of the most confidential secret. Because you are so dear to me, I shall tell you what is good for you.

"Fix your mind in me. Be my devotee. Always worship me, bow down to me. Then you shall come to me. Really this is my promise to you since you are so dear to me"

"Leaving aside all duties just surrender into me alone. I shall liberate you from all sins; worry no more."

The Lord expects that this divine knowledge should continue flowing.

Warning ***Arjuna,*** the Lord tells about the reward one gets by absorbing this knowledge.

Verses 67 to 72

"This divine secret is never to be disclosed to anyone who has no austerity and devotion, also not to him who disobeys his teacher and who despises me.

But he who teaches this supreme secret to my devotees; and thus offers to me his great devotion will certainly come to me.

Amongst men there is no one greater than him who is doing such a good service to me. And in this world there can be no one dearer to me.

And if anyone studies this holy conversation of ours I consider as if he is worshipping me by offering the sacrifice of knowledge.

Even if a man who does listen this with faith and without envy, he will be liberated and placed in the auspicious abode of righteous people."

Finally the Lord wants to know from ***Arjuna*** his response, so he asks: "Oh ***Arjuna,*** have you listened this with concentrated mind? Oh ***Dhananjay,*** has your delusion created by ignorance disappeared?

Without any hesitation Arjuna promptly answers:

Verse 73

Oh Lord, by your grace my delusion is destroyed. I have regained my memory, I am now firm with my doubts totally gone oh Krishna. I shall follow your words."

Here ended the dialogue between the Lord and ***Arjuna.*** ***Sanjay*** who was reporting this dialogue between two great souls to king ***Dhirtarashtra*** concluded this ***adhyãya*** as well as ***Gita*** by expressing his joyful reaction to what he heard and saw. He exclaims:

Verses 74 to 78

"Thus I heard the dialogue between Lord Krishna and Arjuna the great. It was so wondrous that I am extremely thrilled with my hair getting erect.

By the grace of ***Vyãsa,*** I heard this highly mysterious ***Yõga*** at the time when it was delivered directly by the Lord Krishna, the master of ***Yoga***.

"O King, recalling that wonderful and holy dialogue held between ***Keshava*** and ***Arjuna***, I rejoice again and again."

His great astonishment and joy overcoming him again and again at the repeated remembrance of Lord Krishna's most wondrous universal form, made ***Sanjaya*** to proclaim his judgement at the close of this celestial song.

"Wherever there is ***Krishna,*** the master of ***Yoga*** and wherever there is ***Arjuna***, the master of archery, only there I know for certain will be fortune, victory, welfare and morality.

Here ends the science that combines the knowledge of being one with the Supreme Lord and the skill of active participation in the process of evolution that keeps the Lord's creation progressing.

(150 A)

CHAPTER I

धृतराष्ट्र उवाच / *Dhṛtarāṣṭra Uvāca*

धर्मक्षेत्रे कुरूक्षेत्रे समवेता युयुत्सवः ।
Dharma-kṣetre kuru-kṣetre samavetā yuyutsavaḥ
मामकाः पांडवाश्चैव किमकुर्वत संजय ।। (1)
Māmakāḥ pāṇḍavāś-chaiva kimakurvata Sañjaya |

संजय उवाच / *Sañjaya Uvāca*

दृष्ट्वा तु पाण्डवानीकं व्यूढं दुर्योधनस्तदा ।
Dṛṣtvā tu pāṇḍavānīkaṁ vyūḍhaṁ duryodhanastadā
आचार्यमुपसंगम्य राजा वचनमब्रवीत् ।। (2)
Āchāryam-upasangamya rājā vachanamabravīt ||

दुर्योधन उवाच / *Duryodhana Uvāca*

पश्यैतां पाण्डुपुत्राणाम् आचार्य महतीं चमूम् ।
Paśyaitāṁ pāṇḍu-putrāṇāṁ āchārya mahatīm chamūṁ |
व्यूढां द्रुपदपुत्रेण तव शिष्येण धीमता ।। (3)
Vyūḍhāṁ drupada-putreṇa tava śiṣyeṇa dhīmatā ||
अत्र शूरा महेष्वासा भीमार्जुनसमा युधि ।
Atra śūrā maheṣvāsā Bhīmārjunasamā yudhi |
युयुधानो विराटश्च द्रुपदश्च महारथः ।। (4)
Yuyudhāno Virāṭaś-ca Drupadaś-ca mahārathaḥ ||
धृष्ठकेतुश्चेकितानः काशिराजश्च वीर्यवान् ।
Dhṛṣṭaketuśchekitānaḥ Kāśirājaśca viryavān |
पुरूजित्कुन्तिभोजश्च शैब्यश्च नरपुङ्गवः।। (5)
Purujītkuntibhojaśca śaibyaśca narapuṅgavaḥ ||
युधामन्युश्च विक्रांत उत्तमौजाश्च वीर्यवान् ।
Yudhāmanyuśca vikrānta uttamaujāśca vīryavān

सौभद्रो द्रौपदेयाश्च सर्व एव महारथाः ।। (6)
Saubhadro Draupadeyāśca sarva eva Mahārathāḥ ||
अस्माकं तु विशिष्ठा ये तान्निबोध द्विजोत्तम ।
Asmākaṁ tu viśishṭhā ye tānnibodha dvijottama |
नायका मम सैन्यस्य संज्ञार्थं तान्ब्रवीमि ते ।। (7)
Nāyakā mama sainyasya saṁjñārthaṁ tānbravīmi te |
भवान्भीष्मश्च कर्णश्च कृपश्च समितिंजयः ।
Bhavānbhīṣmaśca Karṇaśca Kṛpaśca samitiñjayaḥ |
अश्वत्थामा विकर्णश्च सौमदत्तिस्तथैव च ।। (8)
AśvātthāmāVikarṇaścha Saumadattiśtathaiva ca ||
अन्ये च बहवः शूरा मदर्थे त्यक्तजीविताः ।
Anye ca bahavaḥ śūrā madarthe tyaktajīvitāḥ |
नानाशस्त्रप्रहरणाः सर्वे युद्धविशारदाः ।। (9)
Nānāśastrapraharaṇāḥ sarve yuddhaviśāradāḥ ||
अपर्याप्तं तदस्माकं बलं भीष्माभिरक्षितम् ।
Aparyāptaṁ tadasmākaṁ balaṁ Bhīṣmābhirakṣitaṁ |
पर्याप्तं त्विदमेतेषां बलं भीमाभिरक्षितम् ।। (10)
Paryāptaṁ tvidameteṣāṁ balaṁ Bhīṣmābhirakṣitaṁ |
अयनेषु च सर्वेषु यथाभागमवस्थिताः ।
Anayeshu ca sarveṣu yathābhāgamavasthitāḥ |
भीष्मेवाभिरक्षन्तु भवन्तः सर्व एव हि ।। (11)
Bhīṣmamevābhirakṣantu bhavantaḥ sarva eva hi ||
तस्य संजनयन्हर्षं कुरूवृद्धः पितामहः ।
Tasya sañjanayanharsham Kuruvṛddhaḥ pitāmahaḥ |
सिंहनादं विनद्योच्चैः शंखं दध्मौ प्रतापवान् ।। (12)
Siṁhanādaṁ vinadyoccaiḥ śankhaṁ dadhmau pratāpavān||
ततः शंखाश्च भेर्यश्च पणवानकगोमुखाः ।
Tataḥ śaṅkhāśca, bheryaśca, panavānakagomukhāḥ |
सहसैवाभ्यहन्यंत स शब्दस्तुमुलोऽभवत् ।। (13)
Sahasaivābhyahanyanta sa śabdastumulo-abhavat ||

ततः श्वेतैर्हयैर्युक्ते महति स्यंदने स्थितौ ।
Tataḥ śvetairhayairyukte mahati syandane sthitau |
माधवः पाण्डवश्चैव दिव्यौ शंखौ प्रदध्मतुः ।। (14)
Mādhavaḥ pāṇḍavaśchaiva divyau śaṅkhau pradadhmatuḥ ||
पाञ्चजन्यं हृषीकेशो देवदत्तं धनंजयः ।
Pāñchajanyaṁ Hṛṣikeso devadattaṁ Dhanañjayaḥ |
पौण्ड्रं दध्मौ महाशंखं भीमकर्मा वकोदरः ।। (15)
Pauṇḍraṁ dadhman mahāśaṅkhaṁ bhīmakarmā Vṛkōdaraḥ||
अनंतविजयं राजा कुन्तीपुत्रो युधिष्ठिरः ।
Anantavijayaṁ rājā Kuntīputro Yudhiṣṭhiraḥ |
नकुलः सहदेवश्च सुघोषमणिपुष्पकौ ।। (16)
Nakulaḥ Sahadevaśca Sughoṣamaṇipuspakau ||
काश्यश्च परमेष्वासः शिखण्डी च महारथः ।
Kāśyaśca parameshvāsaḥ Śikhaṇḍī ca mahārathaḥ |
धृष्टद्युम्नो विराटश्य सात्यकिश्चापराजितः ।। (17)
Dhrishṭadyumno Virāṭaśca Sātyakiścāparājitaḥ ||
द्रुपदो द्रौपदेयाश्च सर्वशः पृथिवीपते ।
Drupado Draupadeyāśca sarvaśaḥ prithivīpate |
सौभद्रश्च महाबाहुः शंखान्दध्मुः पृथक् पृथक् ।। (18)
Saubhadraśca Mahābāhuḥ saṅkhāndadhmuḥ prithak prithak||
स घोषो धार्तराष्ट्राणां हृदयानि व्यदारयत ।
Sa ghosho Dhārtārashṭrāṇāṁ hridayāni vyadārayat |
नभश्च पृथिवी चैव तुमुलो व्यनुनादयन् ।। (19)
Nabhaśca prithivīm chaiva tumulo vyanunādayan ||
अथ व्यवस्थितान्दृष्ट्वा धार्तराष्ट्रान कपिध्वजः ।
Atha vyavasthitāndrishṭvā Dhārtarāshṭrān kapidhvajah|
प्रवृते शस्त्रसंपाते धनुरूद्यम्य पाण्डवः ।। (20)
Pravritte śastrasaṁpāte dhanurudyamya pāṇḍavaḥ ||
हृषीकेशं तदा वाक्यमिदमाह महीपते ।
Hrishīkeśaṁ tadā vākyamidamāha mahīpate |

अर्जुन उवाच / *Arjuna uvācha*

सेनयोंरुभयोर्मध्ये रथं स्थापय मेऽच्युत ।। (21)
Senayorubhayor-madhye ratham sthāpaya me-acyuta ||
यावदेतान्निरीक्षेऽहं योद्धुकामानवस्थितान् ।
Yāvadetānnirīkshe-ahaṁ Yoddhukāmānavasthitān |
कैर्मया सह योद्धव्यमस्मिन् रणसमुद्यमे ।। (22)
Kairmayā saha yoddhavyamasmin ranasamudyame ||
योत्स्यमानानवेक्षेऽहं य एतेऽत्र समागताः ।
Yotsyamānānavekshe-ahaṁ ya ete-atra samāgatāḥ |
धार्तराष्ट्रस्य दुर्बुद्धेर्युद्धे प्रियचिकीर्षवः ।। (23)
Dhārtarāṣhṭrasya durbuddheryuddhe priyacikīrshavaḥ ||

संजय उवाच/*Sañjaya Uvācha*

एवमुक्तो हृषीकेशो गुडाकेशेन भारत ।
Evamukto Hriṣīkeśo Gudākeśena Bhārata |
सेनायोरुभयोर्मध्ये स्थापयित्वा रथोत्तमम् ।। (24)
Senayorubhayormadhye sthāpayitvā rathottamaṁ ||
भीष्मदोणप्रमुखतः सर्वेषां च महीक्षिताम् ।
Bhīṣmadroṇa-pramukhataḥ sarveṣāṃ ca mahīkshitāṁ |
उवाच पार्थ पश्यैतान्समवेतान्कुरूनिति ।। (25)
Uvāca Pāṛtha paśyaitānsamavetānkūruniti ||
तत्रापश्यत्स्थितान्पार्थः पितृनथ पितामहान् ।
Tātrāpaśyatsthitānpārthaḥ pitrinatha pitāmahān |
आचार्यान्मातुलान्भ्रातृन् पुत्रान्पौत्रान्सखींस्तथा ।। (26)
Acāryānmātulānbhrātrin putrạnpautrạn sakhinstathā ||
श्वशुरान्सुहृदश्चैव सेनयोरूभयोरपि ।
Śvaśurānsuhridaścaiva senayorubhayorapi |
तान्समीक्ष्य स कौन्तेयः सर्वान्बन्धूनवस्थितान् ।। (27)
Tānsamīkshya sa Kaunteyaḥ sarvānbandhūnavasthitān ||
कृपया परयाविष्टो विषीदन्निदमब्रवीत् ।
Kripayā parayāviṣṭo viṣīdannidamabravīt |

अर्जुन उवाच /*Arjuna uvāca*

दृष्ट्वेमं स्वजनं कृष्ण युयुत्सुं समुपस्थितम् ।। (28)
Drishtvemaṁ svajanaṁ Kṛishṇa yuyutsuṁ samupasthitam ||
सीदंति मम गात्राणि मुखं च परिशुष्यति ।
Sīdanti mama gātrāṇi mukhaṁ ca pariśuṣyati |
वेपथुश्च शरीरे मे रोमहर्षश्च जायते ।। (29)
Vepathuśca śarīre me romaharshaścha jāyate ||
गांण्डीवं स्रंसते हस्तात्त्वक्चैव परिदह्यते ।
Gāṇḍīvam sraṁsate hastāttvakcaiva paridahyate |
न च शक्नोम्यवस्थातुं भ्रमतीव च मे मनः ।। (30)
Na ca śaknomyavasthātuṁ bhramatīva ca me manah ||
निमित्तानि च पश्यामि विपरीतानि केशव ।
Nimittāni ca paśyāmi viparītāni Keśava |
न च श्रेयोऽनुपश्यामि हत्वा स्वजनमाहवे ।। (31)
Na ca śreyo-anupaśyāmi hatvā svajanamāhave ||
न कांक्षे विजयं कृष्ण न च राज्यं सुखानि च ।
Na Kāṅkṣe vijayaṁ Kṛṣṇa na ca rājyaṁ sukhāni ca |
किं नो राज्येन गोविंद किं भोगैर्जीवितेन वा ।। (32)
Kiṁ no rājyena Govinda kiṁ bhogairjīvitena vā ||
येषामर्थे कांक्षितं नो राज्यं भोगाः सुखानि च ।
Yeṣāmarthe kāṅkshitaṁ no rājyaṁ bhogāḥ sukhāni ca |
त इमेऽवस्थिता युद्धे प्राणांस्त्यक्त्वा धनानि च ।। (33)
Ta ime-avasthitā yuddhe prāṇānstyaktvā dhanāni ca ||
आचार्याः पितरः पुत्रास्तथैव च पितामहाः ।
Āchāryāḥ pitaraḥ putrāstathiva ca pitāmahāḥ |
मातुलाः श्वशुराः पौत्राः श्यालाः संबन्धिनस्तथा ।। (34)
Mātulāḥ śvaśurāḥ pautrāḥ śyālāḥ saṁbandhinastathā ||
एतान्न हन्तुमिच्छामि ध्नतोऽपि मधुसूदन ।
Etānna hantumichchhāmi ghnato-api mudhusūdana |

अपि त्रैलोक्यराज्यस्य हेतोः किं नु महीकृते ।। (35)

Api trailokyarājyasya hetoḥ kim nu mahīkrite ||

निहत्य धार्तराष्ट्रान् नः का प्रीतिः स्याज्जनार्दन ।

Nihatya Dhārtarāṣhtrānnaḥ kā prītiḥ syājjanārdana |

पापमेवाश्रयेदस्मान् हत्वैतानाततायिनः ।। (36)

Pāpamevāśrayedasmān hatvaitānatātāyinaḥ ||

तस्मान्नार्हा वयं हन्तुं धार्तराष्ट्रान्स्वबान्धवान् ।

Tasmānnārhā vayaṁ hantuṁ Dhārtarāṣṭrānsvabandhavān |

स्वजनं हि कथं हत्वा सुखिनः स्याम माधव ।। (37)

Svajanam hi kathaṁ hatvā sukhināḥ syāma Mādhava ||

यद्यप्येते न पश्यंन्ति लोभोपहतचेतसः ।

Yadyapyete na paśyanti lobhopahatacetasaḥ |

कुलक्षयकृतं दोषं मित्रद्रोहे च पातकम् ।। (38)

Kulakshayakritaṁ doṣaṁ mitradrohe ca pātakaṁ ||

कथं न ज्ञेयमस्माभिः पापादस्मान्निवर्तितुम् ।

Katham na jñeyamasmābhiḥ pāpādasmānnivartituṁ |

कुलक्षयकृतं दोषं प्रपश्यद्भिर्जनार्दन ।। (39)

Kulakshayakritaṁ doṣam prapaśyadbhirjanārdana ||

कुलक्षये प्रणश्यन्ति कुलधर्माः सनातनाः ।

Kulakshaye praṇaśyanti Kuladarmāh sanātanāh |

धर्मे नष्टे कुलं कृत्स्नमधर्मोऽभिभवत्युत ।। (40)

Dharme naṣṭe kulaṁ kritsnamadharmoabhibhavatyuta ||

अधर्माभिभवात्कृष्ण प्रदुष्यन्ति कुलस्त्रियः ।

Adharmābhibhavātkṛiṣna praduṣyanti Kulastriyaḥ |

स्त्रीषु दुष्टासु वार्ष्णेय जायते वर्णसंकरः ।। (41)

Strīṣu duṣṭāsu vārṣṇeya jāyate varṇasankaraḥ ||

संकरो नरकायैव कुलघ्नानां कुलस्य च ।

Sankaro narakāyaiva Kulaghnānāṁ Kulasya ca |

पतन्ति पितरो ह्येषां लुप्तपिण्डोदकक्रिया: ।। (42)
Patanti pitaro hyeṣāṁ luptapiṇḍodakakriyāḥ ||

दोषैरेतै: कुलघ्नानां वर्णसंकरकारकै: ।
Doshiaretaiḥ Kulaghnānāṁ varṇasankarakārakaiḥ|
उत्साद्यन्ते जातिधर्मा: कुलधर्माश्च शाश्वता: ।। (43)
Utsādyante jātidharmāḥ kuladharmāśca śāśvatāḥ ||

उत्सन्नकुलधर्माणां मनुष्याणां जनार्दन ।
Utsannakuladharmāṇāṁ manusyāṇāṁ Janārdana |
नरके नियतं वासो भवतीत्यनुशुश्रुम ।। (44)
Narake niyataṁ vāso bhavatītyanuśuśruma ||

अहो बत महात्पापं कर्तुं व्यवसिता वयम् ।
Aho bata mahatpāpaṁ kartum vyavasitā vayaṁ |
यद्राज्यसुखलोभेन हन्तुं स्वजनमुद्यता: ।। (45)
Yadrājyasukhalobhena hantum svajanamudyatāḥ ||

यदि मामप्रतीकारमशस्त्रं शस्त्रपाणय: ।
Yadi māmapratīkāramaśastram śastrapāṇayaḥ |
धार्तराष्ट्रा रणे हन्युस्तन्मे क्षेमतरं भवेत् ।। (46)
Dhārtarāshtrā raṇe hanyustanme kshemataraṁ bhavet ||

संजय उवाच / *Sañjaya Uvāca*

एवमुक्त्वार्जुन: संख्ये रथोपस्थ उपाविशत् ।
Evamuktvārjunaḥ saṅkhye rathopastha upāviśat |
विसृज्य सशरं चापं शोकसंविग्नमानस: ।। (47)
Visrijya saśaraṁ chāpaṁ śokasamvignamānasaḥ ||

इति श्रीमद्भगवद्गीतासूपनिषत्सु ब्रह्मविद्यायां
Iti Śrīmadbhagavadgītāsūpanishatshu Brahmavidyāyāṁ
योगशास्त्रे श्रीकृष्णार्जुनसंवादेऽर्जुनविषादयोगो नाम प्रथमोऽध्याय :
Yogasātre Śrikrishṇārjunasamvāde-Arjunavishādayogo nāma prathamodhyāyaḥ||

CHAPTER II

संजय उवाच / *Sañjaya Uvāca*

तं तथा कृपयाविष्टमश्रुपूर्णाकुलेक्षणम् ।

Taṁ tathā kripayāvishṭamaśrūpūrṇākulekshaṇaṁ |

विषीदन्तमिदं वाक्यमुवाच मधुसूदनः ।। (1)

Vishīdantamidaṁ vākyamuvāca Madhusūdanaḥ ||

श्रीभगवानुवाच / *Śrī Bhagavānuvāca*

कुतस्त्वा कश्मलमिदं विषमे समुपस्थितम् ।

Kutastvā Kasmalamidaṁ viṣame samupasthitaṁ |

अनार्यजुष्टमस्वर्ग्यमकीर्तिकरमर्जुन।। (2)

Anāryajushtamasvargyamakīrtikaramarjuna ||

क्लैब्यं मा स्म गमः पार्थ नैतत्त्वय्युपपद्यते ।

Klaibyaṁ mā sma gamaḥ Pārtha naitattvayyupapadyate |

क्षुद्रं हृदयदौर्बल्यं त्यक्तवोत्तिष्ठ परंतप ।। (3)

Kshudraṁ hridayadaurbalyaṁ tyaktvottiṣṭha parantapa ||

अर्जुन उवाच / *Arjuna Uvāca*

कथं भीष्ममहं संख्ये द्रोणं च मधसूदन ।

Kathaṁ Bhīṣmamahaṁ saṁkhye Droṇaṁ ca Madhusūdana |

इषुभिः प्रतियोत्स्यामि पूजार्हावरिसूदन ।। (4)

Iṣubhiḥ pratiyotsyāmi pūjarhāvarisūdana ||

गुरूनहत्वा हि महानुभावान्

Gurūnahatvā hi mahānubhāvān

श्रेयो भोक्तु भैक्ष्यमपीह लोके ।

śreyo bhoktuṁ bhaikshyamapīha loke

हत्वार्थकामांस्तु गुरूनिहैव

hatvārthakāmāmstu gurūnihaiva

भुंजीय भोगान् रूधिरप्रदिग्धान् ।। (5)
bhuñjīya bhogān rudhirapradigdhān ||
न चैतद्विध्मः कतरन्नो गरीया
Na caitadvidmah kataranno garīyo
यद्वा जयेम यदि वा नो जयेयुः ।
Yadvā jayema yadi vā no jayeyuḥ |
यानेव हत्वा न जिजीविषामस्तेऽवस्थिताः प्रमुखे धार्तराष्ट्राः ।। (6)
Yāneva hatvā na jijīviṣāma-ste-avasthitāḥ pramukhe Dhārtarāshṭrāḥ ||
कार्पण्यदोषोपहतस्वभावः
Kārpaṇyadoshopahatasvabhāvaḥ
पृच्छामि त्वां धर्मसंमूढचेताः ।
Prichchhāmi tvāṁ dharmasaṁmūḍhachetāḥ |
यच्छ्रेयः स्यान्निश्चितं ब्रूहि तन्मे
Yachchhreyaḥ syānniścitaṁ brūhi tanme
शिष्यस्तेऽहं शाधि मां त्वां प्रपन्नम् ।। (7)
Śishyaste-'haṁ śādhi māṁ tvām prapannaṁ ||
नहि प्रपश्यामि ममापनुद्याद्-यच्छोकमुच्छोषणमिन्द्रियाणाम् ।
Nahi prapaśyāmi mamāpanudyād
Yachchhokamuchchhosaṇamindriyāṇāṁ |
अवाप्य भूमावसपत्नमृद्धं राज्यं सुराणामपि चाधिपत्यम् ।। (8)
Avāpya bhūmāvasapatnamriddhaṁ rājyaṁ surāṇāmapi cādhipatyaṁ ||

संजय उवाच / *Sañjaya Uvāca*

एवमुक्त्वा हृषीकेशं गुडाकेशः परंतपः ।
Evamuktvā Hriṣīkeśaṁ Guḍākesaḥ paraṅtapaḥ |
न योत्स्य इति गोविन्दमुक्त्वा तूष्णीं बभूव ह ।। (9)
Na yotsya iti Govīndamuktvā tūshṇīṁ babhūva ha ||
तमुवाच हृषीकेशः प्रहसन्निव भारत ।
Tamuvāca Hriṣīkeśaḥ prahasanniva Bhārata |

सेनयोरूभयोर्मध्ये विषीदन्तमिदं वचः ।। (10)
Senayorubhayormadhye vishīdantamidam vachaḥ ||

श्रीभगवानुवाच / *Śrī Bhagavānuvāca*

अशोच्यानन्वशोचस्त्वं प्रज्ञावादांश्च भाषसे ।
Aśocyānanvaśocastvaṁ prajñavādāṁśca bhāshase |
गतासूनगतासूंश्च नानुशोचन्ति पण्डिताः ।। (11)
Gatāsūnagatāsūṁścha nānuśocanti paṇḍitāḥ ||

न त्वेवाहं जातु नासं न त्वं नेमे जनाधिपाः ।
Na tvevāhaṁ jātu nāsaṁ na tvaṁ ne'me janādhipāḥ
न चैव न भविष्यामः सर्वे वयमतः परम् ।। (12)
Na caiva na bhavishyāmaḥ sarve vayamataḥ paraṁ ||

देहिनोऽस्मिन्यथा देहे कौमारं यौवनं जरा ।
Dehino-asminyathā dehe kaumāraṁ yauvanaṁ jarā |
तथा देहान्तरप्राप्तिर्धीरस्तत्र न मुह्यति ।। (13)
Tathā dehāntaraprāptirdhīrastatra na muhyati ||

मात्रास्पर्शास्तु कौन्तेय शीतोष्णसुखदु:खदाः ।
Mātrāsparśāstu Kaunteya śītoshṇasukhaduhkhadāḥ
आगमापायिनोऽनित्यास्तांस्तितिक्षस्व भारत ।। (14)
āgamāpāyino-anityāstāṁstitikshasva Bhārata ||

यं हि न व्यथयंत्येते, पुरूषं पुरूषर्षभ । (15)
yaṁ hi na vyathayantyete Purushaṁ purusharshabha |
समदु:खसुखं धीरं सोऽमृतत्वाय कल्पते ।
Samaduḥkhasukhaṁ dhīraṁ so-amritatvāya kalpate |

नासतो विद्यते भावो नाभावो विद्यते सतः ।। (16)
Nā'sato vidyate bhāvo Nā'bhāvo vidyate sataḥ ||
उभयोरपि दृष्टोऽन्तस्त्वनयोस्तत्त्वदर्शिभिः ।।
Ubhayorapi drishṭoṅtastvanayos tattvadarśibhiḥ ||

अविनाशि तु तद्विद्धि येन सर्वमिदं ततम् ।
Avināśi tu tadviddhi yena sarvamidhaṁ tataṁ |
विनाशमव्ययस्यास्य न कश्चित्कर्तुमर्हति ।। (17)
Vināṣamavyayasyāsya na kaśchit kartumarhati ||

अन्तवन्त इमे देहा नित्यस्योक्ता: शरीरिण: ।

Antavanta ime dehā nityasyoktāḥ śārīriṇaḥ |

अनाशिनोऽप्रमेयस्य तस्माद्युध्यस्व भारत ।। (18)

Anāśino'prameyasya tasmād yudhyasva bhārata ||

य एनं वेत्ति हंतारं यश्चैनं मन्यते हतम् ।

Ya enaṁ vetti hantāraṁ yaśchainam manyate hataṁ

उभौ तौ न विजानीतो नायं हन्ति न हन्यते ।। (19)

Ubhau tau na vijānīto nā'yam hanti na hanyate ||

न जायते म्रियते वा कदाचिन्

Na jāyate mriyate vā kadāchin

नाय भूत्वा भविता वा न भूय: ।

Nā'yaṁ bhūtvā bhavitā vā nu bhūyaḥ |

अजो नित्य: शाश्वतोऽयं पुराणो

Ajo nityaḥ śāśvato'yaṁ purāṇo

न हन्यते हन्यमाने शरीरे ।। (20)

Na hanyate hanyamāne śarīre ||

वेदा— विनाशिनं नित्य य एनमंजमंव्ययम् ।

Vedā 'avināśinaṁ nityaṁ Ya enaṁ ajam avyayaṁ |

कथं स पुरूष: पार्थ कं घातयति हन्ति कम् ।। (21)

Kathaṁ sa purushaḥ pārtha Kaṁ ghātayati hanti kaṁ |

वासांसि जीर्णानि यथा विहाय नवानि गहृणाति नरोऽपराणि ।

Vāsāṁsi jīrṇāni yathā vihāya Navāni gṛhṇāti naro'parāṇi |

तथा शरीराणि विहाय जीर्णान्यन्यानि संयाति नवानि देही ।। (22)

Tathā śarīrāṇi vihāya jīrṇānyanyāni samyāti navāni dehī ||

नैनं छिन्दन्ति शस्त्राणि नैनं दहति पावक: ।

Nainam chindanti śastrāṇi nainam dahati pāvakaḥ |

न चैनं क्लेदयन्त्यापो न शोषयति मारूत: ।। (23)

Na cainaṁ kledayantyāpo na śoṣayati mārutaḥ ||

अच्छेद्योऽयमदाह्योऽयम-

Acchedyo'yam adāhyo'yam

क्लेद्योऽशोष्य एव च ।
akledyo' aśoshya eva ca |
नित्यः सर्वगतः स्थाणुरचलोऽयं सनातनः ।। (24)
Nityaḥ sarvagataḥ sthāṇur achalo'yam sanātanaḥ ||
अव्यक्तोऽयमचिन्त्योऽयमविकार्योऽयमुच्यते ।
Avyakto'ayamacintyo'ayaṁ avikāryo'ayamucyate |
तस्मादेवं विदित्वैनं नानुशोचितुमर्हसि ।। (25)
Tasmādevaṁ viditvainam Nā'anuśocitumarhasi ||
अथ चैनं नित्यजात
Atha cainaṁ nityajātaṁ
नित्यं वा मन्यसे मृतम् ।
nityaṁ vā manyase mṛtaṁ |
तथापि त्वं महाबाहो नैवं शोचितुमर्हसि ।। (26)
Tathāpi tvaṁ mahābāho naivaṁ śocitumarhasi ||
जातस्य हि ध्रुवो मृत्युर्ध्रुवं जन्म मृतस्य च ।
Jātasya hi dhruvo mrityurdhruvaṁ janma mṛtasya ca |
तस्मादपरिहार्येऽर्थे न त्वं शोचितुमर्हसि ।। (27)
Tasmādaparihārye'rthe na tvaṁ śocitumarhasi ||
अव्यक्तादीनि भूतानि व्यक्तमध्यानि भारत ।
Avyaktādīni bhūtāni vyaktamadhyāni bhārata |
अव्यक्तनिधनान्येव तत्र का परिदेवना ।। (28)
Avyakta-nidhanān-yeva tatra kā paridevanā ||
आश्चर्यवत्पश्यति कश्चिदेनमाश्चर्यवद्वदति तथैव चान्यः ।
Āścaryavatpaśyati kaścidenamāścaryavad vadati tathaiva cānyaḥ|
आश्चर्यवच्चैनमन्यः शृणोति
Āścaryavac caina-manyaḥ śṛṇoti
श्रुत्वाप्येनं वेद न चैव कश्चित् ।। (29)
Srutvāpyenaṁ veda na caiva kaścit ||
देही नित्यमवध्योऽयं देहे सर्वस्य भारत
Dehī nityam avadhyo 'ayam dehe sarvasya bhārata |

तस्मात्सर्वाणि भूतानि न त्वं शोचितुमर्हसि ।। (30)
Tasmāt sarvāṇi bhūtāni na tvaṁ śocitum arhasi ||
स्वधर्ममपि चावेक्ष्य न विकम्पितुमर्हसि ।
Svadharmam api cā'-vekṣya na vikampitum arhasi |
धर्म्याद्धि युद्धाच्छ्रेयोऽन्यत्क्षत्रियस्य न विद्यते ।। (31)
Dharmyād-dhi yuddhāc-chreyo- anyat kṣatriyasya na vidyate||
यदृच्छया चोपपन्नं स्वर्गद्वारमपावृतम् ।
Yadṛcchayā co'papannam svargadvāram apāvṛtaṁ |
सुखिनः क्षत्रियाः पार्थ लभन्ते युद्धमीदृशम् ।। (32)
Sukhinaḥ kṣatriyāḥ Pārtha labhante yuddham īdṛśam ||
अथ चेत्त्वमिमं धर्म्यं संग्रामं न करिष्यसि ।
Atha cet tvam imam dharmyaṁ saṁgrāmaṁ na kariṣyasi |
ततः स्वधर्मंकीर्तिं च हित्वा पापमवाप्यसि ।। (33)
Tataḥ svadharmaṁ kīrtiṁ ca hitvā pāpam avāpyasi ||
अकीर्तिं चापि भूतानि कथयिष्यन्ति ते ऽव्ययाम् ।
Akīrtim cā 'pi bhūtāni kathayiṣyanti te avyayām
संभावितस्य चाकीर्तिर्मरणादतिरिच्यते ।। (34)
Sambhāvitasya cākīrtirmaraṇādatiricyate ||
भयाद्रणादुपरतं मंस्यन्ते त्वां महारथाः ।
Bhayād raṇād uparataṁ maṁsyante tvāṁ mahārathāḥ |
येषां च त्वं बहुमतो भूत्वा यास्यसि लाघवम् ।। (35)
Yeṣāṁ ca tvaṁ bahumato bhūtvā yāsyasi lāghavaṁ
अवाच्यवादांश्च बहून्वदिष्यन्ति तवाहिताः ।
Avācyavādāṁśca bahūnvadiṣyanti tavā'hitāḥ |
निन्दन्तस्तव सामर्थ्यं
Nindantas- tava sāmarthyam
ततो दुःखतरं नु किम् ।। (36)
tato duhkhataram nu kim ||
हतो वा प्राप्स्यसि स्वर्गं
Hato vā prāpṣyasi svargaṁ

जित्वा वा भोक्ष्यसे महीम् ।
jitvā vā bhokṣyase mahīm |
तस्मादुत्तिष्ट कौन्तेय
Tasmād uttiṣṭha Kaunteya
युद्धाय कृतनिश्चयः ।। (37)
yuddhāya kritaniścayaḥ ||
सुखदुःखे समे कृत्वा लाभालाभौ जयाजयौ ।
Sukhaduḥkhe same kṛtvā lābhālābhau jayājayau |
ततो युद्धाय युज्यस्व नैवं पापमवाप्स्यसि ।। (38)
Tato yuddhāya yujyasva nai'vaṁ pāpaṁ avāpsyasi ||
एषा ते ऽभिहिता सांख्ये बुद्धिर्योगे त्विमां शृणु ।
Eṣā te 'bhihitā sāṅkhye buddhiryoge tvimāṁ śṛṇu |
बुद्ध्या युक्तो यया पार्थ
Buddhyā yukto yayā Pārtha
कर्मबन्धं प्रहास्यसि ।। (39)
Karmabandhaṁ prahāsyasi ||
नेहाभिक्रमनाशोऽस्ति प्रत्यवायो न विद्यते ।
Ne'hā'bhikramanāśo 'sti pratyavāyo na vidyate |
स्वल्पमप्यस्य धर्मस्य त्रायते महतो भयात् ।। (40)
Svalpamapyasya dharmasya trāyate mahato bhayāt ||
व्यवसायात्मिका बुद्धिरेकेह कुरूनंदन ।
Vyavasāyātmikā buddhirekeha kurunandana |
बहुशाखा ह्यनन्ताश्च बुद्धयोऽव्यवसायिनाम् ।। (41)
Bahuśākhā hyanantāśca buddhayo-avyavasāyināṁ ||
यामिमां पुष्पितां वाचं प्रवदन्त्यविपश्चितः ।
Yāmimāṁ puṣpitāṁ vācaṁ pravadantyavipaścitaḥ |
वेदवादरताः पार्थ नान्यदस्तीति वादिनः ।। (42)
Vedavādaratāḥ Pārtha nānyadastīti vādinaḥ ||
कामात्मानः स्वर्गपरा जन्मकर्मफलप्रदाम् ।
Kāmātmānaḥ svargaparā janmakarmāphalapradāṁ |

क्रियाविशेषबहुलां भोगैश्वर्यगतिं प्रति ।। (43)
Kriyāviśeṣabahulāṁ bhogaiśvaryagatim prati ||
भोगैश्वर्यप्रसक्तानां तयाऽपहृतचेतसां ।
Bhogaiśvaryaprasaktānāṁ tayāpahṛtacetasāṁ |
व्यवसायात्मिका बुद्धिः समाधौ न विधीयते ।। (44)
Vyavasāyātmikā buddhiḥ samādhau na vidhīyate ||
त्रैगुण्यविषया वेदा निस्त्रैगुण्यो भवार्जुन ।
Traiguṇyaviṣayā Vedā nistraiguṇyo bhavārjuna |
निर्द्वन्द्वो नित्यसत्त्वस्थो निर्योगक्षेम आत्मवान् ।। (45)
Nirdvandvo nityasattvastho niryogakṣema ātmavān ||
यावानर्थ उदपाने सर्वतः संप्लुतोदके ।
Yāvānartha udapāne sarvataḥ saṁplutodake |
तावान्सर्वेषु वेदेषु ब्राह्मणस्य विजानतः ।। (46)
Tāvānsarveṣu vedeṣu brāhmaṇasya vijānataḥ ||
कर्मण्येवाधिकारस्ते मा फलेषु कदाचन ।
Karmaṇyevādhikāraste mā phaleṣu kadācana |
मा कर्मफलहेतुर्भूर्मा ते सङ्गोऽस्त्वकर्मणि ।। (47)
Mā karmaphalaheturbhūrmā te saṅgo'stvakarmaṇi ||
योगस्थः कुरू कर्माणि सङ्गं त्यक्त्वा धनंजय ।
Yogasthaḥ kuru karmāṇi saṅgam tyaktvā Dhanañjaya |
सिद्ध्यसिद्ध्योः समो भूत्वा समत्वं योग उच्यते ।। (48)
Siddhyasiddhyoḥ samo bhūtvā samatvaṁ yoga ucyate ||
दूरेण ह्यवरं कर्म बुद्धियोगाद्धनंजय ।
Dūreṇa hyavaraṁ karma buddhiyogāddhanañjaya |
बुद्धौ शरणमन्विच्छ कृपणाः फलहेतवः ।। (49)
Buddhau śaraṇamanviccha kṛpaṇāḥ phalahetavaḥ ||
बुद्धियुक्तो जहातीह उभे सुकृतदुष्कृते ।
Buddhiyukto jahātīha ubhe sukṛtaduṣkṛte |
तस्माद्योगाय युज्यस्व योगः कर्मसु कौशलम् ।। (50)
Tasmādyogāya yujyasva yogaḥ karmasu kauśalaṁ ||

कर्मजं बुद्धियुक्ता हि फलं त्यक्त्वा मनीषिण:
Karmajaṁ buddhiyuktā hi phalaṁ tyaktvā manīṣīṇaḥ |
जन्मबन्धविनिर्मुक्ता: पदं गच्छन्त्यनामयम्: ।। (51)
Janmabandhavinirmuktāḥ padaṁ gacchantyanāmayaṁ ||
यदा ते मोहकलिलं बुद्धिर्व्यतितरिष्यति ।
Yadā te mohakalilam buddhirvyatitariṣyati |
तदा गन्तासि निर्वेदं श्रोतव्यस्य श्रुतस्य च ।। (52)
Tadā gantāsi nirvedam śrotavyasya śrutasya ca ||
श्रुतिविप्रतिपन्ना ते यदा स्थास्यति निश्चला ।
Śrutiviparatipannā te yadā sthāsyati niścalā |
समाधावचला बुद्धिस्तदा योगमवाप्स्यसि ।। (53)
Smādhāvacalā buddhistadā yogamavāpsyasi ||

अर्जुन उवाच /*Arjuna Uvāca*

स्थितप्रज्ञस्य का भाषा समाधिस्थस्य केशव ।
Sthitaprajñasya kā bhāṣā samādhisthasya keśava |
स्थितधी: किं प्रभाषेत किमासीत व्रजेत किम् ।। (54)
Sthitadhīḥ kim prabhāṣeta kimāsīta vrajeta kiṁ ||

श्रीभगवानुवाच /*(Śrībhagavānuvāca)*

प्रजहाति यदा कामान्सर्वान्पार्थ मनोगतान् ।
Prajahātī yadā kāmānsarvạ̄npārtha manogatām
आत्मन्येवात्मना तुष्ट: स्थितप्रज्ञस्तदोच्यते ।। (55)
Ātmanyevātmanā tuṣṭaḥ sthitaprajñastadocyate ||
दु:खेष्वुद्विग्नमना: सुखेषु विगतस्पृह: ।
Duḥkheṣvanudvignamanāḥ sukheṣu vigatasprihaḥ |
वीतरागभयक्रोध: स्थितधीर्मुनिरूच्यते ।। (56)
Vitarāgabhayakrodhaḥ sthitadhīrmunirucyate ||
य: सर्वत्रानभिस्तेहस्तत्तत्प्राप्य शुभाशुभम् ।
Yaḥ sarvatrānabhisnehastattatprāpya śubhāśubhaṁ |

नाभिनन्दति न द्वेष्टि तस्य प्रज्ञा प्रतिष्ठिता ।। (57)

Nābhinaṇdati na dveṣṭi tasya prajñā pratiṣṭhitā ||

यदा संहरते चायं कूर्मोऽङगानीव सर्वशः ।

Yadā samharate cāyam kūrmoangānīva sarvaśah |

इन्द्रियाणीन्द्रियार्थेभयस्तस्य प्रज्ञा प्रतिष्ठिता ।। (58)

Indriyāṇīndriyārthebhyastasya prajñā pratiṣṭhitā ||

विषया विनिवर्तन्ते निराहारस्य देहिनः ।

Viṣayā vinivartante nirahārasya dehinaḥ |

रसवर्ज रसोऽप्यस्य परं दृष्ट्वा निवर्तते ।। (59)

Rasavarjaṁ raso'pyasya paraṁ dṛṣṭvā nivartate ||

यततो ह्यपि कौन्तेय पुरूषस्य विपश्चितः ।

Yatato hyapi kaunteya puruṣasya vipaścitaḥ |

इन्द्रियाणि प्रमाथीनि हरन्ति प्रसभं मनः ।। (60)

Indriyāṇi pramāthīni haranti prasabhaṁ manaḥ ||

तानि सर्वाणि संयम्य युक्त आसीत मत्परः ।

Tāni sarvāṇi saṁyamya yukta āsita matparaḥ |

वशे हि यस्येन्द्रियाणि तस्य प्रज्ञा प्रतिष्ठिता ।। (61)

Vaśe hi yasyendriyāṇi tasya prajñā pratiṣṭhitā ||

ध्यायतो विषयान्पुंसः संगस्तेषूपजायते ।

dhyāyato viṣayānpuṁsaḥ sangasteṣūpajāyate |

संगात्संजायते कामः कामात्क्रोधोऽभिजायते ।। (62)

sangātsañjāyate kāmaḥ kāmātkrodho'bhijāyate ||

क्रोधाद्भवति संमोहः संमोहात्स्मृति विभ्रमः ।

Krodhādbhavati saṁmohaḥ saṁmohātsmṛtivibhramaḥ |

स्मृतिभ्रम शाद्बुद्धिनाशो बुद्धिनाशात्प्रणश्यति ।। (63)

Smṛtibhraṁśādbuddhināśo buddhināśātpraṇaśyati ||

रागद्वेषवियुक्तैस्तु विषयानिन्द्रियैश्चरन् ।

Rāgadveṣaviyuktaistu viṣayānindriyaiścaran |

आत्मवश्यैर्विधेयात्मा प्रसादमधिगच्छति ।। (64)

Ātmavaśyairvidheyātmā prasādamadhigacchati ||

प्रसादे सर्वदु:खानां हानिरस्योपजायते ।
Prasāde sarvaduhkhānāṁ hānirasyopajāyate |
प्रसन्नचेतसो ह्याशु बुद्धि: पर्यवतिष्ठति ।। (65)
Prasannacetaso hyāśu buddhiḥ paryavatiṣṭhati |
नास्ति बुद्धिरयुक्तस्य न चायुक्तस्य भावना ।
Nāsti buddhirayuktasya na cāyuktasya bhāvanā |
न चाभावयत: शांतिरशांतस्य कुत: सुखम् ।। (66)
Na cābhāvayataḥ śāntiraśāntasya kutaḥ sukhaṁ ||
इन्द्रियाणां हि चरतां यन्मनोऽनुविधीयते ।
Indriyāṇāṁ hi caratāṁ yanmano-anuvidhīyate |
तदस्य हरति प्रज्ञां वायुर्नावमिवाम्भसि ।। (67)
Tadasya harati prajñāṁ vāyurnāvamivāṁbhasi ||
तस्माद्यस्य महाबाहो निगृहीतानि सर्वश: ।
Tasmādyasya mahābāho nigrhitāni sarvaśaḥ
इन्द्रियाणीन्द्रियार्थेभ्यस्तस्य प्रज्ञा प्रतिष्ठिता ।। (68)
Indriyāṇīndriyārthebhyastasya prajñā pratiṣṭhita ||
या निशा सर्वभूतानां तस्यां जागर्ति संयमी ।
Yā niśa sarvabhūtānāṁ tasyāṁ jāgarti saṁyamī |
यस्यां जाग्रति भूतानि सा निशा पश्यतो मुने: ।। (69)
Yasyām jāgrati bhūtāni sā niśā paśyatō muneḥ ||
आपूर्यमाणमचलप्रतिष्ठं समुद्रमाप: प्रविशन्ति यद्वत् ।
Āpūryamāṇamacala-pratiṣṭhaṁ Samudramāpaḥ praviśanti yadvat |
तद्वत्कामा यं प्रविशन्ति सर्वे स शान्तिमाप्नोति न कामकामी ।। (70)
Tadvatkāmā yaṁ parviśanti sarve sa śāntimāpnoti na kāmakāmī ||
विहाय कामान्य: सर्वान्पुमांश्चरति नि:स्पृह: ।
Vihāya kāmānyaḥ sarvānpuṁaṁścarati niḥsprihaḥ |
निर्ममो निरहंकार: स शान्तिमधिगच्छति ।। (71)
Nirmamo nirahaṁkāraḥ sa śāntimadhigacchati ||

एषा ब्राह्मी स्थितिः पार्थ नैनां प्राप्य विमुह्यति ।
Eṣā brāhmī sthitiḥ Pārtha naināṁ prāpya vimuhyati |
स्थित्वास्यामन्तकालेऽपि ब्रह्मनिर्वाणमृच्छति ।। (72)
Sthitvāsyāmantakāle 'pi brahmanirvāṇamṛcchati ||
इति श्रीमद्भगवद्गीतासूपनिषत्सु
Iti Śrīmadbhagavadgītasūpaniṣatsu
सांख्ययोगो नाम द्वितीयोऽध्यायः ।।
Sāṅkhyayogo nāma dvitīyo-adhyāyaḥ ||

CHAPTER III

Karma Yoga or Method of Work

अर्जुन उवाच /*Arjuna uvāca*

ज्यायसी चेत्कर्मणस्ते मता बुद्धिर्जनार्दन ।
Jyāyasī cetkarmaṇaste matābuddhirjanārdana |
तत्किं कर्मणि घोरे मां नियोजयसि केशव ।। (1)
Tatkiṁ karmaṇi ghore māṁ niyojayasi Keśava ||
व्यामिश्रेणेव वाक्येन बुद्धिं मोहयसीव मे ।
Vyāmiśreṇeva vākyena buddhiṁ mohayasīva me |
तदेकं वद निश्चित्य येन श्रेयोऽहमाप्नुयाम् ।। (2)
Tadekaṁ vada niścitya yena sreyo 'hamāpnuyāṁ ||

श्रीभगवानुवाच /*(Śrībhagavānuvāca)*

लोकेऽस्मिन् द्विविधा निष्ठा पुरा प्रोक्ता मयानध ।
Loke-asmin dvividhā niṣṭhā purā proktā mayānagha |
ज्ञानयोगेन सांख्यानां कर्मयोगेन योगिनाम् ।। (3)
Jñānayogena sāṅkhyānāṁ karmayogena yogināṁ ||
न कर्मणामनारंभान्नैष्कर्भ्यं पुरूषोऽश्नुते ।
Na karmaṇāmanrambhānnaiṣkarmyaṁ puruṣa 'śnute |
न च संन्यसनादेव सिद्धिं समधिगच्छति ।। (4)
Na ca saṁnyasanādeva siddhiṁ samadhigacchati ||
नहि कश्चित्क्षणमपि जातु तिष्ठत्यकर्मकृत् ।
Nahi kaścitkṣaṇamapi jātu tiṣṭhatyakarmakṛt |
कार्यते ह्यवशः कर्म सर्वः प्रकृतिजैर्गुणैः ।। (5)
Kāryate hyavaśaḥ karma sarvaḥ prakṛtijairguṇaiḥ ||
कर्मेन्द्रियाणि संयम्य य आस्ते मनसा स्मरन् ।
Karmendriyāṇi saṁyamya ya āste manasā smaran |

इन्द्रियार्थान्विमूढात्मा मिथ्याचारः स उच्चते ।। (6)
Indriyārthānvimūḍhātmā mithyācāraḥ sa ucyate
यस्त्विन्द्रियाणि मनसा नियम्यारभतेऽर्जुन ।
Yastvindriyāṇi manasā niyamyārabhate-`rjuna |
कर्मेन्द्रियैः कर्मयोगमसक्तः स विशिष्यते ।। (7)
Karmendriyaiḥ karmayogamasaktaḥ sa viśiṣyate ||
नियतं कुरू कर्म त्वं कर्म जयायो ह्यकर्मणः ।
Niyataṁ kuru karma tvaṁ karma jyāyo hyakarmaṇaḥ |
शरीरयात्रापि च ते न प्रसिध्येदकर्मणः ।। (8)
Śarīrayātrāpi ca te na prasidhyedakarmaṇaḥ ||
यज्ञार्थात्कर्मणोऽन्यत्र लोकोऽयं कर्मबन्धनः ।
Yajñārthātkarmaṇo-anyatra loko-ayam karmabandhanaḥ
तदर्थं कर्म कौन्तेय मुक्तसंगः समाचर ।। (9)
Tadarthaṁ karma Kaunteya muktasangaḥ samāchara ||
सहायज्ञाः प्रजाः सृष्ट्वा पुरोवाच प्रजापतिः ।
Sahayajñāḥ prajāḥ sriṣṭvā purovāca prajāpatiḥ |
अनेन प्रसविष्यध्वमेष वोऽस्त्विष्टकामधक् ।। (10)
Anena prasaviṣyadhvameṣa vo-astviṣṭakāmadhuk ||
देवान्भावयतानेन ते देवा भावयन्तु वः ।
Devānbhāvayatānena te devā bhāvayantu vaḥ |
परस्परं भावयन्तः श्रेयः परमवाप्स्यथ ।। (11)
Parasparaṁ bhāvayantaḥ śreyaḥ paramavāpsyatha ||
इष्टान्भोगान्हि वो देवा दास्यन्ते यज्ञभाविताः ।
Iṣṭānbhogānhi vo devā dāsyante yajñabhāvitāḥ |
तैर्दत्तानप्रदायैभ्यो यो भुङक्ते स्तेन एव सः ।। (12)
Tairdattānapradāyaibhyo yo bhuṅkte stena eva saḥ ||
यज्ञशिष्टाशिनः सन्तो मुच्यन्ते सर्वकिल्बिषैः ।
Yajñaśiṣṭāśinaḥ santo muchyante sarvakilbiṣaiḥ |
भुञ्जते ते त्वघं पापा ये पचन्त्यात्मकारणात् ।। (13)
Bhuñjate te tvaghaṁ pāpā ye pacantyātṁakāraṇāt ||

अन्नाद्भवन्ति भूतानि पर्जन्यादन्नसंभवः ।
Annādbhavanti bhūtāni parjanyādannasambhavaḥ |
यज्ञाद्भवति पर्जन्यो यज्ञः कर्मसमुद्भव ।। (14)
Yajñādbhavati parjanyo yajnaḥ karmasamudbhavaḥ ||
कर्म ब्रह्मोद्भवं विद्धि ब्रह्माक्षरसमुद्भवम् ।
Karma brahmodbhavaṁ viddhi brahmākṣarasamudbhavam |
तस्मात्सर्वगतं ब्रह्म नित्यं यज्ञे प्रतिष्ठितम् ।। (15)
Tasmātsarvagataṁ brahma nityaṁ yajne pratiṣṭhitam ||
एवं प्रवर्तितं चक्रं नानुवर्तयतीह यः ।
Evaṁ pravartitaṁ cakraṁ nānuvartayatīha yaḥ |
अघायुरिन्द्रियारामो मोघं पार्थ स जीवति ।। (16)
Aghāyurindriyārāmo moghaṁ Pārtha sa jīvati ||
यस्त्वात्मरतिरेव स्यादात्मतृप्तश्च मानवः ।
Yastvātmaratireva syādātmatriptaśca mānavaḥ |
आत्मन्येव च सन्तुष्टस्तस्य कार्यं न विद्यते ।। (17)
Ātmanyeva ca santuṣtastasya kāryaṁ na vidyate ||
नैव तस्य कृतेनार्थो नाकृतेनेह कश्चन ।
Naiva tasya kritenārtho nākriteneha kaścana |
न चास्य सर्वभूतेषु कश्चिदर्थव्यपाश्रयः ।। (18)
Na cāsya sarvabhūteṣu kaścidarthavyapāśrayaḥ ||
तस्मादसक्तः सततं कार्यं कर्म समाचर ।
Tasmādasaktaḥ satataṁ kāryaṁ karma samācara |
असक्तो ह्याचरन्कर्म परमाप्नोति पूरुषः ।। (19)
Asakto hyācarankarma paramāpnoti pūruṣaḥ ||
कर्मणैव हि संसिद्धिमास्थिता जनकादयः ।
Karmaṇaiva hi saṁsiddhimāsthitā janakādayaḥ |
लोकसंग्रहमेवापि संपश्यन्कर्तुमर्हसि ।। (20)
Lokasaṁgrahamevāpi saṁpaśyankartumarhasi ||
यद्यदाचरति श्रेष्टस्तत्तदेवेतरो जनः ।
Yadyadācarati śreṣṭhastattadevetaro janaḥ |

स यत्प्रमाणं कुरूते लोकस्तदनुवर्तते ।। (21)

Sa Yatpramāṇaṁ kurute lokastadanuvartate ||

न मे पार्थास्ति कर्तव्यं त्रिषु लोकेषु किंचन ।

Na me Pārthāsti kartavyam triṣu lokeṣu kiñchana |

नानवाप्तमवाप्तव्यं वर्त एव च कर्मणि ।। (22)

Nānavāptamavāptavyaṁ varta eva ca karmaṇi ||

यदि ह्यहं न वर्तेयं जातु कर्मण्यतन्द्रितः ।

Yadi hyahaṁ na varteyaṁ jātu karmaṇyatandritaḥ

मम वर्त्मानुवर्तन्ते मनुष्याः पार्थ सर्वशः ।। (23)

Mama vartmānuvartante manuṣyāḥ Pārtha sarvaśaḥ

उत्सीदेयुरिमे लोका न कुर्यां कर्म चेदहम् ।

Utsīdeyurime lokā na kuryāṁ karma cedahaṁ |

संकरस्य च कर्ता स्यामुपहन्यामिमाः प्रजाः ।। (24)

Saṅkarasya ca kartā syāmupahanyāmimāḥ prajāḥ ||

सक्ताः कर्मण्यविद्वांसो यथा कुर्वन्ति भारत ।

Saktāh karmaṇyavidvāṁso yathā kurvanti Bhārata |

कुर्याद्विद्वांस्तथा— सक्तश्चिकीर्षुर्लोकसंग्रहम् ।। (25)

Kuryādvidvāṁstathā saktaścikīrṣurlokasamgrahaṁ ||

न बुद्धिभेदं जनयेदज्ञानां कर्मसङ्गिनाम् ।

Na buddhibhedam janayedajñanāṁ karmasaṅgināṁ |

जोषयेत्सर्वकर्माणि विद्वान्युक्तः समाचरन् ।। (26)

Joṣayetsarvakarmāṇi vidvānyuktaḥ samācaran ||

प्रकृतेः क्रियमाणानि गुणैः कर्माणि सर्वशः ।

Prakriteḥ kriyamāṇāni guṇaiḥ karmāṇi sarvaśaḥ |

अहंकारविमूढात्मा कर्ताहमिति मन्यते ।। (27)

Ahaṅkāravimūḍhātmā kartāhamiti manyate ||

तत्ववित्तु महाबाहो गुणकर्मविभागयोः ।

Tatvavittu mahābāho guṇakarmavibhāgayoḥ |

गुणा गुणेषु वर्तन्त इति मत्वा न सज्जते ।। (28)

Guṇā guṇeṣu vartanta iti matvā na sajjate ||

प्रकृतेर्गुणसंमूढा: सज्जन्ते गुणकर्मसु ।
Prakriterguṇasaṁmūḍhāḥ sajjante guṇakarmasu |
तानकृत्स्नविदो मन्दान्कृत्स्नविन्न विचालयेत् ।। (29)
Tānakṛtsnavido mandānkṛtsnavinna vicālayet ||
मयि सर्वाणि कर्माणि संन्यस्याध्यात्मचेतसा ।
Mayi sarvāṇi karmāṇi sanyasyādhyātmacetasā |
निराशीर्निर्ममो भूत्वा युध्यस्व विगतज्वर: ।। (30)
Nirāśīrnirmamo bhūtvā yuḍhyasva vigatajvaraḥ ||
ये मे मतमिदं नित्यमनुतिष्ठन्ति मानवा: ।
Ye me matamidaṁ nityamanutiṣṭhanti mānavaḥ
श्रद्धावन्तोऽनसूयन्तो मुच्यन्ते तेऽपि कर्मभि:।। (31)
Śraddhāvanto-anasūyanto mucyante te-api karmabhih||
ये त्वेतदभ्यसूयन्तो नानुतिष्ठन्ति मे मतम् ।
Ye tvetadbhyasūyanto nānutiṣṭhanti me matam |
सर्वज्ञानविमूढांस्तान्विद्धि नष्टानचेतस: ।। (32)
Sarvajñānavimūḍhāṁstānviddhi naṣṭānacetasaḥ ||
सदृशं चेष्टते स्वंस्या: प्रकृतेर्ज्ञनिवानपि ।
Sadṛśam ceṣṭate svasyāḥ prakṛterjñānavānapi |
प्रकृतिं यान्ति भूतानि निग्रह: किं करिष्यति ।। (33)
Prakṛtiṁ yānti bhūtāni nigrahaḥ kiṁ kariṣyati ||
इन्द्रियस्येन्द्रियस्यार्थे रागद्वेषौ व्यवस्थितौ ।
Indriyasyendriyasyārthe rāgadveṣau vyavasthitau ||
तयोर्न वशमागच्छेत्तौ ह्यस्य परिपन्थिनौ ।। (34)
Tayorna vaśamāgacchettau hyasya paripanthinau ||
श्रेयान्स्वधर्मो विगुण: परधर्मात्स्वनुष्ठितात् ।
Śreyānsvadharmo viguṇaḥ paradharmātsvanuṣṭhitāt ||
स्वधर्मे निधनं श्रेय: परधर्मो भयावह: ।। (35)
Svadharme nihanaṁ śreyaḥ paradharmo bhāyavahaḥ ||

अर्जुन उवाच / *Arjuna uvāca*

अथ केन प्रयुक्तोऽयं पापं चरति पूरुष: ।
Atha kena prayukto-ayaṁ pāpaṁ carati pūruṣaḥ |

अनिच्छन्नपि वार्ष्णेय बलादिव नियोजितः ।। (36)

Anicchannapi vārṣṇeya balādiva niyojitaḥ ||

श्रीभगवानुवाच / *Śrï Bhagavānuvāca*

काम एष क्रोध एष रजोगुणसमुद्भवः

Kāma eṣa krodha eṣa rajoguṇasamudbhavaḥ |

महाशनो महापाप्मा विद्ध्येनमिह वैरिणाम् ।। (37)

Mahāśano mahāpāpmā viddhyenamiha vairiṇaṁ ||

धूमेनाव्रियते वह्निर्यथादर्शो मलेन च ।

Dhūmenāvriyate vahniryathādarśo malena ca |

यथोल्बेनावृतो गर्भस्तथा तेनेदमावृतम ।। (38)

Yatholbenāvṛto garbhastathā tenedamāvṛtaṁ ||

आवृतं ज्ञानमेतेन ज्ञानिनो नित्यवैरिणा ।

Āvṛtaṁ jñānametena jñanino nityavairiṇā |

कामरूपेण कौन्तेय दुष्पूरेणानलेन च ।। (39)

Kāmarūpeṇa kaunteya duṣpūreṇānalena ca ||

इन्द्रियाणि मनो बुद्धिरस्याधिष्टानमुच्यत ।

Indriyāṇi mano budhirasyādhiṣṭānamucyate |

एतैर्विमोहयत्येष ज्ञानमावृत्य देहिनम् ।। (40)

Etairvimohayatyeṣa jñānamāvṛtya dehinaṁ ||

तस्मात्त्वमिन्द्रियाण्यादौ नियम्य भरतर्षभ ।

Tasmāttvamindriyāṇyāḍau niyamya bharatarṣabha |

पाप्मानं प्रजहि ह्येनं ज्ञानविज्ञाननाशनम् ।। (41)

Pāpmānaṁ prajahi hyenaṁ jñānavijñānanāśanaṁ ||

इन्द्रियाणि पराण्याहुरिन्द्रियेभ्यः परं मनः ।

Indriyāṇi parāṇyāhurindriyebhyaḥ paraṁ manaḥ |

मनसस्तु परा बुद्धिर्यो बुद्धेः परतस्तु सः ।। (42)

Manasastu parā buddhiryo buddheḥ paratastu saḥ ||

एवं बुद्धेः परं बुद्धवा संस्तभ्यात्मानमात्मना ।

Evaṁ buddheḥ paraṁ buddhvā samstabhuyātmānamātmanā||

जहि शत्रुं महाबाहो कामरूपं दुरासदम् ।। (43)
Jahi śatruṁ mahābāho kāmarūpaṁ durāsadaṁ ||
इति श्रीमद्भगवद्गीतायां कर्मयोगो नाम तृतीयोऽध्यायः ।।
Iti śrīmadbhagavadgītā karmayogo nāma Tritiyo-adhyāyah.

CHAPTER IV

The Path of Knowledge

श्री भगवानुवाच / *Śri Bhagavān-uvāca*

इमं विवस्वते योगं प्रोक्तवानहमव्ययम् ।
Imam vivasvate yogaṁ proktavānahamavyayaṁ |
विवस्वान्मनवे प्राह मनुरिक्ष्वाकवेऽब्रवीत् ।। (1)
Vivasvānamanave prāha manurikṣvākave-'bravīt ||
एवं परम्पराप्राप्तमिमं राजर्षयो विदुः ।
Evam paramparāprāptamimaṁ rājarṣayo viduḥ |
स कालेनेह महता योगो नष्टः परन्तप ।। (2)
Sa Kāleneha mahatā yogo naṣṭaḥ parantapa ||
स एवायं मया तेऽद्य योगः प्रोक्तः पुरातनः ।
Sa evāyaṁ mayā te-'dya yogaḥ proktaḥ purātanaḥ |
भक्तोऽसि मे सखा चेति रहस्यं ह्येतदुत्तमम् ।। (3)
Bhakto-'si me sakhā ceti rahasyaṁ hyetaduttamaṁ ||

अर्जुन उवाच / *Arjuna uvāca*

अपरं भवतो जन्म परं जन्म विवस्वतः ।
Aparaṁ bhavato janma paraṁ janma Vivasvataḥ |
कथमेतद्विजानीयां त्वमादौ प्रोक्त्तवानिति ।। (4)
Kathametadvijānīyāṁ tvamādau proktavāniti ||

श्री भगवानुवाच / *Śrībhagavānuvāca*

बहूनि मे व्यतीतानि जन्मानि तव चार्जुन ।
Bahūni me vyatītāni janmāni tava cārjuna |
तान्यहं वेद सर्वाणि न त्वं वेत्थ परन्तप ।। (5)
Tānyahaṁ veda sarvāṇi na tvaṁ vettha parantapa ||

अजोऽपि सन्व्ययात्मा भूतानामीश्वरोऽपि सन् ।
Ajo'pi sannavyāyatmā bhūtānamīsvaro-'pi san |
प्रकृतिं स्वामधिष्टाय सम्भवाम्यात्ममायाया ।। (6)
Prakritiṁ svāmadhistāya sambhavāmyātmamāyayā ||
यदा यदा हि धर्मस्य ग्लानिर्भवति भारत ।
Yadā Yadā hi dharmasya glānirbhavati Bhārata |
अभ्युत्थानमधर्मस्य तदात्मानं सृजाम्यहम् ।। (7)
Abhyutthānamadharmasya tadātmānaṁ sṛjāmyahaṁ ||
परित्राणाय साधूनां विनाशाय च दुष्कृताम ।
Paritrāṇāya sādhūnāṁ vināśāya ca duṣkritāṁ |
धर्मसंस्थापनार्थाय सम्भवामि युगे युगे ।। (8)
Dharmasamsthāpanārthāya sambhavāmi yuge yuge ||
जन्म कर्म च मे दिव्यमेवं यो वेत्ति तत्त्वतः ।
Janma karma ca me divyamevaṁ yo vetti tattvataḥ |
त्यक्त्वा देहं पुनर्जन्म नैति मामेति सोऽर्जुन ।। (9)
Tyaktvā dehaṁ punarjanma naiti māmeti so-arjuna |
वीतरागभयक्रोधा मन्मना मामुपाश्रिताः ।
Vītarāgabhayakrodhā manmanā māmupāśritāḥ |
बहवो ज्ञानतपसा पूता मद्भावमागताः ।। (10)
Bahavo jñānatapasā pūtā madbhāvamāgatāḥ ||
ये यथा मां प्रपद्यन्ते तांस्तथैव भजाम्यहम् ।
Ye yathā mām prapadyante tāṁstathaiva bhajāmyahaṁ |
मम वर्त्मानुवर्तन्ते मनुष्या पार्थ सर्वशः ।। (11)
Mama vartmānuvartante manuṣyāḥ Pārtha sarvaśaḥ ||
काङ:क्षन्तः कर्मणः सिद्धिं यजन्त इह देवताः ।
Kāṅkṣantaḥ karmaṇaḥ siddhiṁ yajanta iha devatāḥ |
क्षिप्रं हि मानुषे लोके सिद्धिर्भवति कर्मजा ।। (12)
Kṣipraṁ hi mānuṣe loke siddhirbhavati karmajā ||
चातुर्वर्ण्यं मया सृष्टं गुणकर्मविभागशः ।
Cāturvarṇyam mayā sṛṣṭaṁ guṇakarmavibhāgaśaḥ |

तस्य कर्तारमपि मां विद्ध्यकर्तारमव्ययम् ।। (13)
Tasya kartāramapi mām viddhyakartāramavyayam ||
न मां कर्माणि लिम्पन्ति न मे कर्मफले स्पृहा ।
Na māṁ karmāṇi limpanti na me karmaphale spṛhā |
इति मां योऽभिजानाति कर्मभिर्न स विध्यते ।। (14)
Iti māṁ yo-'bhijānāti karmabhirna sa vidhyate ||
एवं ज्ञात्वा कृतं कर्म पूर्वैरपि मुमुक्षभिः ।
Evaṁ jñātvā kṛtaṁ karma pūrvairapi mumukṣubhiḥ |
कुरू कर्मैव तस्मात्त्वं पूर्वैः पूर्वतरं कृतम् ।। (15)
Kuru karmaiva tasmāttvaṁ pūrvaih pūrvataraṁ kṛtaṁ ||
किं कर्म किमकर्मेति कवयोऽप्यत्र मोहिताः ।
Kim karma kimakarmeti kavayo-'pyatra mohitāh |
तत्ते कर्म प्रवक्ष्यामि यज्ज्ञात्वा मोक्ष्यसेऽशुभात् ।। (16)
Tatte karma pravakṣyāmi yajjñātvā mokṣyase-'śubhāt ||
कर्मणो ह्यपि बोद्धव्यं बोद्धव्यं च विकर्मणः ।
Karmaṇo hyapi boddhavyaṁ boddhavyaṁ ca vikarmaṇaḥ |
अकर्मणश्च बोद्धव्यं गहना कर्मणो गतिः ।। (17)
Akarmaṇaśca boddhavyaṁ gahanā karmaṇo gatiḥ ||
कर्मण्यकर्म यः पश्येदकर्मणि च कर्म यः ।
Karmaṇyakarma yaḥ paśyedakarmaṇi ca karma yaḥ |
स बुद्धिमान्मनुष्येषु स युक्तः कृत्स्नकर्मकृत् ।। (18)
Sa buddhimānmanuṣyeṣu sa yuktaḥ kṛtsnakarmakrit ||
यस्य सर्वे समारम्भाः कामसंकल्पवर्जिताः ।
Yasya sarve samārambhāḥ kāmasaṁkalpavarjitāḥ |
ज्ञानाग्निदग्धकर्माणं तमाहुः पण्डितं बुधाः ।। (19)
Jñānāgnidagdhakarmāṇaṁ tamāhuḥ paṇḍitaṁ budhāḥ||
त्यक्त्वा कर्मफलासङ्गं नित्यतृप्तो निराश्रयः ।
Tyaktvā karmaphalāsaṅgaṁ nityatripto nirāśrayaḥ |
कर्मण्यभिप्रवृत्तोऽपि नैव किंचित्करोति सः ।। (20)
Karmaṇyabhipravṛtto-'pi naiva kiṅcitkaroti saḥ ||

निराशीर्यतचित्तात्मा त्यक्तसर्वपरिग्रहः ।
Nirāsīryatacittātmā tyaktasarvaparigrahaḥ |
शरीरं केवलं कर्म कुर्वन्नाप्नोति किल्बिषम् ।। (21)
Śarīraṁ kevalaṁ karma kurvannāpnoti kilbiṣaṁ ||
यदृच्छालाभसंतुष्टो द्वन्द्वातीतो विमत्सरः ।
Yadṛcchālābhasantuṣṭo dvandvātīto vimatsaraḥ |
समः सिद्धावसिद्धौ च कृत्वापि न निबद्ध्यते ।। (22)
Samaḥ siddhāvasiddhau ca kṛtvāpi na nibaddhyate ||
गतसङ्गस्य मुक्तस्य ज्ञानावस्थितचेतसः ।
Gatasaṅgasya muktasya jñānāvasthitacetasaḥ |
यज्ञायाचरतः कर्म समग्रं प्रविलीयते ।। (23)
Yajñāyācarataḥ karma samagraṁ pravilīyate ||
ब्रह्मार्पणं ब्रह्म हविर्ब्रह्माग्नौ ब्रह्मणा हुतम् ।
Brahmārpaṇaṁ brahma havirbrahmāgnau brahmaṇā hutaṁ
ब्रह्मैव तेन गन्तव्यं ब्रह्मकर्मसमाधिना ।। (24)
Brahmaiva tena gantavyaṁ brahmakarmasamādhinā ||
दैवमेवापरे यज्ञं योगिनः पर्युपासते ।
Daivamevāpare yajñaṁ yoginaḥ paryupāsate |
ब्रह्माग्नावपरे यज्ञं यज्ञेनैवोपजह्वति ।। (25)
Brahmagnavapare yajnam yajñenaivopajuhvati ||
श्रोत्रादीनीन्द्रियाण्यन्ये संयमाग्निषु जुह्वति।
Śrotrādīnīndriyāṇyanye samyamāgniṣu juhvati |
शब्दादीन्विषयानन्य इन्द्रियाग्निषु जुह्वति ।। (26)
Śabdādīnviṣayānanya indriyāgniṣu juhvāti.
सर्वाणीन्द्रियकर्माणि प्राणकर्माणि चापरे ।
Sarvāṇīndriyakarmāṇi prāṇakarmāṇi chāpare |
आत्मसंयमयोगाग्नौ जुह्वति ज्ञानदीपिते ।। (27)
Ātmasamyamayogāgnau juhvati jñānadīpite ||
द्रव्ययज्ञास्तपोयज्ञा योगयज्ञास्तथापरे ।
Dravyayajñāstapoyajñā Yogayajñāstathāpare |

स्वाध्यायज्ञानयज्ञाश्च यतयः संशितव्रताः ।। (28)

Svādhyāyajñānayajñāśca yatayaḥ saṁśitavratāḥ ||

अपाने जुह्वति प्राणं प्राणेऽपानं तथापरे ।

Apāne juhvati prāṇaṁ prāṇe-apānaṁ tathāpare |

प्राणापानगती रूद्ध्वा प्राणयामपरायणाः ।। (29)

Prāṇāpānagatī ruddhā prāṇāyāmaparāyaṇāḥ ||

अपरे नियताहाराः प्राणान्प्राणेषु जुह्वति ।

Apare niyatāhārāḥ prāṇānprāṇeṣu juhvati |

सर्वेऽप्येते यज्ञविदो यज्ञक्षपितकल्मषाः ।। (30)

Sarve-'pyete yajñavido yajñaksupitakalmaṣāḥ ||

यज्ञशिष्टामृतभुजो यान्ति ब्रह्म सनातनम् ।

Yajñaśiṣṭāmṛtabhujo yānti Brahma sanātanaṁ |

नायं लोकोऽस्त्ययज्ञस्य कुतोऽन्यः कुरूसत्तम ।। (31)

Nāyaṁ loko-styayajñasya kuto-'nyah kurusattama ||

एवं बहुविधा यज्ञा वितता ब्रह्मणो मुखे ।

Evaṁ bahuvidhā yajñā vitatā Brahmaṇo mukhe |

कर्मजान्विद्धि तान्सर्वानेवं ज्ञात्वों विमोक्ष्यसे ।। (32)

Karmajānviddhi tānsarvānevaṁ jñātvā vimokṣyase ||

श्रेयान्द्रव्यमयाद्यज्ञाज्ज्ञानयज्ञः परन्तप ।

Śreyāndravyamayādyajñājjñānāyajnaḥ parantapa |

सर्व कर्माखिलं पार्थ ज्ञाने परिसमाप्यते ।। (33)

Sarvaṁ Karmākhilaṁ Pārtha jñāne parisamāpyate ||

तद्विद्धि प्रणिपातेन परिप्रश्नेन सेवया ।

Tadviddhi praṇipātena paripraśnena sevayā |

उपदेक्ष्यन्ति ते ज्ञानं ज्ञानिनस्तत्त्वदर्शिनः ।। (34)

Upadekṣyanti te jñānaṁ jñāninastattvadarśinaḥ ||

यज्ज्ञात्वा न पुनर्मोहमेवं यास्यसि पाण्डव ।

Yajjñātvā na punarmohamevaṁ yāsyasi Pāṇḍava |

येन भूतान्यशेषेण दक्ष्यस्यात्मन्यथो मयि ।। (35)

Yena bhūtānyaśeseṇa drakṣyasyātmanyatho mayi ||

अपि चेदसि पापेभ्यः सर्वेभ्यः पापकृत्तमः ।
Api cedasi pāpebhyaḥ sarvebhyaḥ pāpakrittamaḥ |
सर्वं ज्ञानप्लवेनैव वृजिनं संतरिष्यसि ।। (36)
Sarvaṁ jñānaplavenaiva vṛjinaṁ santariṣyasi ||
यथैधांसि समिधोऽग्निर्भस्मसात्कुरूतेऽर्जुन ।
Yathaidhāṁsi samidho-'gnirbhasmasātkurute-'rjuna |
ज्ञानाग्निः सर्वकर्माणि भस्मसात्कुरूते तथा ।। (37)
Jñānāgniḥ sarvakarmāṇi bhasmasātkurute tathā ||
नहि ज्ञानेने सदृशं पवित्रमिह विद्यते ।
Nahi Jñānena sadṛśaṁ pavitramiha vidyate |
तत्स्वयं योगसंसिद्धः कालेनात्मनि विन्दति ।। (38)
Tatsvayam yogasaṁsiddhaḥ kālenātmani vindati ||
श्रद्धावाँल्लभते ज्ञानं तत्परः संयतेन्द्रियः ।
Śraddhāvānllabhate jñānaṁ tatparaḥ saṁyatendriyaḥ |
ज्ञानं लब्ध्वा परां शान्तिमचिरेणाधिगच्छति ।। (39)
Jñānaṁ labdhvā parāṁ śāntimacireṇādhigacchati ||
अज्ञश्चाश्रद्दधानश्च संशयात्मा विनश्यति ।
Aiñaścāśraddadhānaśca saṁśayātmā vinaśyati |
नायं लोकोऽस्ति न परो न सुखं संशयात्मनः ।। (40)
Nāyaṁ loko-asti na paro na sukhaṁ saṁśayātmanaḥ ||
योगसंन्यस्तकर्माणं ज्ञानसंछिन्नसंशयम।
Yogasaṁnyastakarmāṇaṁ jñānasaṁchinnasaṁśayaṁ |
आत्मवन्तं न कर्माणि निबध्नन्ति धनंजय ।। (41)
Ātmavantaṁ na karmāṇi nibadhnanti Dhanañjaya ||
तस्मादज्ञानसंभूतं हृत्स्थं ज्ञानासिनात्मनः ।
Tasmādajñānasaṁbhūtaṁ hṛisthaṁ jñānāsinātmanaḥ |
छित्त्वैनं संशयं योगमातिष्ठोत्तिष्ट भारत ।। (42)
Chitvainaṁ saṁśayaṁ yogamātiṣṭottiṣṭa Bhārata ||
इति श्रीमद्भगवद्गीता ...ज्ञानयोगो नाम चतुर्थोऽध्यायः ।।
Iti Śrīmadbhagavadgītā ...Jñānayogo nāma caturtho-adhyāyaḥ ||

CHAPTER V

अर्जुन उवाच / *Arjuna uvāca*

संन्यासं कर्मणां कृष्ण पुनर्योगं च शंससि ।
Saṁnyāsaṁ karmaṇāṁ Kṛṣṇa punaryogaṁ śaṁsasi |
यच्छ्रेय एतयोरेकं तन्मे ब्रूहि सुनिश्चितम् ।। (1)
Yacchreya etayorekaṁ tanme brūhi suniścitaṁ ||

श्रीभगवानुवाच / *Srībhagavānuvāca*

संन्यासं कर्मयोगश्च निःश्रेयसकरावुभौ ।
Saṁnyāsaṁ karmayogaśca niśreyasakarāvubhau |
तयोस्तु कर्मसंन्यासात्कर्मयोगो विशिष्यते ।। (2)
Tayostu karmasaṁnyāsātkarmayogo viśiṣyate ||
ज्ञेयः स नित्यसंन्यासी यो न द्वेष्टि न काङ्क्षति ।
Jñeyaḥ sa nityasaṁnyāsī yo na dveṣṭi na kāṅkṣati |
निर्द्वन्दो हि महाबाहो सुखं बन्धात्प्रमुच्यते ।। (3)
Nirdvando hi manābāho sukhaṁ bandhātpramucyate ||
सांख्ययोगो पृथग्बालाः प्रवदन्ति न पण्डिताः ।
Sāṅkhyayogo pṛthagbālāḥ pravadanti na paṇḍitāḥ |
एकमप्यास्थितः सम्यगुभयोर्विन्दते फलम् ।। (4)
Ekamapyāsthitaḥ samyayubhayorvindate phalaṁ ||
यत्सांख्यैः प्राप्यते स्थानं तद्योगैरपि गम्यते ।
Yatsāṅkhyaiḥ prāpyate sthānaṁ tadyogairapi gamyate
एकं सांख्यं च योगं च यः पश्यति स पश्यति ।। (5)
Ekaṁ Sāṅkhyaṁ ca Yogaṁ ca yaḥ paśyati sa paśyati ||
संन्यास्तु महाबाहो दुःखमाप्तुमयोगतः ।
Saṁnyāsatu Mahābāho duḥkhamāptumayogataḥ |
योगयुक्तो मुनिर्ब्रह्म नचिरेणाधिगच्छति ।। (6)
Yogayukto munirbrahma nacireṇādhigacchati ||

योगयुक्तो विशुद्धात्मा विजितात्मा जितेन्द्रियः ।
Yogayukto viśuddhātmā vijitātmā jitendriyaḥ |
सर्तभूतात्मभूतात्मा कुर्वन्नपि न लिप्यते ।। (7)
Sarvabhūtātmabhutātmā kurvannapi na lipyate ||
नैव किंचित्करोमीति युक्तो मन्येत तत्ववित् ।
Naiva kincitkaromīti yukto manyeta tatvavit|
पश्यन्श्रृण्वन्स्पृशञ्जिघ्रन्नश्नन्गाच्छन्स्वपन्श्वसन् ।। (8)
Paśyan-śṛṇvan-spṛśañ-jighran-aśnan-gacchan-śvapan-svasan||
प्रलपन्विसृजन्गृह्ण न्नुन्मिषन्निमिषन्नपि ।
Pralapan-visṛjan-gṛhṇan- nunmiṣan-nimiṣan-napi |
इन्द्रियाणीन्द्रियार्थेषु वर्तन्त इति धारयन् ।। (9)
Indriyāṇīndriyārtheṣu vartanta iti dhārayan ||
ब्रह्मण्याधाय कर्माणि सङ्गं त्यक्त्वा करोति यः।
Brahmaṇyādhāya karmāṇi saṅgaṁ tyaktvā karoti yaḥ |
लिप्यते न स पापेन पद्मपत्रमिवाम्भसा ।। (10)
Lipyate na sa pāpena padmapatramivāmbhasā ||
कायेन मनसा बुद्ध्या केवलैरिन्द्रियैरपि ।
Kāyena manasā buddhyā kevalairindriairapi |
योगिनः कर्म कुर्वन्ति सङ्गं त्यक्त्वात्मशुद्धये ।। (11)
Yogniḥ karma kurvanti sangaṁ Tyaktvātmaśuddhaye ||
युक्तः कर्मफलं त्यक्त्वा शान्तिमाप्नोति नैष्टिकीम् ।
Yuktaḥ karmaphalaṁ tyaktvā śāntimāpnoti naiṣṭikīm
अयुक्तः कामकारेण फले सक्तो निबद्ध्यते ।। (12)
Ayuktaḥ kāmakāreṇa phale sakto nibadhyate ||
सर्वकर्माणि मनसा संन्यस्यास्ते सुखं वशी ।
Sarvakarmāṇi manasā sannyasyāste sukhaṁ vaśī |
नव द्वारे पुरे देही नैव कुर्वन्न कारयन् ।। (13)
Nava dvāre pure dehī naiva kurvanna kārayan ||
न कर्तृत्वं न कर्माणि लोकस्य सृजति प्रभुः ।
Na kartṛtvaṁ na karmāṇi lokasya sṛjati Prabhuḥ |

न कर्मफलसंयोगं स्वभावस्तु प्रवर्तते ।। (14)

Na karmaphalasaṁyogaṁ svabhāvastu pravartate ||

नादत्ते कस्यचित्पापं न चैव सुकृतं विभुः ।

Nādatte kasyacitpāpaṁ na caiva sukṛtaṁ vibhuḥ |

अज्ञानेनावृतं ज्ञानं तेन मुह्यन्ति जन्तवः ।। (15)

Ajñānenāvṛtaṁ jñānaṁ tena muhyanti jantavaḥ ||

ज्ञानेन तु तदज्ञानं येषां नाशितमात्मनः ।

Jñānena tu tadajñānaṁ yeṣāṁ nāśitamātmanaḥ |

तेषामादित्यवज्ज्ञानं प्रकाशयति तत्परम् ।। (16)

Teṣāmādityavajjñanaṁ prakāśayati tatparaṁ ||

तद्बुद्धयस्तदात्मानस्तन्निष्टास्तत्परायणाः ।

Tadbuddhayastadātmānas-tanniṣṭās-tatparāyaṇāḥ ||

गच्छन्त्यपुनरावृतिं ज्ञाननिर्धूतकल्मषाः ।। (17)

Gacchantyapunarāvṛttiṁ jñānanirdhūtakalmaṣāḥ ||

विद्या विनयसंपन्ने ब्राह्मणे गवि हस्तिनि ।

Vidyā vinayasaṁpanne brāhmaṇe gavi hastini |

शुनि चैव श्वपाके च पण्डिताः समदर्शिनः ।। (18)

Śuni caiva śvapāke ca paṇḍitāḥ samadarśinaḥ ||

इहैव तैर्जितः सर्गो येषां साम्ये स्थितं मनः ।

Ihaiva tairjitaḥ sargo yesāṁ sāmye sṭhitaṁ manaḥ |

निर्दोषं हि समं ब्रह्म तस्मादब्रह्मणि ते स्थिताः ।। (19)

Nirdoṣaṁ hi samaṁ brahma tasmādbrahmani te sthitāḥ ||

न प्रहस्येत्प्रियं प्राप्य नोद्विजेत्प्राप्य चाप्रियम् ।

Na prahasyetpriyaṁ prāpya nodvijet-prapyā cāpriyam |

स्थिरबुद्धिरसंमूढो ब्रह्मविद्ब्रह्मणि स्थितः ।। (20)

Sthirabuddhirasaṁmūḍho brahmavidbrahmaṇi sthitaḥ ||

बाह्यस्पर्शेष्वसक्तात्मा विन्दत्यात्मनि यत्सुखम् ।

Bāhyaspareśvaṣaktātmā vindatyātmani yastsukhaṁ |

स ब्रह्मयोगयुक्तात्मा सुखमक्षय्यमश्नुते ।। (21)

Sa brahmayogayuktātmā sukhamakṣayyamaśnute ||

ये हि संस्पर्शजा भोगा दुःखयोनय एव ते ।
Ye hi samsparśajā bhogā duhkhayonaya eva te |
आद्यन्तवन्तः कौन्तेय न तेषु रमते बुधः ।। (22)
Ādyantavantaḥ kaunteya na teṣu ramate budhaḥ ||
शक्नोतीहैव यः सोढुं प्राक् शरीरविमोक्षणात् ।
Śaknotīhaiva yaḥ soḍhuṁ prāk śarīravimokṣaṇāt |
कामक्रोधोद्भवं वेगं स युक्तः स सुखी नरः ।। (23)
Kāmakrodhodbhavaṁ vegam sa yuktaḥ sa sukhī Narah||
योऽन्तः सुखोऽन्तरारामस्तथान्तर्ज्योतिरेव यः ।
Yo-'antaḥ-sukho-antarārāma-stathāntarjyoti reva yaḥ |
स योगी ब्रह्मनिर्वाणं ब्रह्मभूतोऽधिगच्छति ।। (24)
Sa yogī brahma-nirvāṇam brahmabhūto-'dhigacchati ||
लभन्ते ब्रह्मनिर्वाणमृषयः क्षीगकल्मषाः ।
Labhante brahmanirvāṇamṛṣayaḥ kṣīṇa kalmaṣāḥ |
छिन्नद्वैधा यतात्मानः सर्वभूतहिते रताः ।। (25)
Chinnadvaidhā yatātmānaḥ sarvabhūtahite ratāḥ ||
कामक्रोधवियुक्तानां यतीनां यतचेतसाम् ।
Kāmakrodhaviyuktānāṁ yatīnāṁ yatacetasāṁ |
अभितो ब्रह्मनिर्वाणं वर्तते विदितात्मनाम् ।। (26)
Abhito brahmanirvāṇaṁ vartate viditātmanāṁ||
स्पर्शान्कृत्वा बहिर्बाह्यांश्चक्षुश्चैवान्तरे भ्रुवोः ।
Sparśānkṛtvā bahiṛbāhyāṁścakṣuścaivāntare bhruvoḥ |
प्राणापानौ समौ कृत्वा नासाभ्यन्तरचारिणौ ।। (27)
Prāṇāpānau samau kṛtvā nāsābhyantaracāriṇau ||
यतेन्द्रियमनोबुद्धिर्मुनिर्मोक्षपरायणः ।
Yatendriyamanobuddhirmunirmokṣaparāyaṇaḥ |
विगतेच्छाभयक्रोधो यः सदा मुक्त एव सः ।। (28)
Vigatecchābhayakrodho yaḥ sadā mukta eva saḥ |
भोक्तारं यज्ञतपसां सर्वलोकमहेश्वरम् ।
Bhoktāraṁ yajña tapasāṁ sarvalokamaheśvaraṁ |

सुहृदं सर्वभूतानां ज्ञात्वा मां शान्तिमृच्छति ।। (29)

Suhṛdaṁ sarvabhūtānāṁ jñatvā māṁ śāntimṛcchati ||

इति श्रीमद्भगवद्गीता कर्मसंन्यासयोगो नाम पंञ्चमोऽध्यायः ।।

Iti śrīmadbhagavad gītā........ karmasaṁnyasa yogo nāma Pañcamo-adhyāyaḥ||

CHAPTER VI

श्रीभगवानुवाच / Śrībhagāvanuvāca

अनाश्रितः कर्मफलं कार्यं कर्म करोति यः ।
Anāśritaḥ karmaphalaṁ kāryaṁ karma karoti yaḥ |
स सन्यासी च योगी च न निरग्निर्न चाक्रियः ।। (1)
Sa sanyāsī ca yagī ca na niragnirna cākriyaḥ ||
यं संन्यासमिति प्राहुर्योगं तं विद्धि पाण्डव ।
Yam saṁṅyāsamiti prāhuryogaṁ taṁ viddhi Pāṇḍava
न ह्यसंन्यस्तसंकल्पो योगी भवति कश्चन ।। (2)
Na hyasaṁnyastasṁkalpo yogi bhavati kaś-cana ||
आरूरूक्षोर्मुनेर्योगं कर्म कारणमुच्यते ।
Āruruksor-muner-yogaṁ karma kāraṇa-mucyate |
योगारूढस्य तस्यैव शमः कारणमुच्यते ।। (3)
Yogārūḍhasya tasyaiva śamaḥ kāraṇamucyate ||
यदा हि नेन्द्रियार्थेषु न कर्मस्वनुषज्जते ।
Yadā hi nendriyārtheṣu na karmasvanuṣajjate |
सर्वसंकल्पसंन्यासी योगारूढस्तदोच्यते ।। (4)
Sarvasaṁkalpasaṁnyāsi yogārūḍha stadocyate ||
उद्धरेदात्मनात्मानं नात्मानमवसादयेत् ।
Uddhared-ātmanā-tmānaṁ nātmāna-mava-sādayet |
आत्मैव ह्यात्मनो बन्धुरात्मैव रिपुरात्मनः ।। (5)
Ātmaiva hyātmano bandhu-rātmaivā ripurātmanaḥ ||
बन्धुरात्मात्मनस्तस्य येनात्मैवात्मना जितः ।
Bandhurātmātmanastasya yenātmaivātmanā jitaḥ |
अनात्मनस्तु शत्रुत्वे वर्तेतात्मैव शत्रुवत् ।। (6)
Anātmanastu śatrutve vartetātmaiva śatruvat ||

जितात्मनः प्रशान्तस्य परमात्मा समाहितः ।
Jitātmanaḥ praśāntasya paramātmā samāhitaḥ |
शीतोष्णसुखदुःखेषु तथा मानापमानयोः ।। (7)
Śītoṣṇasukhaduḥkheṣu tathā mānāpamānayoḥ ||
ज्ञानविज्ञान तृप्तात्मा कूटस्थो विजितेन्द्रियः ।
Jñānavijñāna tṛptātmā kūṭastho vijitendriyaḥ |
युक्त इत्युच्यते योगी समलोष्टाश्मकाञ्चनः ।। (8)
Yukta ityucyate yogī samaloṣṭāśma kāñcanaḥ ||
सुहृन्मित्रार्युदासीनमध्यस्थद्वेष्यबन्धुषु ।
Suhṛnmitrāryudāsīna madhyasṭhadveṣya bandhuṣu |
साधुष्वपि च पापेषु समबुद्धिर्विशिष्यते ।। (9)
Sādhuṣvapi ca pāpeṣu samabuddhirviśiṣyate ||
योगी युंञ्जीत सततमात्मानं रहसि स्थितः ।
Yogī yuñjīta satatamātmānaṁ rahasi sṭhitaḥ |
एकाकी यतचित्तात्मा निराशीरपरिग्रहः ।। (10)
Ekākī yatacittātmā nirāśīraparigrahaḥ ||
शुचौ देशे प्रतिष्टाप्य स्थिरमासनमात्मनः ।
Sucau deśe pratiṣṭāpya sthiramāsanamātmanaḥ |
नात्युच्छ्रूतं नातिनीचं चैलाजिन कुशोत्तरम् ।। (11)
Nātyucchritaṁ nāti-nīcaṁ cailājina kuśottaraṁ ||
तत्रैकाग्रं मनः कृत्वा यतचित्तेन्द्रियक्रियः ।
Tatraikāgraṁ manaḥ kṛtvā yatacittendriya kriyaḥ |
उपविश्यासने युञ्ज्याद्योगमात्मविशुद्धये ।। (12)
Upaviśyāsane yuñjyādyogamātmaviśuddhaye ||
समं कायशिरोग्रीवं धारयन्नचलं स्थिरः ।
Samaṁ kāyaśirogrīvaṁ dhārayannacalaṁ sṭhiraḥ |
संप्रेक्ष्य नासिकाग्रं स्वं दिश श्चानवलोकयन् ।। (13)
Saṁprekṣya nāsikāgraṁ svaṁ diśaścānavalokayan ||
प्रशान्तात्मा विगतभीर्ब्रह्मचारिव्रते स्थितः।
Praśāntātmā vigatabhīr-brahmacārivrate sṭhitaḥ |

मनः संयम्य मच्चित्तो युक्त आसीत मत्परः ।। (14)
Manaḥ saṁyamya maccitto yukta āsīta matparaḥ ||
युञ्जन्नैवं सदात्मानं योगी नियतमानसः।
Yuñjannaivaṁ sadatmānaṁ Yogī niyatamānasaḥ |
शान्तिं निर्वाणपरमां मत्संस्थामधिगच्छति ।। (15)
Śāntiṁ nirvāṇaparamāṁ matsaṁsthāmadhigacchati |
नात्यश्नतस्तु योगोऽस्ति न चैकान्तमनश्नतः ।
Nātyaśnatastu yogo-asti na caikāntamanaśnataḥ
न चातिस्वप्नशीलस्य जाग्रतो नैव चार्जुन ।। (16)
Na cātisvapanaśīlasya jāgrato naiva cārjuna ||
युक्ताहारविहारस्य युक्तचेष्टस्य कर्मसु ।
Yuktāhāravihārasya yuktaceṣṭasya karmasu |
युक्तास्वप्नावबोधस्य योगो भवति दुःखहा ।। (17)
Yuktāsvapnāvabodhasya yogo bhavati duḥkhahā
यदा विनियतं चित्तमात्मन्येवावतिष्टते ।
Yadā viniyataṁ cittamātmanyevāvatiṣṭate |
निःस्पृहः सर्वकामेभ्यो युक्त इत्युच्यते तदा ।। (18)
Nihspṛhaḥ sarvakāmebhyo yukta ityucyate tadā ||
यथा दीपो निवातस्थो नैञ्जते सोपमा स्मृता ।
Yathā dīpo nivātastho naiñjate sopamā smṛtā |
योगिनो यतचित्तस्य युञ्जतो योगमात्मनः ।। (19)
Yogino yatacittasya yuñjato yogamātmanaḥ ||
यत्रोपरमते चितं निरूद्धं योगसेवया ।
Yatroparamate cittaṁ niruddhaṁ yogasevayā
यत्र चैवात्मनात्मानं पश्यन्नात्मनि तुष्यति ।। (20)
Yatra caivātmanātmānaṁ paśyannātmani tuṣyati |
सुखमात्यन्तिकं यत्तद्बुद्धिग्राह्यमतीन्द्रियम् ।
Sukhamātyantikaṁ yattadbuddhigrāhyamatīndriyam
वेत्ति यत्र न चैवायं स्थितश्चलति तत्त्वतः ।। (21)
Vetti yatra na caivāyaṁ sṭhitaścalati tattvataḥ ||

यं लब्ध्वा चापरं लाभं मन्यते नाधिकं ततः ।
Yaṁ labdhvā cāparaṁ lābhaṁ manyate nādhikaṁ tataḥ |
यस्मिन्स्थितो न दुःखेन गुरूणापि विचाल्यते ।। (22)
Yasminsthito na duhkhena gurūṇāpi vīcālyate ||
तं विद्याद्दुःखसंयोगवियोगं योगसंज्ञितम् ।
Taṁ vidyādduḥkhasaṁyogaviyogaṁ Yogasaṁjñitaṁ |
स निश्चयेन योक्तव्यो योगोऽनिर्विण्णचेतसा ।। (23)
Sa niścayena yoktavyo yogo'nirviṇṇacetasā |
संकल्पप्रभवान्कामांस्त्यक्त्वा सर्वानिशेषतः ।
Saṁkalpaprabhavān-kāmaṁstyaktvā sarvānaśeṣataḥ |
मनसैवेन्द्रियग्रामं विनियम्य समन्ततः ।। (24)
Manasaivendriyagrāmaṁ viniyamya samantataḥ ||
शनैः शनैरूपरमेद्बुद्ध्या धृतिगृहीतया ।
Śanaiḥ sanairuparamed-buddhyā dhṛtigṛhītayā |
आत्मसंस्थं मनः कृत्वा न किंचिदपि चिन्तयेत् ।। (25)
Ātmasaṁsthaṁ manaḥ kṛtvā na kincidapi cintayet |
यतो यतो निश्चरति मनश्चञ्चलमस्थिरम् ।
Yato yato niścarati manaścañcalam-asthiraṁ |
ततस्ततो नियम्यैतदात्मन्येव वशं नयेत् ।। (26)
Tatastato niyamyaitadātmanyeva vaśaṁ nayet ||
प्रशान्तमनसं ह्येनं योगिनं सुखमुत्तमम् ।
Praśāntamanasaṁ hyenaṁ yoginaṁ Sukhamuttamaṁ |
उपैति शान्तरजसं ब्रह्मभूतमकल्मषम् ।। (27)
Upaiti śāntarajasaṁ brahmabhūtamakalmaṣaṁ ||
युञ्जन्नैवं सदात्मानं योगी विगतकल्मषः ।
Yuñjannaivaṁ sadātmānaṁ yogī vigatakalmaṣaḥ |
सुखेन ब्रह्मसंस्पर्शमत्यन्तं सुखमश्नुते ।। (28)
Sukhena brahmasaṁsparśamatyantaṁ sukhamaśnute ||
सर्वभूतस्थमात्मानं सर्वभूतानि चात्मनि ।
Sarvabhūtasthamātmānaṁ sarvabhūtāni cātmaṇi |

ईक्षते योगयुक्तात्मा सर्वत्र समदर्शनः ।। (29)
Ikṣate yogayuktātmā sarvatra samadarśanaḥ ||
यो मां पश्यति सर्वत्र सर्वं च मयि पश्यति ।
Yo māṁ paśyati sarvatra sarvaṁ ca mayi paśyati |
तस्याहं न प्रणश्यामि स च मे न प्रणश्यति ।। (30)
Tasyāhaṁ na praṇaśyāmi sa ca me na praṇaśyati |
सर्वभूतस्थितं यो मां भजत्येकत्वमास्थितः ।
Sarvabhūtasthitaṁ yo māṁ bhajatyekatvamāsthitaḥ |
सर्वथा वर्तमानोऽपि स योगी मयि वर्तते ।। (31)
Sarvathā vartamāno'pi'sa yogī mayi vartate ||
आत्मौपम्येन सर्वत्र समं पश्यति योऽर्जुन ।
Ātmaupamyena sarvatra samaṁ paśyati yo'rjuna |
सुखं वा यदि वा दुःखं स योगी परमो मतः ।। (32)
Sukhaṁ vā yadi vā duhkhaṁ sa yogī paramo mataḥ ||

अर्जुन उवाच / Arjuna uvāca

योऽयं योगस्त्वया प्रोक्तः साम्येन मधुसूदन ।
Yo'yaṁ yogastvayā proktaḥ sāmyena Madhusūdana |
एतस्याहं न पश्यामि चञ्चलत्वात्स्थितिं स्थिराम् ।। (33)
Etasyāhaṁ na paśyāmi cañcalatvātsṭhitim sṭhirāṁ ||
चञ्चलं हि मनः कृष्ण प्रमाथि बलवद्दृढम् ।
Cañcalaṁ hi manaḥ Kṛṣṇa pramāthi balavaddṛḍhaṁ |
तस्याहं निग्रहं मन्ये वायोरिव सुदुष्करम् ।। (34)
Tasyāhaṁ nigrahaṁ manye vāyoriva suduṣkaraṁ ||

श्रीभगवानुवाच / Srībhagavānuvāca

असंशयं महाबाहो मनो दुर्निग्रहं चलम् ।
Asaṁśayaṁ mahābāho mano durnigrahaṁ calaṁ |
अभ्यासेन तु कौन्तेय वैराग्येण च गृह्यते ।। (35)
Abhyāsena tu Kaunteya vairāgyeṇa ca gṛhyate ||

असंयतात्मना योगो दुष्प्राप इति मे मतिः ।
Asaṁyatātmanā yogo duṣprāpa iti me matiḥ |
वश्यात्मना तु यतता शक्योऽवाप्तुमुपायतः ।। (36)
Vaśyātmanā tu yatatā śakyo'vāptumupāyataḥ ||

अर्जुन उवाच / Arjuna uvāca

अयतिः श्रद्धयोपेतो योगाच्चलितमानसः ।
Ayatiḥ śraddhayopeto yogāccalitamānasaḥ |
अप्राप्य योगसंसिद्धिं कां गतिं कृष्ण गच्छति ।। (37)
Aprāpya yogasmsiddhiṁ kām gatiṁ Kṛṣṇa gacchati ||
कच्चिन्नोभयविभ्रष्टश्छिन्नाभ्रमिव नश्यति ।
Kaccinnobhayavibhraṣṭaśchinnābhra-miva naśyati |
अप्रतिष्टो महाबाहो विमूढो ब्रह्मणः पथि ।। (38)
Apratiṣto mahābāho vimūḍho brahmaṇaḥ pathi ||
एतन्मे संशय कृष्ण छेत्तुमर्हस्यशेषतः ।
Etanme saṁśayaṁ Kṛṣṇa chettumarhasyaśeṣataḥ |
त्वदन्यः संशयस्यास्य छेत्ता नह्युपपद्यते ।। (39)
Tvadanyaḥ saṁśayasyāsya chettā nahyupapadyate ||

श्रीभगवानुवाच / Śrībhagavānuvāca

पार्थ नैवेह नामुत्र विनाशस्तस्य विद्यते ।
Pārtha naiveha nāmutra vināśastasya vidyate |
नहि कल्याणकृत्कश्चिदद्दुर्गतिं तात गच्छति ।। (40)
Nahi kalyāṇakṛtkaściddurgatiṁ tāta gacchati ||
प्राप्य पुण्यकृतांल्लोकानुषित्वा शाश्वतीः समाः ।
Prāpya puṇyakṛtāṁllokānuṣitvā śāśvatīḥ
शुचीनां श्रीमतां गेहे योगभ्रष्टोऽभिजायते ।। (41)
Śucīnāṁ śrīmatāṁ gehe yogabhraṣṭo'bhijāyate ||
अथवा योगिनामेव कुले भवति धीमताम् ।
Athavā yogināmeva kule bhavati dhīmatāṁ |
एतद्धि दुर्लभतरं लोके जन्म यदीदृशम् ।। (42)
Etaddhi durlabhataraṁ loke janma yadīdṛśaṁ ||

तत्र तं बुद्धिसंयोगं लभते पौर्वदेहिकम् ।

Tatra taṁ buddhisamyogaṁ labhate paurvadehikaṁ|

यतते च ततो भूयः संसिद्धौ कुरूनन्दन ।। (43)

Yatate ca tato bhūyaḥ saṁsiddhau kurunadana ||

पूर्वाभ्यासेन तेनैव ह्रियते ह्यवशोऽपि सः ।

Pūrvābhyāsena tenaiva hṛyate hyavaśo'pi saḥ |

जिज्ञासुरपि योगस्य शब्दब्रह्मातिवर्तते ।। (44)

Jijñāsurapi yogasya śabdabrahmātivartate ||

प्रयत्नाद्यतमानस्तु योगी संशुद्धकिल्बिषः ।

Prayatnādyatamānastu yogī saṁsūddhakilbiṣaḥ |

अनेक जन्मसंसिद्धस्ततो याति परां गतिम् ।। (45)

Anekajanma-saṁsiddhastato yāti parāṁ gatiṁ |

तपस्विभ्योऽधिको योगी ज्ञानिभ्योऽपि मतोऽधिकः ।

Tapasvibyo'dhiko yogī jñānibhyo'pi mato'dhikaḥ |

कर्मभ्यश्चाधिको योगी तस्माद्योगी भवार्जुन ।। (46)

Karmabhyaścādhiko yogī tasmādyogī bhavārjuna ||

योगिनामपि सर्वेषां मद्गतेनान्तरात्मना । (47)

Yogināmapi sarveṣāṁ madgatenāntarātmanā ||

श्रृद्धावान्भजते यो मां स मे युक्ततमो मतः ।।

Śraddhāvānbhajate yo māṁ sa me yuktatamo matah ||

इति श्रीमद्भगवद्गीताः ध्यानयोगो नाम षष्टोऽध्यायः ।।

Iti Śrīmadbhagavadgītā: dhyānayogo nāma ṣaṣṭo'dyyāyaḥ ||

CHAPTER VII

श्रीभगवानुवाच / *Śrībhagavānuvāca*

मय्यसक्तमनाः पार्थ योगं युञ्जन्मदाश्रयः ।
Mayyasaktamanāḥ Pārth yogaṁ yuṅjanmadāśrayaḥ |
असंशयं समग्रं मां यथा ज्ञास्यसि तच्छृणु ।। (1)
Asaṁśayaṁ samagraṁ māmyathā jñāsyasi tacchṛṇu |

ज्ञानं तेऽहं सविज्ञानमिदं वक्ष्याम्यशेषतः ।
Jñānaṁ te'haṁ savijñānamidaṁ vakṣyāmyaśeṣataḥ |
यज्ज्ञात्वा नेह भूयोऽन्यज्ज्ञातव्यमवशिष्यते ।। (2)
Yajjñātvā neha bhūyo'nyajjñātavyamavaśiṣyate ||

मनुष्याणां सहस्रेषु कश्चिद्यतति सिद्धये ।
Manuṣyāṇāṁ sahasreṣu kaścidyatati siddhaye |
यततामपि सिद्धानां कश्चिन्मां वेत्ति तत्त्वतः ।। (3)
Yatatāmapi siddhānāṁ kaścinmāṁ vetti tattvataḥ ||

भूमिरापोऽनलो वायुः खं मनो बुद्धिरेव च ।
Bhūmirāpo 'nalo vāyuḥ khaṁ mano buddhireva ca |
अहंकार इतीयं मे भिन्ना प्रकृतिरष्टधा ।। (4)
Ahaṁkāra itīyam me bhinnā prakṛtiraṣṭadhā ||

अपरेयमितस्त्वन्यां प्रकृतिं विद्धि मे पराम् ।
Apareyamitastvanyāṁ prakṛtiṁ viddhi me parām |
जीवभूतां महाबाहो ययेदं धार्यते जगत् ।। (5)
Jīvabhūtāṁ mahābāho yayedaṁ dhāryate jagat ||

एतद्योनीनि भूतानि सर्वाणीत्युपधारय ।
Etadyonīni bhūtāni sarvāṇītyupadhāraya |
अहं कृत्स्नस्य जगतः प्रभवः प्रलयस्तथा ।। (6)
Ahaṁ kṛtsnasya jagataḥ prabhavaḥ pralayastathā ||

मत्तः परतरं नान्यत्किंचिदस्ति धनंजय ।
Mattaḥ parataraṁ nānyatkiñcidasti Dhanañjaya
मयि सर्वमिदं प्रोतं सूत्रे मणिगणा इव ।। (7)
Mayi sarvamidaṁ protaṁ sūrte maṇigaṇā iva |
रसोऽहमप्सु कौन्तेय प्रभास्मि शशिसूर्ययोः ।
Raso'hamapsu Kaunteya prabhāsmi śaśisūryayoḥ |
प्रणवः सर्ववेदेषु शब्दः खे पौरूषं नृषु ।। (8)
Praṇavaḥ sarvavedeṣu śabdaḥ khe pauruṣaṁ nṛṣu |
पुण्यो गन्धः पृथिव्यां च तेजश्चास्मि विभावसौ ।
Puṇyo gaṅdhaḥ pṛthivyāṁ ca tejaścāsmi vibhāvasau |
जीवनं सर्वभूतेषु तपश्चास्मि तपस्विषु ।। (9)
Jīvanaṁ sarvabhūteṣu tapaścāsmi tapasviṣu ||
बीजं मां सर्वभूतानां विद्धि पार्थ सनातनम् ।
Bījaṁ māṁ sarvabhūtānāṁ viddhi Pārtha sanātanaṁ |
बुद्धिर्बुद्धिमतामस्मि तेजस्तेजस्विनामहम् ।। (10)
Buddhirbuddhimatāmasmi tejastejasvināmahaṁ ||
बलं बलवतामस्मि कामरागविवर्जितम् ।
Balaṁ balavatāmasmi kāmarāgavivarjitaṁ |
धर्माविरूद्धो भूतेषु कामोऽस्मि भरतर्षभ ।। (11)
Dharmāviruddho bhūteṣu kāmo'smi bharatarṣabha ||
ये चैव सात्विका भावा राजसास्तामसाश्च ये ।
Ye caiva sātvikā bhāvā rājasāstāmasāśca ye |
मत्त एवेति तान्विद्धि न त्वहं तेषु ते मयि ।। (12)
Matta eveti tānviddhi na tvahaṁ teṣu te mayi ||
त्रिभिर्गुणमयैर्भावैरेभिः सर्वमिदं जगत् ।
Tribhirguṇamayairbhāvairebhiḥ sarvamidaṁ jagat |
मोहितं नाभिजानाति मामेभ्यः परमव्ययम् ।। (13)
Mohitaṁ nābhijānāti māmebhyaḥ paramavyayaṁ ||
दैवी ह्येषा गुणमयी मम माया दुरत्यया ।
Daivī hyeṣā guṇamayī mama māyā duratyayā |

मामेव ये प्रपद्यन्ते मायामेतां तरन्ति ते ।। (14)
Māmeva ye prapadyante māyāmetāṁ taranti te ||
न मां दुष्कृतिनो मूढाः प्रपद्यन्ते नराधमाः ।
Na māṁ duṣkṛtino mūḍhāḥ prapadyante narādhamāḥ
माययापहृतज्ञाना आसुरं भावमाश्रिताः ।। (15)
Māyayāpahṛtajñānā āsuraṁ bhāvamāśritāḥ ||
चतुर्विधा भजन्ते मां जनाः सुकृतिनोऽर्जुन ।
Caturvidhā bhajante māṁ janāḥ sukṛtino'rjuna |
आर्तो जिज्ञासुरर्थार्थी ज्ञानी च भरतर्षभ ।। (16)
Ārto jijñāsurarthārthī jñānī ca bharatarṣabha ||
तेषां ज्ञानी नित्ययुक्त एकभक्तिर्विशिष्यते ।
Teṣāṁ jñāni nityayukta ekabhaktirviśiṣyate |
प्रियो हि ज्ञानिनोऽत्यर्थमहं स च मम प्रियः ।। (17)
Priyo hi jñānino'tyarthamahaṁ sa ca mama priyaḥ ||
उदाराः सर्व एवै ते ज्ञानी त्वात्मैव मे मतम् ।
Udārāḥ sarva evai te jñānī tvātmaiva me matam |
आस्थितः स हि युक्तात्मा मामेवानुत्तमां गतिम् ।। (18)
Āsthitaḥ sa hi yuktātmā māmevānuttamāṁ gatiṁ ||
बहूनां जन्मनामन्ते ज्ञानवान्मां प्रपद्यते ।
Bahūnāṁ janmanāmante jñānavānmāṁ prapadyate |
वासुदेवः सर्वमिति स महात्मा सुदुर्लभः ।। (19)
Vāsudevaḥ sarvamiti sa mahātmā sudurlabhaḥ |
कामैस्तैस्तैर्हृतज्ञानाः पद्यन्तेऽन्यदेवताः ।
Kāmaistaistairhṛtajñānāḥ prapadyante'nyadevatāḥ |
तं तं नियममास्थाय प्रकृत्या नियताः स्वया ।। (20)
Taṁ taṁ niyamamāsthāya prakṛtyā niyatāḥ svayā ||
यो यो यां यां तनुं भक्ताः श्रद्धयार्चितुमिच्छति ।
Yo yo yāṁ yāṁ tanuṁ bhaktāḥ śraddhayārcitumicchati|
तस्य तस्याचलां श्रद्धां तामेव विदधाम्यहम् ।। (21)
Tasya tasyācalāṁ śraddhāṁ tāmeva vidadhāmyaham ||

स तया श्रद्धया युक्तस्तस्याराधनमीहते ।
Sa tayā śraddhayā yuktastasyārādhanamīhate |
लभते च ततः कामान्मयैव विहितान्हि तान् ।। (22)
Labhate ca tataḥ Kāmānmayaiva vihitānhi tān ||
अन्तवत्तु फलं तेषां तद्भवत्यल्पमेधसाम् ।
Antavattu phalaṁ teṣāṁ tadbhavatyalpamedhasāṁ |
देवान्देवयजो यान्ति मद्भक्ता यान्ति मामपि ।। (23)
Devāndevayajo yānti madbhaktā yānti māmapi ||
अव्यक्तं व्यक्तिमापन्नं मन्यन्ते मामबुद्धयः ।
Avyaktaṁ vyaktimāpannaṁ manyante māmabuddhayaḥ |
परं भावमजानन्तो ममाव्ययमनुत्तमम् ।। (24)
Paraṁ bhāvamajānanto mamāvyayamanuttamaṁ ||
नाहं प्रकाशः सर्वस्य योगमायासमावृतः ।
Nāhaṁ prakāśaḥ sarvasya yogamāyāsamāvṛtaḥ |
मूढोऽयं नाभिजानाति लोको मामजमव्ययम् ।। (25)
Mūḍho'yaṁ nābhijānāti loko māmajamavyayaṁ ||
वेदाहं समतीतानि वर्तमानानि चार्जुन ।
Vedāhaṁ samatītāni vartamānāni cārjuna |
भविष्याणि च भूतानि मां तु वेद न कश्चन ।। (26)
Bhaviṣyāṇi ca bhūtāni māṁtu veda na kaścana ||
इच्छाद्वेषसमुत्थेन द्वन्द्वमोहेन भारत ।
Icchādveṣasamutthena dvaṅdvamohena bhārata |
सर्वभूतानि संमोहं सर्गे यान्ति परन्तप ।। (27)
Sarvabhūtāni sammohaṁ sarge yānti parantapa ||
येषां त्वन्तगतं पापं जनानां पुण्यकर्मणाम् ।
Yesāṁ tvantagataṁ pāpaṁ janānāṁ puṇyakarmaṇāṁ |
ते द्वन्द्वमोहनिर्मुक्ता भजन्ते मां दृढव्रताः ।। (28)
Te dvandvamohanirmuktā bhajante māṁ dṛḍhavratāḥ ||
जरामरणमोक्षाय ममाश्रित्य यतन्ति ये ।
Jarāmaraṇamokṣāya mamāśritya yatanti ye |

ते ब्रह्म तद्विदुः कृत्स्नमध्यात्मं कर्म चाखिलम् ।। (29)
Te brahma tadviduḥ kṛtsnamadhyātma karma cākhilaṁ |
साधिभूताधिदैवं मां साधियज्ञं च ये विदुः ।
Sādhibhūtādhidaivaṁ māṁ sādhiyajñaṁ ca ye viduḥ |
प्रयाणकालेऽपि च मां ते विदुर्युक्तचेतसः ।। (30)
Prayāṇakāle'pi ca māṁ te viduryuktacetasaḥ ||
इति श्रीमद्भगवद्गीता... विज्ञानयोगो नाम सप्तमोऽध्यायः ।।
Iti Śrīmadbhagavadgītā... Vijñānayogo nāma saptamo'adhyāyaḥ ||

CHAPTER VIII

अर्जुन उवाच /*Arjuna uvāca*

किं तद्ब्रह्म किमध्यात्मं किं कर्म पुरूषोत्तम ।
Kim tadbrahma kimadhyātmaṁ kim karma puruṣottama
अधिभूतं च किं प्रोक्तमधिदैवं किमुच्यते ।। (1)
Adhibhūtaṁ ca kim proktamadhidaivaṁ kimucyate ||
अधियज्ञः कथं कोऽत्र देहेऽस्मिन्मधूसुदन ।
Adhiyajñaḥ kathaṁ ko'tra dehe'smin-madhusūdana |
प्रयाणकाले च कथं ज्ञेयोऽसिस नियतात्मभिः ।। (2)
Prayāṇakāle ca kathaṁ jñeyo'si niyatātmabhiḥ ||

श्रीभगवानुवाच /*Śrobhagavānuvāca*

अक्षरं ब्रह्म परमं स्वभावोऽध्यात्ममुच्यते ।
Akṣaraṁ brahma paramaṁ *Svabhāvo'dhyātmamucyate |*
भूतभावोद्भवकरो विसर्गः कर्मसंज्ञितः ।। (3)
Bhūtabhāvodbhavakaro visargaḥ karmasaṁjñitaḥ |
अधिभूतं क्षरो भावः पुरूषश्चाधिदैवतम् ।
Adhibhūtaṁ ksaro bhāvaḥ puruṣaścādhidaivataṁ |
अधियज्ञोऽहमेवात्र देहे देहभृतां वर ।। (4)
Adhiyajño'hamevātra dehe dehabhṛtāṁ vara ||
अन्तकाले च मामेव स्मरन्मुक्त्वा कलेवरम् ।
Antakāle ca māmeva smaranmuktvā kalebaraṁ |
यः प्रयाति स मद्भावं याति नास्त्यत्र संशयः ।। (5)
Yaḥ prayāti sa madbhāvaṁ yāti nāstyatra saṁśayaḥ |
यं यं वापि स्मरन्भावं त्यजत्यन्ते कलेवरम् ।
Yaṁ Yaṁ vāpi smaranbhāvaṁ tyajatyantekalevaraṁ |

त तमेवैति कौन्तेय सदा तद्भावभावितः ।। (6)

Taṁ tamevaiti Kaunteya sadā sadbhāvabhāvitaḥ ||

तस्मात्सर्वेषु कालेषु मामनुस्मर युद्धय च ।

Tasmāt-sarveṣu kāleṣu māmanusmara yudhya ca |

मय्यर्पितमनाबुद्धिर्मामेवैष्यस्यसंशयम् ।। (7)

Mayyarpitamanobuddhirmāmevaiṣyasyasaṁśayaṁ |

अभ्यासयोगयुक्तेन चेतसा नान्यगामिना ।

Abhyāsayogayuktena cetasā nānyagāminā |

परमं पुरूषं दिव्यं याति पार्थानुचिन्तयन ।। (8)

Paramaṁ puruṣaṁ divyaṁ yāti pārthānucintayan

कविं पुराणमनुशासितार मणोरणीयांसमनुस्मरेद्यः ।

Kaviṁ purāṇamanuśāsitāra maṇoraṇīyāṁ-samanusmaredyaḥ|

सर्वस्य धातारमचिन्त्यरूपं आदित्यवर्ण तमसः परस्तात् ।। (9)

Sarvasya dhātāramacintyarūpaṁ ādityavarṇaṁ tamasaḥ parastāt ||

प्रयाणकाले म साचलेन भक्त्या युक्तो योगबलेन चैव ।

Prayāṇakāle manasācalena Bhaktyā yukto yogabalena caiva|

भ्रुवोर्मध्ये प्राणमावेश्य सम्यक् स तं परं पुरूषमुपैति दिव्यम् ।। (10)

Bhruvormadhye prāṇamāveśya samyak sa taṁ paraṁ puruṣamupaiti divyaṁ ||

यदक्षरं वेदविदो बदन्ति विशन्ति यद्यतयां वीतरागाः ।

Yadakṣaraṁ vedavido vadantyi Viśanti yadyatayo vītarāgāḥ!

यदिच्छन्ती ब्रह्मचर्यं चरन्ति तते पदं संग्रहेण प्रवक्ष्ये ।। (11)

Yadicchantī brahmacaryaṁ caranti Tatte padaṁ saṁgraheṇa pravakṣye ||

सर्वद्वाराणि संयम्य मनो हृदि निरूध्य च ।

Sarva dvārāṇi saṁyaṁya mano hṛdi nirudhya ca ||

मुध्न्र्याधायात्मनः प्राणमस्थितो योगधारणाम् ।। (12)

Mūrdhnyādhāyātmanaḥ prāṇamāsthito yogadhāraṇaṁ ||

ओमित्येकाक्षरं ब्रह्म व्याहरन्मामनुस्मरन् ।

Omityekākṣaraṁ Brahma vyāharanmāmanusmaran

यः प्रयाति त्यजन्देहं स याति परमां गतिम् ।। (13)
Yaḥ prayāti tyajandehaṁ sa yāti paramāṁ gatim ||
अनन्यचेताः सततं यो मां स्मरति नित्यशः ।
Ananyacetāḥ satataṁ yo māṁ smarati nityaśaḥ
तस्याहं सुलभः पार्थ नित्ययुक्तस्य योगिनः ।। (14)
Tasyāhaṁ sulabhaḥ pārtha nityayuktasya yoginaḥ |
मामुपेत्य पुनर्जन्म दुःखालयमशाश्वतम् ।
Māmupetya punarjanma duhkhālayamaśāśvataṁ |
नाप्नुवन्ति महात्मानः संसिद्धिं परमां गताः ।। (15)
Nāpnuvanti mahātmānaḥ samsiddhim paramāṁ gatāḥ ||
आ ब्रह्मभुवनाल्लोकाः पुनरावर्तिनोऽर्जुन ।
Ā Brahmabhuvanāllokāḥ punarāvartino'rjuna |
मामुपेत्य तु कौन्तेय पुनर्जन्म न विद्यते ।। (16)
Māmupetya tu Kaunteya punarjanma na vidyate ||
सहस्त्रयुगपर्यन्तमहर्यद्ब्रह्मणो विदुः ।
Sahasrayugaparyantamaharyadbrahmaṇo viduḥ |
रात्रिं युगसहस्रां तां तेऽहोरात्रविदो जनाः ।। (17)
Rātriṁ Yugasahasrāṁ tāṁ te'horātravido janāḥ ||
अव्यक्ताद्व्यक्तयः सर्वाः प्रभवन्त्यहरागमे ।
Avyaktādvyaktayaḥ sarvāḥ prabhavantyaharāgame |
रात्र्यागमे प्रलीयन्ते तत्रैवाव्यक्तसंज्ञके ।। (18)
Rātryāgame pralīyante tatraivāvyaktasamjñake ||
भूतग्रामः स एवायं भूत्वा भूत्वा प्रलीयते ।
Bhūtagrāmaḥ sa evāyaṁ bhūtvā bhūtvā pralīyate |
रात्र्यागमेऽवशः पार्थ प्रभवत्यहरागमे ।। (19)
Rātryāgame'vaśaḥ Pārtha prabhavatyaharāgame ||
परस्तस्मात्तु भावोऽन्योऽव्यक्तोऽव्यक्तात्सनातनः ।
Parastasmāttu bhāvo'nyo'vyakto'vyaktātsanātanaḥ |
यः स सर्वेषु भूतेषु नश्यत्सु न विनश्यति ।। (20)
Yaḥ sa sarveṣu bhūteṣu naśyatsu na vinaśyati ||

अव्यक्तोऽक्षर इत्युक्तस्तमाहुः परमां गतिम् ।

Avyakto'kṣara ityuktastamāhuḥ paramāṁ gatiṁ |

यं प्राप्य न निवर्तन्ते तद्धाम परमं मम ।। (21)

Yaṁ prāpya na nivartante taddhāma paramaṁ mama ||

पुरूषः स परः पार्थ भक्त्या लभ्यस्त्वनन्यया ।

Puruṣaḥ sa paraḥ Pārtha bhaktyā labhyastvananyayā।

यस्यान्तःस्थानि भूतानि येन सर्वमिदं ततम् ।। (22)

Yasyāntaḥsthāni bhūtāni yena sarvamidaṁ tataṁ ||

यत्र काले त्वनावृत्तिमावृत्तिं चैव योगिनः ।

Yatra kāle tvanāvṛttimāvṛttiṁ caiva yoginaḥ ||

प्रयाता यान्ति तं कालं वक्ष्यामि भरतर्षभ ।। (23)

Prayātā yānti taṁ kālaṁ vakṣyāmi bharatarṣabha ||

अग्निर्ज्योतिरहः शुक्लः षण्मासा उत्तरायणम् ।

Agnīrjyotirahaḥ śuklaḥ ṣaṇmāsā uttarāyaṇaṁ |

तत्र प्रयाता गच्छन्ति ब्रह्म ब्रह्मविदो जनाः ।। (24)

Tatra prayātā gacchanti brahma brahmavido janāḥ |

धूमो रात्रिस्तथा कृष्णः षण्मासा दक्षिणायनम् ।

Dhūmo rātristathā kṛṣṇaḥ ṣaṇmāsā dakṣiṇāyanaṁ |

तत्र चान्द्रमसं ज्योतिर्योगी प्राप्य निवर्तते ।। (25)

Tatra cāndramasaṁ jyotiryogī prāpya nivartate ||

शुक्लकृष्णे गती ह्येते जगतः शाश्वते मते ।

Śuklakṛṣṇe gatī hyete jagataḥ śāśvate mate |

एकया यात्यनावृत्तिमन्ययावर्तते पुनः ।। (26)

Ekayā yātyanāvṛttimanyayāvartate punaḥ ||

नैते सृती पार्थ जानन्योगी मुह्यति कश्चन ।

Naite sṛtī pārtha jānanyogī muhyati kaścana |

तंस्मात्सर्वेषु कालेषु योगयुक्तो भवार्जुन ।। (27)

Tasmātsarveṣu kāleṣu yogayukto bhavārjuna ||

वेदेषु यज्ञेषु तपःसु चैव दानेषु यत्पुण्यफलं प्रदिष्टम् ।

Vedeṣu yajñeṣu tapaḥsu caiva dāneṣi yatpuṇyaphalaṁ pradiṣṭaṁ |

अत्येति तत्सर्वमिदं विदित्वा योगी परं स्थानमुपैति चाद्यम् ।। (28)

Atyeti tatsarvamidaṁ viditvā yogī paraṁ sthānamupaiti cādyaṁ |

इति श्रीमद्भगवद्गीता योगशास्त्रेऽक्षरेब्रह्मयोगो नामाष्टमोऽध्याय: ।।

Itī śrīmadbhagavadgītā yogaśāstre'kṣarabrahmayogo nāmāṣṭamo'dhyāyaḥ ||

CHAPTER IX

श्री-भगवानुवाच / *Śri Bhagavān-uvāca*

इदं तु ते गुह्यतमं प्रवक्ष्याम्यनसूयवे ।
Idaṁ tu te guhyatmaṁ pravakṣyāmyanasūyave |
ज्ञानं विज्ञानसहितं यज्ज्ञात्वा मोक्ष्यसेऽशुभात् ।। (1)
Jñānaṁ vijñānasahitaṁ yajjñātvā mokṣyase'subhāt ||

राजविद्या राजगुह्यं पवित्रमिदमुत्तमम् ।
Rājavidyā rājaguhyaṁ pavitramidamuttamaṁ
प्रत्यक्षावगमं धर्म्यं सुसुखं कर्तुमव्ययम् ।। (2)
Pratyakṣāvagamaṁ dharmyaṁ susukhaṁ kartumavyayaṁ ||

अश्रद्दधानाः पुरूषा धर्मस्यास्य परंतप ।
Aśraddadhānāḥ puruṣā dharmasyāsya Parantapa |
अप्राप्य मां निवर्तन्ते मृत्युसंसारवर्त्मनि ।। (3)
Aprāpya māṁ nivartante mṛtyusaṁsāravartmani ||

मया ततमिदं सर्व जगदव्यक्तमूर्तिना ।
Mayā tatamidaṁ sarvaṁ jagadavyaktamūrtinā |
मत्स्थानि सर्वभूतानि न चाहं तेष्ववस्थितः ।। (4)
Matsthāni sarvabhūtāni na cāhaṁ teṣvavasthitaḥ ||

न च मत्स्थानि भूतानि पश्य मे योगमैश्वरम् ।
Na ca matsthāni bhūtāni paśya me yogamaiśvaraṁ |
भूतभृन्न च भूतस्थो ममात्मा भूतभावनः ।। (5)
Bhūtabhṛnna ca bhūtastho mamātmā bhutabhāvanaḥ |

यथाकाशस्थितो नित्यं वायुः सर्वत्रगो महान् ।
Yathākāśasthito nityaṁ vāyuḥ sarvatrago mahān |
तथा सर्वाणि भूतानि मस्थानीत्युपधारय ।। (6)
Tathā sarvāṇi bhūtāni matsthānītyupadhāraya ||

सर्वभूतानि कौन्तेय प्रकृतिं यान्ति मामिकाम् ।
Sarvabhūtāni Kaunteya prakṛtiṁ yānti māmikāṁ |

कल्पक्षये पुनस्तानि कल्पादौ विसृजाम्यहम् ।। (7)
Kalpakṣaye punasthāni kalpādau visṛjāmyahaṁ ||

प्रकृतिं स्वामवष्टभ्य विसृजामि पुनः पुनः ।
Prakṛtiṁ svāmavaṣṭabhya visṛjāmi punaḥ punaḥ |
भूतग्राममिमं कृत्स्नमवशं प्रकृतेर्वशात् ।। (8)
Bhūtagrāmamimaṁ kṛtsnamavaśaṁ prakṛtervasāt ||

न च मां तानि कर्माणि निबध्नन्ति धनंजय ।
Na ca māṁ tāni karmāṇi nibadhnanti dhanañjaya |
उदासीनवदासीन मसक्तं तेषु कर्मसु ।। (9)
Udāsīnavadāsīna masaktaṁ teṣu karmasu ||

मयाध्यक्षेण प्रकृतिं सूयते सचराचरम् ।
Mayādhyakṣeṇa prakṛtiḥ sūyate sacarācaraṁ |
हेतुनानेन कौन्तेय जगद्विपरिवर्तते ।। (10)
Hetunānena Kaunteya jagadviparivartate ||

अवजानन्ति मां मूढा मानुषीं तनुमाश्रितम् ।
Avajānanti māṁ mūḍhā mānuṣīṁ tanumāśritaṁ |
परं भावमजानन्तो मम भूतमहेश्वरम् ।। (11)
Paraṁ bhāvamajānanto mama bhūtamaheśvaraṁ ||

मोघाशा मोघकर्मणो मोघज्ञाना विचेतसः ।
Moghāśa moghakarmāṇo moghajñānā vicetasaḥ |
राक्षसीमासुरीं चैव प्रकृतिं मोहिनीं श्रिताः ।। (12)
Rākṣasīmāsurīṁ caiva prakṛtiṁ mohinīṁ śritāḥ ||

महात्मनस्तु मां पार्थ दैवी प्रकृतिमाश्रिताः ।
Mahātmanastu māṁ pārtha daivīṁ prakṛtimāśritāḥ |
भजन्त्यनन्यमनसो ज्ञात्वा भूतादिमव्ययम् ।। (13)
Bhajantyananyamanaso jñatvā bhūtādimavyayaṁ ||

सततं कीर्तयन्तो मां यतन्तश्च दृढव्रताः ।
Satataṁ kīrtayanto māṁ yatantaśca dṛḍhavratāḥ |
नमस्यन्तश्च मा भक्त्या नित्ययुक्ता उपासते ।। (14)
Namasyantaśca māṁ bhaktyā nityayuktā upāsate ||

ज्ञानयज्ञेन चाप्यन्ये यजन्तो मामुपासते ।
Jñānayajñena cāpyanye yajanto māmupāsate |
एकत्वेन पृथक्त्वेन बहुधा विश्वतोमुखम् ।। (15)
Ekatvena pṛthaktvena bahudhā viśvatomukhaṁ ||

अहंक्रतुरहं यज्ञः स्वधाहमहमौषधम् ।
Ahaṁ kraturahaṁ yajñaḥ svadhāhamahamauṣadhaṁ
मन्त्रोऽहमहमेवाज्यमाहमग्निरहं हुतम् ।। (16)
Mantro'hamahamevājyamāhamagniraham hutaṁ ||

पिताहमस्य जगतो माता धाता पिमामहः ।
Pitāhamasya jagato mātā dhātā pitāmahaḥ |
वेद्यं पवित्रमोंकार ऋक्साम यजुरेव च ।। (17)
Vedyaṁ pavitramomkāra ṛk sāma yajureva ca ||

गतिर्भर्ता प्रभुः साक्षी निवासः शरणं सुहृत् ।
Gatirbhartā prabhuḥ sākṣī nivāsaḥ śaraṇaṁ suhṛt |
प्रभवः प्रलयः स्थानं निधानं बीजमव्ययम् ।। (18)
Prabhavaḥ pralayaḥ sthānaṁ nidhānaṁ bījamavyayaṁ ||

तपाम्यहमहं वर्ष निगृह्णाम्युत्सृजामि च ।
Tapāmyahamahaṁ varṣaṁ nigṛhṇāmyutsṛjāmi ca |
अमृतं चैव मृत्युश्च सदसच्चाहमर्जुन ।। (19)
Amṛtaṁ caiva mṛtyuśca sadasaccāhamarjuna ||

त्रैविद्या मां सोमपाः पूतपापा यज्ञैरिष्ट्वा स्वर्गतिं प्रार्थयन्ते ।
Traividyā māṁ somapāḥ pūtapāpā Yajñairiṣṭvā svargatiṁ prārthayante |
ते पुण्यमासाद्य सुरेन्द्रलोक-मश्नन्ति दिव्यान्दिवि देवभोगान् ।। (20)
Te puṇyamāsādya surendraloka-maśnanti divyāndivi devabhogān ||

ते तं भुक्त्वा स्वर्गलोकं विशालं क्षीणे पुण्ये मर्त्यलोकं विशन्ति।
Te taṁ bhuktvā svargalokaṁ viśālaṁ Kṣīṇe puṇye martyalokaṁ viśanti|
एवं त्रयी धर्ममनुप्रपन्ना गतागतं कामकामा लभन्ते ।। (21)
Evaṁ trayī dharma-manuprapannā Gatāgataṁ kāmakāmā labhante ||

अनन्याश्चिन्तयन्तो मां ये जनाः पर्युपासते ।
Ananyāścintayanto māṁ ye janāḥ paryupāsate |
तेषां नित्याभियुक्तानां योगक्षेमं वहाम्यहम् ।। (22)
Teṣāṁ nityābhiyuktānāṁ yogakṣemaṁ vahāmyahaṁ ||
येऽप्यन्यदेवताभक्ता यजन्ते श्रद्धयान्विताः ।
Ye'pyanyadevatābhaktā yajante śraddhayānvitāḥ |
तेऽपि मामेव कौन्तेय यजन्त्यविधिपूर्वकम् ।। (23)
Te'pi māmeva Kaunteya yajantyavidhipūrvakaṁ ||
अहं हि सर्वयज्ञानां भोक्ता च प्रभुरेव च ।
Ahaṁ hi sarvayajñānāṁ bhoktā ca prabhureva ca |
न तु मामभिजानन्ति तत्त्वैतातश्च्यवन्ति ते ।। (24)
Na tu māmabhijānanti tattvaitātaścyavanti te ||
यान्ति देवव्रता देवान्पितृन्यान्ति पितृव्रताः ।
Yānti devavratā devān-pitṛnyānti pitṛvratāḥ |
भूतानि यान्ति भूतेज्या यान्ति मद्याजिनोऽपि माम् ।। (25)
Bhūtāni yānti bhūtejyā yānti madyājino'pi māṁ ||
पत्रं पुष्पं फलं तोयं यो मे भक्त्या प्रयच्छति ।
Patraṁ puṣpaṁ phalaṁ toyaṁ yo me bhaktyā prayacchati|
तदहं भक्त्युपहृतमश्नामि प्रयतात्मनः ।। (26)
Tadahaṁ bhaktyupahṛtamaśnāmi prayatātmanaḥ ||
यत्करोषि यदश्नासि यज्जुहोषि ददासि यत् ।
Yatkaroṣi yadaśnāsi yajjuhoṣi dadāsi yat |
यत्तपस्यसि कौन्तेय तत्कुरूष्व मदर्पणम् ।। (27)
Yattapasyasi Kaunteya tatkuruṣva madarpaṇaṁ ||
शुभाशुभफलैरेवं मोक्ष्यसे कर्मबन्धनैः ।
Śubhāṣubhaphalairevaṁ mokṣyase karmabandhanaiḥ |
संन्यासयोगयुक्तात्मा विमुक्तो मामुपैष्यसि ।। (28)
Saṁnyāsayogayuktātmā vimukto māṁ upaiṣyasi ||
समोऽहं सर्वभूतेषु न मे द्वेष्योऽस्ति न प्रियः ।
Samo'haṁ sarvabhūteṣu na me dveṣyo'sti na priyaḥ |

ये भजन्ति तु मां भक्त्या मयि ते तेषु चाप्यहम् ।। (29)
Ye bhajanti tu māṁ bhaktyā mayi te teṣu cāpyahaṁ ||

अपि चेत्सुदुराचारो भजते मामनन्यभाक् ।
Api cet-sudurācāro bhajate māṁ-ananyabhāk |
साधुरेव स मन्तव्यः सम्यग्व्यवसितो हि सः ।। (30)
Sādhureva sa mantavyaḥ samyag-vyavasito hi saḥ ||

क्षिप्रं भवति धर्मात्मा शश्वच्छान्तिं निगच्छति ।
Kṣipraṁ bhavati dharmātmā śaśvacchāntiṁ nigacchati |
कौन्तेय प्रतिजानीहि न मे भक्तः प्रणश्यति ।। (31)
Kaunteya pratijānīhi na me bhaktaḥ praṇaśyati ||

मां हि पार्थ व्यपाश्रित्य येऽपि स्युः पापयोनयः ।
Māṁ hi Pārtha vyapāśritya ye'pi syuḥ pāpayonayaḥ |
स्त्रियो वैश्यास्तथा शूद्रास्तेऽपि यान्ति परां गतिम् ।। (32)
Striyo vaiśyāstathā śūdrās-te'pi yānti parāṁ gatiṁ ||

किं पुनर्ब्राह्मणाः पुण्या भक्ता राजर्षयस्तथा ।
Kiṁ punar-brāhmaṇāḥ pūṇyā bhaktā rājarṣayastathā |
अनित्यमसुखं लोकमिमं प्राप्य भजस्व गाम् ।। (33)
Anityaṁ-asukhaṁ lokaṁ-imaṁ prāpya bhajasva māṁ ||

मन्मना भव मद्भक्तो मद्याजी मां नमस्कुरू ।
Manmanā bhava madbhakto madyājī māṁ namaskuru |
मामेवैष्यसि युक्त्वैवमात्मानं मत्परायणः ।। (34)
Mām-evaiṣyasi yuktvai'vamātmānaṁ matparāyaṇaḥ |

इति श्रीमद्भगवद्गीता राजविद्याराजगुह्ययोगो नाम नवमोध्यायः ।।
Iti śrīmadbhagavadgītā: rājavidyā-rājaguhyayogo nāma navamo'dhyāyaḥ

CHAPTER X

श्री भगवानुवाच /*Sri Bhagavān-uvāca*

भूय एव महाबाहो श्रृणु मे परमं वचः ।
Bhūya eva mahābāho śṛṇu me paramaṁ vacaḥ |
यत्तेऽहं प्रीयमाणाय वक्ष्यामि हितकाम्यया ।। (1)
Yat-te'haṁ prīyamāṇāya vakṣyāmi hitakāmyayā ||

न मे विदुः सुरगणाः प्रभवं न महर्षयः ।
Na me viduḥ suragaṇāḥ prabhavāṁ maharṣayaḥ |
अहमादिर्हि देवानां महर्षीणां च सर्वशः ।। (2)
Ahamādirhi devānāṁ maharṣiṇāṁ ca sarvaśaḥ ||

यो मामजमनादिं च वेत्ति लोकमहेश्वरम् ।
Yo māṁ-ajam-anādiṁ ca vetti lokamaheśvaraṁ |
असंमूढः स मर्त्येषु सर्वपापै प्रमुच्यते ।। (3)
Asaṁmūḍhaḥ sa martyeṣu sarvapāpaiḥ pramucyate ||

बुद्धिर्ज्ञानमसंमोहः क्षमा सत्यं दमः शमः ।
Buddhir-jñānam-sammohaḥ kṣamā satyaṁ damaḥ śamaḥ |
सुखं दुखं भवोऽभावो भयं चाभयमेव च ।। (4)
sukhaṁ duḥkhaṁ bhavo'bhāvo bhayaṁ cā'bhayameva ca ||

अहिंसा समता तुष्टिस्तपो दानं यशोऽयशः ।
Ahiṁsā samatā tuṣṭis-tapo dānaṁ yaśo'yaśaḥ |
भवन्ति भावा भूतानां मत्त एव पृथग्विधाः ।। (5)
Bhavanti bhāvā bhūtānāṁ matta eva pṛthagvidhāḥ ||

महर्षयः सप्त पूर्वे चत्वारो मनवस्तथा ।
Maharṣayaḥ sapta pūrve catvāro manavas-tathā |
मद्भावा मनसा जाता येषां लोक इमाः प्रजाः ।। (6)
Madbhāvā manasā jatā yesāṁ loka imāḥ prajāḥ |

एतां विभूति योगं च मम यो वेत्ति तत्त्वतः ।
Etāṁ vibhūtiṁ yogaṁ ca mama yo vetti tattvataḥ |

सोऽविकम्पेन योगेन युज्यते नात्र संशयः ।। (7)
So'vikampena yogena yujyate nā'tra saṁśayaḥ ||

अहं सर्वस्य प्रभवो मत्तः सर्वं प्रवर्तते ।
Ahaṁ sarvasya prabhavo mattaḥ sarvaṁ pravartate |
इति मत्वा भजन्ते मां बुधा भावसमन्विताः ।। (8)
Iti matvā bhajante māṁ budhā bhāvasamanvitāḥ ||

मच्चित्ता मद्गतप्राणा बोधयन्तः परस्परम् ।
Maccittā madgataprāṇā bodhayantaḥ parasparaṁ |
कथयन्तश्च मां नित्यं तुष्यन्ति च रमन्ति च ।। (9)
Kathayantaśca māṁ nityaṁ tuṣyanti ca ramanti ca ||

तेषां सततयुक्तानां भजतां प्रीतिपूर्वकम् ।
Teṣāṁ satatayuktānāṁ bhajatāṁ prītipūrvakaṁ
ददामि बुद्धियोगं तं येन मामुपयान्ति ते ।। (10)
Dadāmi buddhiyogaṁ taṁ yena māmupayānti te ||

तेषामेवाऽनुकम्पार्थमहमज्ञानजं तमः ।
Teṣāṁ-evā'nukampārtham-aham-ajñānajaṁ tamaḥ |
नाशयाम्यात्मभावस्थो ज्ञानदीपेन भास्वता ।। (11)
Nāśayāmyātmabhāvastho jñānadīpena bhāsvatā ||

अर्जुन उवाच / Arjuna Uvāca

परं ब्रह्म परं धाम पवित्रं परमं भवान् ।
Paraṁ Brahma paraṁ dhāma pavitraṁ paramam bhavān |
पुरूषं शाश्वतं दिव्यमादिदेवमजं विभुम् ।। (12)
Puruṣaṁ śāśvataṁ divyam-ādidevaṁ-ajaṁ vibhuṁ ||

आहुस्त्वामृषयः सर्वे देवर्षिर्नारदस्तथा ।
Āhus-tvāṁ-ṛṣayaḥ sarve devarṣir-nāradas-tathā |
असितो देवलो व्यासः स्वयं चैव ब्रवीषि मे ।। (13)
Asito devalo vyāsah svayaṁ caiva braviṣi me ||

सर्वमेतदृतं मन्ये यन्मां वदसि केशव ।
Sarvaṁ-etad-ṛtaṁ manye yan-māṁ vadasi Keśava |

न हि ते भगवन् व्यक्तिं विदुर्देवा न दानवाः।। (14)
Na hi te bhagavan-vyaktiṁ vidur-devā na dānavāḥ ||
स्वयमेंवात्मनात्मानं वेत्थ त्वं पुरूषोत्तम ।
Svayam-evā-'tmanā-tmānaṁ vettha tvaṁ puruṣottama|
भूतभावन भूतेश देवदेव जगत्पते ।। (15)
Bhūtabhāvana bhūteśa devadeva jagatpate ||
वक्तुमर्हस्यशेषेण दिव्या ह्यात्मविभूतयः ।
Vaktum-arhasy-aśeṣeṇa divyā hyātmavibhūtayaḥ |
याभिर्विभूतिभिर्लोकानिमांस्त्वं व्याप्य तिष्ठसि ।। (16)
Yābhir-vibhūtibhir-lokān-imāṁs-tvaṁ vyāpya tiṣṭhasi ||
कथं विद्यामहं योगिस्त्वां सदा परिचिन्तयन् ।
Kathaṁ vidyāmahaṁ yogiṁstvāṁ sadā paricinatayan |
केषु केषु च भावेषु चिन्त्योऽसि भगवन्मया ।। (17)
Keṣu keṣu ca bhāveṣu cintyo'si bhagavan-mayā ||
विस्तरेणात्मनो योगं विभूतिं च जनार्दन ।
Vistareṇā-tmano yogaṁ vibhūtiṁ ca Janārdana |
भूयः कथय तृप्तिर्हि शृण्वतो नास्ति मेऽमृतम् ।। (18)
Bhūyaḥ kathaya tṛptir hi śṛṇvato nā-sti me-mṛtaṁ ||

श्रीभगवानुवाच /*Sri bhagavān-uvāca*

हन्त ते कथयिष्यामि दिव्या ह्यात्मविभूतयः ।
Hanta te kathayiṣyāmi divyā hyātmavibhūtayaḥ |
प्राधान्यतः कुरूश्रेष्ठ नास्त्यन्तो विस्तरस्य मे ।। (19)
prādhānyataḥ kuruśreṣtha nā-sty-anto vistarasya me ||
अहमात्मा गुडाकेश सर्वभूताशयस्थितः ।
Ahamātmā guḍākeśa sarvabhūtāśayasthitaḥ |
अहमादिश्च मध्यं च भूतानामन्त एव च ।। (20)
Ahaṁ-ādiś-ca madhyaṁ ca bhūtānāṁ-anta eva ca ||
आदित्यानामहं विष्णुर्ज्योतिषां रविरंशुमान् ।
Ādityānām-ahaṁ Viṣṇur-jyotiṣāṁ ravir-aṁśumān
मरीचिर्मरूतामस्मि नक्षत्राणामहं शशी ।। (21)
Marīcir-marutām-asmi nakṣatrāṇāmahaṁ śaśi ||

वेदानां सामवेदोऽस्मि देवानामस्मि वासवः ।
Vedānāṁ sāmavedo'smi devānām-asmi Vāsavaḥ |
इन्द्रियाणां मनश्चास्मि भूतानामस्मि चेतना ।। (22)
Indriyāṇāṁ manaś-cā-smi bhūtānām asmi cetanā ||
रूद्राणां शंकरश्चास्मि वित्तेशो यक्षरक्षसाम् ।
Rudrāṇāṁ Śaṁkaras-ca-smi vitteśo yakṣarakṣasāṁ |
वसूनां पावकश्चास्मि मेरूः शिखरिणामहम् ।। (23)
Vasūnāṁ pāvakaś-cā-smi meruḥ śikhariṇāṁ-ahaṁ ||
पुरोधसां च मुख्यं मां विद्धि पार्थ बृहस्पतिम् ।
Purodhasāṁ ca mukhyaṁ māṁ viddhi pārtha bṛhaspatiṁ |
सेनानीनामहं स्कन्दः सरसामस्मि सागरः ।। (24)
Senānīnām-ahaṁ skandaḥ sarasāṁ asmi sāgaraḥ ||
महर्षीणां भृगुरहं गिरामस्म्येकमक्षरम् ।
Maharṣīṇāṁ bhṛgur-ahaṁ girām-asmy-ekaṁ-akṣaraṁ |
यज्ञानां जपयज्ञोऽस्मि स्थावराणां हिमालयः ।। (25)
Yajñānāṁ japayajño'smi sthāvarāṇāṁ himālayaḥ |
अश्वत्थः सर्ववृक्षाणां देवर्षीणां च नारदः ।
Aśvatthaḥ sarvavṛkṣāṇāṁ devarṣīṇāṁ ca nāradaḥ ||
गन्धर्वाणां चित्ररथः सिद्धानां कपिलो मुनिः ।। (26)
Gandharvāṇāṁ citrarathaḥ siddhānāṁ kapilo muniḥ ||
उच्चैःश्रवसमश्वानां विद्धि माममृतोद्भवम् ।
Uccaiḥśravasam-aśvānāṁ viddhi māṁ-amṛtodbhavaṁ
ऐरावतं गजेन्द्राणां नराणां च नराधिपम् ।। (27)
Airāvataṁ gajendrāṇāṁ narāṇāṁ ca narādhipaṁ ||
आयुधानामहं वज्रं धेनूनामस्मि कामधुक् ।
Āyudhānām-ahaṁ vajraṁ dhenūnāṁ asmi kāmadhuk |
प्रजनश्चास्मि कन्दर्पः सर्पाणामस्मि वासुकिः ।। (28)
Prajanaś-cā-smi kandarpaḥ sarpāṇām-asmi vāsukiḥ ||
अनन्तश्चास्मि नागानां वरुणो यादसामहम् ।
Anantas-cā-smi nāgānāṁ Varuṇo yādasāṁ-ahaṁ |

पितृणामर्यमा चास्मि यमः संयमतामहम् ।। (29)
Pitṛṇām-aryamā cā-smi yamaḥ saṁyamatām-ahaṁ ||
प्रह्लादश्चास्मि दैत्यानां कालः कलयतामहम् ।
Pahlādaś-cā-smi daityānāṁ kālaḥ kalayatām-ahaṁ |
मृगाणां च मृगेन्द्रोऽहं वैनतेयश्च पक्षिणाम् ।। (30)
Mṛgāṇāṁ ca mṛgendro'haṁ vainateyas-ca pakṣiṇāṁ ||
पवनः पवतामस्मि रामः शस्त्रभृतामहम् ।
Pavanaḥ pavatām-asmi rāmaḥ śastrabhṛtām-ahaṁ |
झषाणां मकरश्चास्मि स्त्रोतसामस्मि जान्हवी ।। (31)
Jhasāṇāṁ makaras-ca-smi srotasām-asmi jāhnavī ||
सर्गाणामादिरन्तश्च मध्यं चैवाहमर्जुन ।
Sargāṇāṁ-ādir-antaś-ca madhyaṁ cai-vā-ham-arjuna |
अध्यात्मविद्या विद्यानां वादः प्रवदतामहम् ।। (32)
Adhyātmavidyā vidyānāṁ vādaḥ pravadatām-ahaṁ ||
अक्षराणामकारोऽस्मि द्वन्द्वः सामासिकस्य च ।
Akṣarāṇām-akāro-'smi dvandvaḥ sāmāsikasya ca |
अहमेवाक्षयः कालो धाताऽहं विश्वतोमुखः ।। (33)
Aham-evā-kṣayaḥ kālo dhātā'haṁ viśvatomukhaḥ ||
मृत्युः सर्वहरश्चाहमुद्भवश्च भविष्यताम् ।
Mṛtyuḥ sarvaharaś-cā-ham-udbhavaś-ca bhaviṣyatāṁ |
कीर्तिः श्रीर्वाक्च नारीणां स्मृतिर्मेधा धृतिः क्षमा ।। (34)
Kīrtiḥ śrir-vāk-ca nārīṇāṁ smṛtir-medhā dhṛtiḥ kṣamā ||
बृहत्साम तथा साम्नां गायत्री छन्दसामहम् ।
Bṛhatsāma tathā sāmnāṁ gāyatri chandasāmahaṁ |
मासानां मार्गशीर्षोऽहमृतूनां कुसुमाकरः ।। (35)
Māsānāṁ Mārgaśīrṣo-haṁ-ṛtúnāṁ kusumākaraḥ ||
द्यूतं छलयतामस्मि तेजस्तेजस्विनामहम् ।
Dyūtaṁ chalayatām-asmi tejas-tejasvinām-ahaṁ |
जयोऽस्मि व्यवसायोऽस्मि सत्त्वं सत्त्ववतामहम् ।। (36)
Jayo 'smi vyavasāyo 'smi sattvaṁ sattvavatāmahaṁ ||

वृष्णीनां वासुदेवोऽस्मि पाण्डवानां धनंजयः ।
Vṛṣṇīnāṁ Vāsudevo'smi Pāṇḍavānāṁ Dhananjayaḥ !
मुनीनामप्यहं व्यासः कवीनामुशना कविः ।। (37)
Munīnāṁ-apy-ahaṁ Vyāsaḥ kavīnām-uśanā kaviḥ ||
दण्डो दमयतामस्मि नीतिरस्मि जिगीषताम् ।
Daṇḍo damayatāṁ asmi nītir asmi jigīṣatāṁ |
मौनं चैवास्मि गुह्यानां ज्ञानं ज्ञानवतामहम् ।। (38)
Maunaṁ cai-vā-smi guhyānāṁ jñānaṁ jñānavatām-ahaṁ ||
यच्चापि सर्वभूतानां बीजं तदहमर्जुन ।
Yac-cā-pi sarvabhūtānāṁ bījaṁ tadahamarjuna |
न तदस्ति विना यत्स्यान्मया भूतं चराचरम् ।। (39)
Na tad-asti vinā yat-syān-mayā bhūtaṁ carācaraṁ ||
नान्तोऽस्ति मम दिव्यानां विभूतीनां परंतप ।
Nā-'nto-'sti mama divyānāṁ vibhūtīnāṁ parantapa |
एष तूद्देशतः प्रोक्तो विभूतेर्विस्तरो मया ।। (40)
Eṣa tūddeśataḥ prokto vibhūter-vistaro mayā ||
यद्यद्विभूतिमत्सत्वं श्रीमदूर्जितमेव वा ।
Yad-yad vibhūtimat sattvaṁ śrimad-ūrjitaṁ eva vā |
तत्तदेवावगच्छ त्वं मम तेजोंशसंभवम् ।। (41)
Tad-tad evā'vagaccha tvaṁ mama tejoṁśasambhavaṁ ||
अथवा बहुनैतेन किं ज्ञातेन तवार्जुन ।
Athavā bahunai tena kiṁ jñātena tavā-rjuna |
विष्टभ्याहमिदं कृत्स्नमेकांशेन स्थितो जगत् ।। (42)
Viṣṭabhyā 'ham idaṁ kṛtsnaṁ ekāmśena sthito jagat ||
इति श्रीमद्भगवद्गीता विभूतियोगो नाम दशमोऽध्यायः ।।
Iti Śrīmad-Bhagavadgītā-Vibhūtiyogo nāma daśamo'dhyāyaḥ|

CHAPTER XI

अर्जुन उवाच / *Arjuna Uvāca*

मदनुग्रहाय परमं गुह्यमध्यात्मसंज्ञितम् ।
Mad-anugrahāya paramaṁ guhyaṁ-adhyātm asaṁjñitaṁ |
यत्त्वयोक्तं वचस्तेन मोहोऽयं विगतो मम ।। (1)
Yat-tvyo-ktaṁ vacas-tena moho'yaṁ vigato mama ||
भवाप्ययौ हि भूतानां श्रुतौ विस्तरशो मया ।
Bhavāpyayau hi bhūtānāṁ śrutau vistaraśo mayā |
त्वत्तः कमलपत्राक्ष माहात्म्यमपि चाव्ययम् ।। (2)
Tvattaḥ kamalapatrākṣa māhātmyam api cā 'vyayam ||
एवमेतद्यथात्थ त्वमात्मानं परमेश्वर ।
Evam-etad-yathā 'ttha tvam-ātmānaṁ parameśvara |
द्रष्टुमिच्छामि ते रूपमैश्वरं पुरूषोत्तम ।। (3)
Draṣṭum-icchāmi te rūpam-aiśvaraṁ puruṣottama |
मन्यसे यदि तच्छक्यं मया द्रष्टुमिति प्रभो ।
Manyase yadi tacchakyaṁ mayā draṣṭuṁ iti, prabho
योगेश्वर ततो मे त्वं दर्शयात्मानमव्ययम् ।। (4)
Yogeśvara tato me tvaṁ darśayātmānaṁ-avyayaṁ ||

श्री भगवानुवाच / *Śrī Bhagavān-uvāca*

पश्य मे पार्थ रूपाणि शतशोऽथ सहस्रशः ।
Paśya me pārtha rūpāṇi śataśo'tha sahasraśaḥ |
नानाविधानि दिव्यानि नानावर्णाकृतीनि च ।। (5)
Nānāvidhāni divyāni nānāvarṇākṛtīni ca ||
पश्यादित्याम्वसून्रुद्रानश्विनौ मरूतस्तथा ।
Paśy-ādityān-vasūn-rudrān aśvinau marutas-tathā |

बहून्यदृष्टपूर्वाणि पश्याश्चर्याणि भारत ।। (6)
Bahūny-aḍṛṣṭapūrvāṇi paśyā-ścaryāṇi Bhārata |
इहैकस्थं जगत्कृस्नं पश्याद्य सचराचरम् ।
Ihaikasthaṁ jagat-kṛtsnaṁ paśyā-dya sacarācaram |
मम देहे गुडाकेश यच्चान्यद्दृष्टुमिच्छसि ।। (7)
Mama dehe guḍākeśa yac-cā'nyad draṣṭuṁ icchasi ||
न तु मां शक्यसे द्रष्टुमनेनैव स्वचक्षुषा ।
Na tu māṁ śakyase draṣṭum anenai'va svacakṣuṣā |
दिव्यं ददामि ते चक्षुः पश्य मे योगमैश्वरम् ।। (8)
Divyaṁ dadāṁi te cakṣuḥ paśya me yogam-aiśvaraṁ ||

संजय उवाच / *Sañjaya Uvācha*

एवमुक्त्वा ततो राजन् महायोगेश्वरो हरिः ।
Evam-uktvā tato Rājan mahāyogeśvaro Hariḥ |
दर्शयामास पार्थाय परमं रूपमैश्वरम् ।। (9)
Darśayāmāsa Pārthāya paramaṁ rūpam-aiśvaraṁ ||
अनेक वक्त्रनयनमनेकाद्भुतदर्शनम् ।
Anekavaktra-nayanam-anekād-bhuta-darśanaṁ |
अनेक दिव्याभरणं दिव्यानेकोद्यतायुधम् ।। (10)
Anekadivyābharaṇaṁ divyāneko-dyatāyudhaṁ ||
दिव्यमाल्याम्बरधरं दिव्यगन्धानुलेपनम् ।
Divyamālyāmbaradharaṁ divyagandhānulepanaṁ |
सर्वाश्चर्यमयं देवमनन्तं विश्वतोमुखम् ।। (11)
Sarvāścaryamayaṁ devaṁ anantaṁ viśvatomukhaṁ ||
दिवि सूर्यसहस्रस्य भवेद्युगपदुत्थिता ।
Divi sūryasahasrasya bhavedyugapad-utthitā |
यदि भाः सदृशी सा स्याद्भासस्तस्य महात्मनः ।। (12)
Yadi bhāḥ sadṛśī sā syād-bhāsas-tasya mahātmanaḥ |
तत्रैकस्थं जगत्कृत्सनं प्रविभक्तमनेकधा ।
Tatraikasthaṁ jagatkṛtsnaṁ pravibhaktam-anekadhā ||

अपश्यद्देव देवस्य शरीरे पाण्डवस्तदा ।। (13)
Apaśyad-deva devasya śarīre Pāṇḍavas-tadā ||
ततः स विस्मयाविष्टो हृष्टरोमा धनंजयः ।
Tataḥ sa vismayāviṣṭo hṛṣṭaromā Dhanañjayaḥ |
प्रणम्य शिरसा देवं कृतांञ्जलिरभाषत ।। (14)
Praṇamya śirasā devaṁ kṛtāñjalir-abhāṣata ||

अर्जुन उवाच / *Arjuna Uvāca*

पश्यामि देवांस्तव देव देहे सर्वास्तथा भूतविशेषसंघान् ।
Paśyāmi devāṁs-tava deva dehe Sarvāṁs-tathā bhūtaviśeṣasaṁghān |
ब्रह्माणमीशं कमलासनस्थ मृषींश्च सर्वानुरगांश्च दिव्यान् ।। (15)
Brahmāṇam-īśaṁ kamalāsanastha mṛṣīṁś-ca sarvān-uragāṁś-ca divyān ||
अनेकबाहूदरवक्त्र नेत्रं पश्यामि त्वां सर्वतोऽनन्तरूपम् ।
Anekabāhūdaravaktra netraṁ paśyāmi tvāṁ sarvato'nantarūpaṁ |
नान्तं न मध्यं न पुनस्तवादिं पश्यामि विश्वेश्वर विश्वरूपम् ।। (16)
Nā-ntaṁ na madhyaṁ na punas-tavā-diṁ paśyāmi viśveśvara viśvarūpaṁ ||
किरीटिनं गदिनं चक्रीणं च तेजोराशिं सर्वतो दीप्तिमन्तम् ।
Kirīṭinaṁ gadinaṁ cakriṇaṁ ca tejorāśiṁ sarvato dīptimantaṁ|
पश्यामि त्वां दुर्निरीक्ष्यं समन्ता द्दीप्तानलार्कद्युतिमप्रमेयम् ।। (17)
Paśyāmi tvāṁ durnirikṣyaṁ samantād dīptānalārkadyutimaprameyaṁ ||
त्वमक्षरं परमं वेदितव्यं त्वमस्य विश्वस्य परं निधानम् ।
Tvam-akṣaraṁ paramaṁ veditavyaṁ Tvaṁ-asya viśvasya paraṁ nidhānaṁ ||
त्वमव्ययः शाश्वतधर्मगोप्ता सनातनस्त्वं पुरूषो मतो मे ।। (18)
Tvam-avyayaḥ śāśvata dharma-goptā Sanātanas-tvaṁ puruṣo mato me ||

अनादिमध्यान्तमनन्तवीर्य-मनन्तबाहुं शशिसूर्यनेत्रम् ।
Anādimadhyāntaṁ anantavīrya ananta bāhum śaśisūryanetram |
पश्यामि त्वां दीप्तहुताशवक्त्रं स्वतेजसा विश्वमिदं तपन्तम् ।। (19)
Paśyāmi tvāṁ dīptahutāśavaktraṁ svatejasā viśvam-idaṁ tapantaṁ ||

द्यावापृथिव्योरिदमन्तरं हि व्याप्तं त्वयैकेन दिशश्च सर्वाः ।
Dyāvā-pṛthivyor-idam-antaraṁ hi vyāptaṁ tvayaikena diśaś-ca sarvāḥ |
दृष्टाद्भूतं रूपमुग्रं तवेदं लोकत्रयं प्रव्यथितं महात्मन् ।। (20)
Dṛṣṭvābhutaṁ rūpam-ugraṁ tave-daṁ loka-trayaṁ pravyathitaṁ mahātman ||
अमी हि त्वां सुरसंघा विशन्ति केचिद्भीता प्राञ्जलयो गृणन्ति ।
Ami hi tvāṁ surasaṁghā viśanti Kecid-bhītaḥ prāñjalayo gṛṇanti |
स्वस्तीत्युक्त्वा महर्षिसिद्धसंघाः स्तुवन्ति त्वां स्तुतिभिः पुष्कलाभिः।। (21)

Svastītyuktvā maharṣisiddhasamghāḥ stuvanti tvāṁ stutibhiḥ puṣkalābhiḥ ||
रूद्रादित्या वसवो ये च साध्या विश्वेऽश्विनौ मरूतश्चोष्मपाश्च ।
Rudrādityā vasavo ye ca sādhyā Visve 'śvinau marutas-coṣmapāś-ca |
गन्धर्वयक्षासुरसिद्धसंघा वीक्ष्यन्ते त्वां विस्मिताश्चैव सर्वे ।। (22)
Gandharva-yakṣāsura-siddha-saṁghā vīkṣyante tvāṁ vismitās-caiva sarve ||
रूपं महत्ते बहुवक्त्रनेत्रं महाबाहो बहुबाहूरुपादम् ।
Rūpaṁ mahatte bahu-vaktra-netraṁ mahābāho bahu-bāhū-rupādaṁ |
बहूदरं बहुदंष्ट्राकरालं दृष्ट्वा लोकाः प्रव्यथितास्तथाहम् ।। (23)
Bahūdaraṁ bahudamṣṭrākarālaṁ dṛṣṭvā lokāḥ pravyathitās-tathā-haṁ ||

नभस्पृशं दीप्तमनेकवर्णं व्यात्ताननं दीप्तविशाल नेत्रं । (24)
Nabhaspṛśaṁ dīptam-anekavarṇaṁ vyāttānanaṁ dīptaviśāla-netraṁ |
दृष्ट्वा हि त्वां प्रव्यथितान्तरात्मा धृति न विन्दामि शमं च विष्णो ।।
Dṛṣṭvā hi tvāṁ pravyathitāntarātmā Dhṛtiṁ na vindāmi śamaṁ ca viṣṇo ||

दंष्ट्राकरालाानि च ते मुखानि दृष्ट्वैव कालानलसंनिभानि । (25)
Daṁṣṭrākarālāni ca te mukhāni dṛṣṭvaiva kālānalasaṁnibhāni|
दिशो न जाने न लभे च शर्म प्रसीद देवेश जगन्निवास ।।
Diśo na jāne na labhe ca śarma prasīda deveśa jagannivāsa ||

अमी च त्वां धृतराष्ट्रस्य पुत्राः सर्वे सहैवावनिपालसंघैः ।
Amī ca tvāṁ dhṛtarāṣṭrasya putrāḥ sarve sahai-vā-vanipālasaṁghaiḥ |
भीष्मो द्रोणः सूतपुत्रस्तथासौ सहास्मदीयैरपि योधमुख्यैः ।। (26)
Bhīṣmo droṇaḥ sūtaputras-tathā-sau Sahāsmadīyair-api yodhamukhyaiḥ ||

वक्त्राणि ते त्वरमाणा विशन्ति दंष्ट्राकरालानि भयानकानि ।
Vaktrāṇi te tvaramāṇā viśanti daṁṣṭrākarālāni bhayānakāni |
केचिद्विलग्ना दशनान्तरेषु संदृश्यन्ते चूर्णितैरुत्तमाङ्गैः ।। (27)
Kecid-vilagnā daśanāntareṣu saṁdṛśyante cūrṇitairuttamāṅgaiḥ ||

यथा नदीनां बहवोऽम्बुवेगाः समुद्रमेवाभिमुखा द्रवन्ति ।
Yathā nadīnāṁ bahavo'mbuvegāḥ samudramevā-bhimukhā dravanti |
तथा तवामी नरलोकवीरा विशन्ति वक्त्राण्यभिविज्वलन्ति ।। (28)
Tathā tavā-mi naralokavīrā viśanti vaktrāṇy-abhivijvalanti ||

यथा प्रदीप्तं ज्वलनं पतङ्गा विशन्ति नाशाय समृद्धवेगाः ।
Yathā pradīptaṁ jvalanaṁ pataṅgā viśanti nāśāya samṛddhavegāḥ |
तथैव नाशाय विशन्ति लोका-स्तवापि वक्त्राणि समृद्धवेगाः ।। (29)
Tathai'va nāśāya viśanti lokā-stavā'pi vaktrāṇi samṛddhavegāḥ ||

लेलिह्यसे ग्रसमानः समन्ता ल्लोकान्समग्रान्वदनैर्ज्वलद्भिः।
Lelihyase grasamānaḥ samantā- Ilokān-samagrān-vadanair-jvaladbhiḥ |
तेजोभिरापूर्य जगत्समग्रं भासस्तवोग्राः प्रतपन्ति विष्णो ।। (30)
Tejobhirāpūrya jagat samagraṁ bhāsas tavo'grāḥ pratapanti viṣṇo ||
आख्याहि मे को भवांनुग्ररूपो नमोऽस्तु ते देववर प्रसीद ।
Ākhyāhi me ko bhavān-ugrarūpo namo'stu te devavara prasīda|
विज्ञातुमिच्छामि भवन्तमाद्यं ।
Vijñātum icchāmi bhavantam ādyaṁ
न हि प्रजानामि तव प्रवृत्तिम् ।। (31)
na hi prajānāmi tava pravṛttiṁ ||

श्रीभगवानुवाच / *Śri bhagavān-uvāca*

कालोऽस्मि लोकक्षयकृत्प्रवृद्धो
Kālo'smi lokakṣayakṛt-pravṛddho
लोकान्समाहर्तुमिह प्रवृतः ।
lokān samāhartum-iha pravṛttaḥ |
ऋतेऽपि त्वां न भविष्यन्ति सर्वे ।
ṛte'pi twāṁ na bhaviṣyanti sarve |
येऽवस्थिताः प्रत्यनीकेषु योधाः ।। (32)
Ye'vasthitāḥ pratyanīkeṣu yodhāḥ ||
तस्मात्त्वमुत्तिष्ठ यशो लभस्व जित्वा शत्रून्भुङक्ष्व राज्यं समृद्धम् ।
Tasmāt-tvaṁ uttiṣṭha yaśo labhasva jitvā śatrūn-bhuṇkṣva rājyam samṛddhaṁ |
मयैवैते निहताः पूर्वमेव निमित्तमात्रं भव सव्यसाचिन् ।। (33)
Mayai'vai-te nihatāḥ pūrvam-eva nimittamātraṁ bhava savyasācin ||
द्रोणं च भीष्मं च जयद्रथं च कर्णं तथान्यानि च योधवीरान् ।
Droṇaṁ ca bhīṣmaṁ ca jayadrathaṁ ca karṇaṁ tathānyāni ca yodhavīrān |

मया हतांस्त्वं जहि मा व्यथिष्ठा
Mayā hatāms-tvaṁ jahi mā vyathiṣṭhā
युद्धस्व जेतासि रणे सपत्नान् ।। (34)
yuddhasva jetā si raṇe sapatnān ||

संजय उवाच / *Sañjaya Uvāca*

एतच्छ्रूत्वा वचनं केशवस्य कृतांञ्जलिर्वेपमानः किरीटी ।
Etac-chrutvā vacanaṁ keśavasya
कृतांजलिर्वेपमानः किरीटी ।
kṛtānjalīr-vepamānaḥ kirītī |
नमस्कृत्वा भूय एवाह कृष्णं सगद्गदं भीतभीतः प्रणम्य ।। (35)
Namaskṛtvā bhūya evā-ha kṛṣṇaṁ Sagadgadaṁ bhītabhītaḥ praṇamya ||

अर्जुन उवाच / *Arjuna Uvāca*

स्थाने हृषीकेश तव प्रकीर्त्या जगत्प्रहृष्यत्यनुरज्यते च ।
Sthāne Hṛsīkeśa tava prakīrtyā jagatprahṛṣyaty-anurajyate ca|
रक्षांसि भीतानि दिशो द्रवन्ति सर्वे नमस्यन्ति च सिद्धसंघाः ।। (36)
Rakṣāṁsi bhītāni diśo dravanti sarve namasyanti ca siddhasaṁghāḥ ||
कस्माच्च ते न नमेरन्महात्मत् गरीयसे ब्रह्मणोऽप्यादिकर्त्रे ।
Kasmāc-ca te na nameran-mahātman garīyase brahmaṇo-py-ādikartre |
अनन्त देवेश जगन्निवास त्वमक्षरं सदसत्तत्परं यत् ।। (37)
Ananta deveśa jagannivāsa Tvamakṣaraṁ sadasattatparam yat||
त्वमादिदेवः पुरूषः पुराण-स्त्वमस्य विश्वस्य परं निधानम् ।
Tvaṁ-ādidevaḥ puruṣaḥ purāṇas Tvaṁ-asya viśvasya paraṁ nidhānaṁ|

वेत्तासि वेद्यं च परं च धाम त्वया ततं विश्वमनन्तरूप ।। (38)
vettā-si vedyaṁ ca paraṁ ca dhāma Tvayā tataṁ viṣvamanantarūpa ||
वायुर्यमोऽग्निर्वरुण: शशाङ्क:
Vāyur yamo `gnir Varuṇaḥ śāśāṅkah
प्रजापतिस्त्वं प्रपितामहश्च ।
Prajāpatis-tvam prapitāmahaśca |
नमो नमस्तेऽस्तु सहस्रकृत्व:
Namo namaste'śtu sahasra-kṛtvaḥ
पुनश्च भूयोऽपि नमो नमस्ते ।। (39)
punaś-ca bhūyo'pi namo namaste ||
नम: पुरस्तादथ पृष्ठतस्ते नमोऽस्तु ते सर्वत एव सर्वे ।
Namaḥ purastād-atha pṛṣthatas-te Namo'stu te sarvata eva sarve|
अनन्तवीर्यामितविक्रमस्त्वं सर्वं समाप्नोषि ततोऽसि सर्व: ।। (40)
Anantavīryāmitavikramas-tvam Sarvaṁ samāpnoṣi tato'si sarvaḥ||
सखेति मत्वा प्रसभं यदुक्तं
Sakhe-ti matvā prasabhaṁ yaduktaṁ
हे कृष्णा हे यादव हे सखेति ।
He kṛṣna he yādava he sakhe-ti |
अजानता महिमानं तवेदं मया प्रमादात्प्रणयेन वापि ।। (41)
Ajānatā mahimānaṁ tave-daṁ Mayā pramādāt-praṇayena vā'pi ||
यच्चावहासार्थमसत्कृतोऽसि विहारशय्यासनभोजनेषु ।
Yac-cā-vahāsārthaṁ-asatkṛto-asi Vihāra-śayyāsana-bhojaneṣu
एकोऽथवाप्यच्युत तत्समक्षं तत्क्षामये त्वामहमप्रमेयम् ।। (42)
Eko 'thavā py-acyuta tatsamakṣaṁ Tat-kṣāmaye tvām-aham-aprameyaṁ ||
पितासि लोकस्य चराचरस्य त्वमस्य पूज्यश्च गुरूर्गरीयान् ।
Pitāsi lokasya carā-carasya Tvaṁ-asya pūjyaś-ca gurur-garīyān |

न त्वत्समोऽस्त्यभ्यधिकः कुतोऽन्यो लोकत्रयेऽप्यप्रतिमप्रभावः ।। (43)

Na tvatsamo-sty-abhyadhikaḥ kuto-nyo Lokatraye-py-apratimaprabhāvaḥ ||

तस्मात्प्रणम्य प्रणिधाय कायं

Tasmāt-praṇamya praṇidhāya kāyaṁ

प्रसादये' त्वामहमीशमीड्यम् ।

Prasādaye Tvām-aham-īśamīḍyaṁ |

पितेव पुत्रस्य सखेव सख्युः प्रियः प्रियायार्हसि देव सोढुम् ।। (44)

Pite'va putrasya sakhe-va sakhyuḥ Priyaḥ priyāyārhasi deva soḍhuṁ ||

अदृष्टपूर्वं हृषितोऽस्मि दृष्टवा भयेन च प्रव्यथितं मनो मे ।

Adṛṣṭa pūrvaṁ hṛṣito-smi dṛṣṭvā Bhayena ca pravyathitaṁ mano me

तदेव मे दर्शय देवरूपं प्रसीद देवेश जगन्निवास ।। (45)

Tad-eva me darśaya devarūpaṁ Prasīda deveśā jagannivāsa||

किरीटिनं गदिनं चक्रहस्त-मिच्छामि त्वां द्रष्टुमहं तथैव ।

Kirīṭinaṁ gadinaṁ cakrahastaṁ Icchāmi tvāṁ draṣṭum-ahaṁ tathai-va |

तेनैव रूपेण चतुर्भुजेन सहस्रबाहो भव विश्वमूर्त्ते ।। (46)

Tenai-va rūpeṇa caturbhujena Schasra-bāho bhava viśvamūrte ||

श्री भगवानुवाच / *Sribhagavān-uvāca*

मया प्रसन्नेन तवार्जुनेदं रूप परं दर्शितमात्मयोगात् ।

Mayā prasannena tavārjune-daṁ Rūpaṁ paraṁ darśitaṁ-ātmayōgāt |

तेजोमयं विश्वमनन्तमाद्यं यन्मे त्वदन्येन न दृष्टपूर्वम् ।। (47)

Tejomayaṁ viśvaṁ-anantaṁ-ādyaṁ yan-me tvadanyena na dṛṣṭapūrvaṁ ||

न वेदयज्ञाध्ययनैनं दानै नं च क्रियाभिनं तपोभिरूग्रैः ।

Na vedayajñādhyayanair-na dānair Na ca kriyābhir-na tapobhir-ugraiḥ |

एवंरूप शक्य अहं नृलोके ।
Evaṁrūpaḥ śakya ahaṁ nṛloke
द्रष्टुं त्वदन्येन कुरूप्रवीर ।। (48)
draṣṭum tvadanyena kurupravira
मा ते व्यथा मा च विमूढभावो दृष्ट्वा रूपं धोरमीदृङममेदम् ।
Mā te vyathā mā ca vimūḍhabhāvo Dṛṣṭvā rūpam ghoramīdṛṅ-mame-daṁ |
व्यपेतभीः प्रीतमनाः पुनस्त्वं
Vyapetabhīḥ Prītamanāḥ punas-tvaṁ
तदेव मे रूपमिदं प्रपश्य ।। (49)
Tad-eva me rūpam-idaṁ prapaśya ||

संजय उवाय / *Sañjaya Uvācha*

इत्यर्जुन वासुदेवस्तथोक्त्वा स्वकं रूपं दर्शयामास भूयः ।
Ity-arjunaṁ Vāsudevastatho'ktvā Svakaṁ rūpaṁ darśayāmāsa bhūyaḥ |
आश्वासयामास च भीतमेनं भूत्वा पुनः सौम्यवपुर्महात्मा ।। (50)
Āśvsayā-māsa ca bhītam-enaṁ Bhūtvā punaḥ saumyavapur-mahātmā ||

अर्जुन उवाच / *Arjuna Uvāca*

दृष्ट्वेदं मानुषं रूपं तव सौम्यं जनार्दन ।
Drṣṭve 'daṁ mānuṣaṁ rūpaṁ tava saumyaṁ janārdana |
इदानीमस्मि संवृतः सचेताः प्रकृतिं गतः ।। (51)
Idānīm-asmi samvṛttaḥ sacetāḥ prakṛtiṁ gataḥ ||

श्री भगवानुवाच / *Sribhagavān-uvāca*

सुदुर्दर्शमिदं रूपं दृष्टवानसि यन्मम ।
Sudurdarśam-idaṁ rūpaṁ dṛṣṭavān-asi yaṇ-mama
देवा अप्यस्य रूपस्य नित्यं दर्शनकाङ्क्षिणः ।। (52)
Devā-apy-asya rūpasya nityaṁ darśana-kāṅkṣiṇaḥ ||

नाहं वेदैर्न तपसा न दानेन न चेज्यया ।
Nāhaṁ vedair-na tapasā na dānena na ce-jyayā |
शक्यं एवंविधो द्रष्टुं दृष्टवानसि मां यथा ।। (53)
Śakyaṁ evaṁvidho draṣṭuṁ dṛṣṭavān-asi māṁ yathā ||
भक्त्या त्वनन्यया शक्यं अहमेवंविधोऽर्जुन ।
Bhaktyā tv-ananyayā śakyaṁ aham-evamvidho-rjuna
ज्ञातुं दृष्टुं च तत्त्वेन प्रवेष्टुं च परंतप ।। (54)
Jñātuṁ drṣtuṁ ca tatvena praveṣṭuṁ ca parantapa ||
मत्कर्मकृन्मत्परमो मद्भक्त: सङ्गवर्जित: ।
Matkarmakṛn-matparamo madbhaktaḥ sangavarjitaḥ
निर्वैर: सर्वभूतेषु य: स मामेति पाण्डव ।। (55)
Nirvairaḥ sarvabhūteṣu yaḥ sa māṁ-eti pāṇḍava ||
इति श्रीमद्भगवद्गीता .... विश्वरूपयोगो नामैकादशोऽध्याय:।।
Iti Śrīmadbhagavadgītā .... Viśvarūpayogo nāmaikādaśo-dhyāyaḥ ||

CHAPTER XII

अर्जुन उवाच / Arjuna Uvāca

एवं सततयुक्ता ये भक्तास्त्वां पर्युपासते ।
Evaṁ satatayuktā ye bhaktās-tvāṁ paryupāsate |
ये चाप्यक्षरमव्यक्तं तेषां के योगवित्तमाः ।। (1)
Ye cā-py-akṣaraṁ-avyaktaṁ teṣāṁ ke yogavittamāḥ ||

श्री भगवानुवाच / Śri bhagavān-uvāca

मय्यावेश्य मनो ये मां नित्ययुक्ता उपासते ।
Mayy-āveśya mano ye māṁ nityayuktā upāsate |
श्रद्धया परयोपेतास्ते मे युक्ततमा मताः ।। (2)
Śraddhayā parayo-petās-te me yuktatamā matāḥ ||
ये त्वक्षरमनिर्देश्यमव्यक्तं पर्युपासते ।
Ye tv-akṣaram-anirdesyam-avyaktam paryupāsate|
सर्वत्रगमचिन्त्यं च कूटस्थमचलं ध्रूवम् ।। (3)
Sarvatragam-acintyaṁ ca kūṭastham-acalam dhruvaṁ ||
संनियम्येन्द्रियग्रामं सर्वत्र समबुद्धयः ।
Saṁniyamye-ndriyagrāmaṁ sarvatra samabuddhayaḥ
ते प्राप्नुवन्ति मामेव सर्वभूतहिते रताः ।। (4)
Te prāpnuvanti māṁ-eva sarvabhūtahite ratāḥ ||
क्लेशोऽधिकतरस्तेषामव्यक्तासक्तचेतसाम् ।
Kleśo-'dhikataras-teṣāṁ-avyaktāsaktacetasāṁ |
अव्यक्ता हि गतिर्दुःखं देहवद्भिरवाप्यते ।। (5)
Avyaktā hi gatir-duhkhaṁ dehavadhīr-avāpyate ||
यं तु सर्वाणि कर्माणि मयि संन्यस्य मत्पराः ।
Ye tu sarvāṇi karmāṇi mayi samnyasya matparāḥ |
अनन्येनैव योगेन मां ध्यायन्त उपासते ।। (6)
Ananyenai-va yogena māṁ dhyāyanta upāsate ||

तेषामहं समुद्धर्ता मृत्युसंसारसागरात् ।
Teṣāṁ-ahaṁ samuddhartā mṛtyusaṁsārasāgarāt |
भवामि नचिरात्पार्थ मय्यावेशितचेतसाम ।। (7)
Bhavāmi nacirāt-pārtha mayy-āveśitacetasāṁ |
मय्येव मन आधत्स्व मचि बुद्धिं निवेशय।
Mayy-eva mana ādhatsva mayi buddhim niveśaya |
निवसिष्यसि मय्येव अत ऊर्ध्वं न संशयः ।। (8)
Nivasiṣyasi mayy-eva ata ūrdhvaṁ na saṁśayaḥ ||
अथ चित्तं समाधातुं न शक्नोषि मयि स्थिरम् ।
Atha cittaṁ samādhātuṁ na saknoṣi mayi sthiraṁ |
अभ्यासयोगेन ततो मामिच्छाप्तुं धनंजय ।। (9)
Abhyāsayogena tato mām-icchā'ptuṁ dhananjaya ||
अभ्यासेऽप्यसमर्थोऽसि मत्कर्मपरमो भव ।
Abhyāse'py asamartho'si matkarmaparamo bhava |
मदर्थमपि कर्माणि कुर्वन्सिद्धिमवाप्स्यसि ।। (10)
Madarthaṁ-api karmāṇi kurvan-siddhim-avāpsyasi ||
अथैतदप्यशक्तोसि कर्तुं मद्योगमाश्रितः
Athai-tad-apy-aśakto-si kartuṁ madyogam-āśritaḥ |
सर्वकर्मफलत्यागं ततः कुरु यतात्मवान् ।। (11)
Sarvakarmaphalatyāgaṁ tataḥ kuru yatātmavān ||
श्रेयो हि ज्ञानमभ्यासाज्झानाद्ध्यानं विशिष्यते ।
Śreyo hi jñānam-abhyāsāṅ-jñānād-dhyānaṁ viśiṣyate |
ध्यानात्कर्मफलत्यागस्त्यागाच्छान्तिरनन्तरम् ।। (12)
Dhyānāt-karmaphalatyāgas-tyāgāc chāntir-anantaraṁ||
अद्वेष्टा सर्वभूतानां मैत्रः करूण एव च ।
Adveṣṭā sarva-bhūtānāṁ maitraḥ karuṇa eva ca
निर्ममो निरहंकारः समदुःखसुखःक्षमी ।। (13)
Nirmamo nirahaṁkāraḥ samaduḥkha-sukhaḥkṣamī ||
संतुष्ट सततं योगी यतात्मा दृढनिश्चयः ।
Saṁtuṣṭaḥ satataṁ yogī yatātmā dṛdhaniścayaḥ |

मय्यर्पितमनोबुद्धिर्यो मे भक्तः स मे प्रियः ।। (14)
Mayy-arpitamanobuddhir-yo me bhaktaḥ sa me priyaḥ ||

यस्मान्नोद्विजते लोको लोकान्नोद्विजते च यः ।
Yasmān-no dvijate loko lokān-no-dvijate ca yaḥ |
हर्षामर्षभयोद्वेगैर्मुक्तो यः स च मे प्रियः ।। (15)
Harṣāmarṣabhayodvegair-mukto yaḥ sa ça me priyaḥ ||

अनपेक्षः शुचिर्दक्ष उदासीनो गतव्यथः ।
Anapekṣaḥ śucir-dakṣa udāsīno gatavyathaḥ |
सर्वारम्भपरित्यागी यो मद्भक्तः स मे प्रियः ।। (16)
Sarvārambhaparityāgi yo madbhaktaḥ sa me priyaḥ ||

यो न हृष्यति न द्वेष्टि न शोचति न काङक्षति ।
Yo na hṛṣyati na dveṣṭi na śocati na kāṅkṣati |
शुभाशुभपरित्यागी भक्तिमान्यः स मे प्रियः ।। (17)
Subhāśubha-parityāgī bhaktimān-yaḥ sa me priyaḥ ||

समः शत्रौ च मित्रे च तथा मानापमानयोः ।
Samaḥ śatrau ca mitre ca tathā mānāpamānayoḥ |
शीतोष्णसुखदुःखेषु समः सङगविवर्जितः ।। (18)
Śītoṣṇasukhaduḥkheṣu samaḥ saṅgavivarjitaḥ ||

तुल्यनिन्दास्तुतिर्मौनी संतुष्टो येन केनचित् ।
Tulya-nindāstutir-maunī saṁtuṣṭo yena-kenacit |
अनिकेतः स्थिरमतिर्भक्तिमा मे प्रियो नरः ।। (19)
Aniketaḥ sthiramatir-bhaktimān-me priyo naraḥ ||

ये तु धर्म्यामृतमिदं यथोक्तं पर्युपासते ।
Ye tu dharmyāmṛtaṁ-idaṁ yathoktaṁ paryupāsate ||
श्रद्दधाना मत्परमा भक्तास्तेऽतीव मे प्रियाः ।। (20)
Śraddadhānā mutparamā bhaktās-te-'tiva me priyaḥ ||

इति श्रीमद्भगवद्गीता ......भक्तियोगो नाम द्वादशोऽध्यायः ।।
Iti Śrīmadbhagavadgītā ...... Bhaktiyogo nāma dvādaśo'dhyayaḥ ||

CHAPTER XIII

अर्जुन उवाच / *Arjuna Uvāca*

प्रकृतिं पुरूषं चैव क्षेत्रं क्षेत्रज्ञमेव च ।
Prakṛtiṁ puruṣaṁ caivakshetraṁ kṣhetrajñam-eva ca |
एतद् वेदितुमिच्छामि ज्ञानं ज्ञेयं च केशव ।।
Etad veditum-icchāmi jñānam jñeyaṁ ca keśava ||

श्रीभगवानुवाच / *Sribhagavān-uvāca*

इदं शरीरं कौन्तेय क्षेत्रमित्यभिधीयते ।
Idaṁ śarīraṁ kaunteya kṣetram-ity-abhidhīyate |
एतद्यो वेत्ति तं प्राहू: क्षेत्रज्ञ इति तद्विद: ।। (1)
Etad-yo vetti taṁ prāhūḥ kṣetrajña iti tadvidaḥ ||
क्षेत्रज्ञं चापि मां विद्धि सर्वक्षेत्रेषु भारत ।
Kṣetrajñaṁ cāpi māṁ viddhi sarvakṣetreṣu bhārata |
क्षेत्रक्षेत्रज्ञयोर्ज्ञानं यत्तज्ज्ञानं मतं मम ।। (2)
Kṣetrakṣetrajñayor-jñanaṁ yat taj jñānaṁ mataṁ mama ||
तत्क्षेत्रं यच्च यादृक् च यद्विकारि यतश्च यत् ।
Tat-kṣetraṁ yac ca yādṛk ca yadvikāri yataś-ca yat |
स च यो यत्प्रभावश्च तत्समासेन मे शृणु ।। (3)
Sa ca yo yatprabhāvaś ca tat samāsena me śṛṇu ||
ऋषिभिर्बहुधा गीतं छन्दोभिर्विविधै: पृथक्।
Ṛṣibhir-bahudhā gītaṁ chandobhir-vividhaiḥ pṛthak |
ब्रह्मसूत्रपदैश्चैव हेतुमद्भिर्विनिश्चितै: ।। (4)
Brahmasūtrapadais-cai-va hetumadbhir viniścitaiḥ ||
महाभूतान्यहंकारो बुद्धिरव्यक्तमेव च ।
Mahābhūtāny-ahaṁkāro buddhir avyktam eva ca |
इन्द्रियाणि दशैकं च पञ्च चेन्द्रिगोचरा: ।। (5)
Indriyāṇi daśaikaṁ ca pañca cendriyagocarāḥ ||

इच्छा द्वेषः सुखं दुःखं संघातश्चेतना धृतिः ।
Icchā dveṣaḥ sukhaṁ duhkhaṁ samghātaś-cetanā dhrtiḥ |
एतत्क्षेत्रं समासेन सविकारमुदाहृतम् ।। (6)
Etat kṣetraṁ samāsena savikāram-udāhṛtaṁ ||
अमानित्वमदम्भित्वमहिंसा क्षान्तिरार्जवम् ।
Amānitvaṁ-adambhitvaṁ-ahiṁsā kṣāntir-ārjavaṁ |
आचार्योपासनं शौचं स्थैर्यमात्मविनिग्रहः ।। (7)
Ācāryopāsanaṁ śaucaṁ sthairyam-ātmavinigrahaḥ ||
इन्द्रियार्थेषु वैराग्यमनहंकार एव च ।
Indriyārtheṣu vairāgyam-anahaṁkāra eva ca |
जन्ममृत्युजराव्याधिदुःखदोषानुदर्शनम् ।। (8)
Janma-mṛtyu-jarā-vyādhi-duhkhadoṣānudarśanaṁ ||
असक्तिरनभिष्वंङ्गः पुत्रदारगृहादिषु ।
Asaktir-anabhiṣvangaḥ putra-dāra-gṛhādiṣu |
नित्यं च समचित्तत्वमिष्टानिष्टोपपत्तिषु ।। (9)
Nityaṁ ca samacittatvaṁ-iṣṭāniṣṭopapattiṣu ||
मयि चानन्ययोगेन भक्तिरव्यभिचारिणी ।
Mayi cā-nanyayogena bhaktir-avyabhicāriṇī |
विविक्तदेश सेवित्मरतिर्जनसंसदि ।। (10)
Viviktadeśa-sevitvam-aratir-jānasamsadi ||
अध्यात्मज्ञाननित्यत्वं तत्वज्ञानार्थदर्शनम् ।
Adhyātmajñānanityatvaṁ tattvajñānārthadarśanaṁ |
एतज्ज्ञानमिति प्रोक्तमज्ञानं यदतोऽन्यथा ।। (11)
Etaj-jñānaṁ-iti proktaṁ-ajñānaṁ yad-ato'nyathā ||
ज्ञेयं यत्तत्प्रवक्ष्यामि यज्ज्ञात्वामृतमश्नुते ।
Jñeyaṁ yat-tat-pravakṣyāmi yaj-jñātvā-mṛtamaśnute |
अनादिमत्परं ब्रह्म न सत्तन्नासदुच्यते ।। (12)
Anādimat-paraṁ brahma na sat-tan-nā-sad-ucyate ||
सर्वतः पाणिपादं तत्सर्वतोऽक्षिशिरोमुखम् ।
Sarvataḥ pāṇipādaṁ tat-sarvato-akṣi-śiro-mukhaṁ |

सर्वतः श्रुतिमल्लोके सर्वमावृत्य तिष्ठति ।। (13)
Sarvataḥ śrutimal-loke sarvam-āvṛtya tiṣṭhati ||
सर्वेन्द्रियगुणाभासं सर्वेन्द्रियविवर्जितम् ।
Sarvendriya-guṇābhāsaṁ sarvendriyavivarjitaṁ |
असक्तं सर्वभृच्चैव निर्गुणं गुणभोक्तृ च ।। (14)
Asaktaṁ sarvabhṛc-cai-va nirguṇaṁ guṇabhoktṛ ca ||
बहिरन्तश्च भूतानामचरं चरमेव च ।
Bahir-antaś-ca bhūtānāṁ-acaraṁ caraṁ-eva ca |
सूक्ष्मत्वात्तदविज्ञेयं दूरस्थं चान्तिके च तत् ।। (15)
Sūkṣmatvāt-tad-avijñeyaṁ dūrasthaṁ cā-ntike ca tat ||
अविभक्तं च भूतेषु विभक्तमिव च स्थितम् ।
Avibhaktaṁ ca bhūteṣu vibhaktam-iva ca sthitaṁ
भूतभर्तृ च तज्ज्ञेयं ग्रसिष्णु प्रभविष्णु च ।। (16)
Bhūtabhartṛ ca taj-jñeyaṁ grasiṣṇu prabhaviṣṇu ca ||
ज्योतिषामपि तज्जयोतिस्तमसः परमुच्यते ।
Jyotiṣām-api taj-jyotis-tamasaḥ paraṁ-ucyate |
ज्ञानं ज्ञेयं ज्ञानगम्यं हृदि सर्वस्य धिष्ठितग् ।। (17)
Jñānaṁ jñeyaṁ jñānagamyaṁ hṛdi sarvasya-dhiṣṭitaṁ ||
इति क्षेत्रं तथा ज्ञानं ज्ञेयं चोक्तं समासतः ।
Itī kṣetraṁ tathā-jñānaṁ jñeyaṁ co-ktaṁ samāsataḥ ||
मद्भक्त एतद्विज्ञाय मद्भावायोपपद्यते ।। (18)
madbhakta etad-vijñāya madbhāvāyo-papadyate ||
प्रकृतिं पुरूषं चैव विद्ध्यनादी उभावपि ।
Prakṛtiṁ puruṣaṁ cai-va viddhy-anādī ubhāv-api |
विकाराश्च गुणांश्चैव विद्धि प्रकृतिसंभवान् ।। (19)
Vikārāṁs-ca guṇāṁś-cai-va viddhi prakṛtisaṁbhavān ||
कार्यकारणकर्तृत्वे हेतुः प्रकृतिरूच्यते ।
Kārya-kāraṇa-kartṛtve hetuḥ prakṛtir-ucyate |
पुरूषः सुखदुःखानां भोक्तृत्वे हेतुरूच्यते ।। (20)
Puruṣaḥ sukha-duḥkhānāṁ bhoktṛtve-hetur-ucyate ||

पुरूषः प्रकृतिस्थो हि भुङक्ते प्रकृतिजान्गुणान् ।
Puruṣaḥ prakṛtistho hi bhuṅkte prakṛtijān-guṇān |
कारणं गुणसङगोऽस्य सदसद्योनिजन्मसु ।। (21)
Kāraṇaṁ guṇasango-'sya sadasad-yonijanmasu ||
उपद्रष्टानुमन्ता च भर्ता भोक्ता महेश्वरः ।
Upadraṣṭā-numantā ca bhartā bhoktā maheśvaraḥ |
परमात्मेति चाप्युक्तो देहेऽस्मिन्पुरूषः परः ।। (22)
Paramātme-ti cā-py-ukto dehe-'smin-puruṣaḥ paraḥ ||
य एवं वेत्ति पुरूषं प्रकृतिं च गुणैः सह ।
Ya evaṁ vetti puruṣaṁ prakṛtiṁ ca guṇaiḥ saha |
सर्वथा वर्तमानोऽपि न स भूयोऽभिजायते ।। (23)
Sarvathā vartamāno-'pi na sa bhūyo-'bhijāyate ||
ध्यानेनात्मनि पश्यन्ति केचिदात्मानमात्मना ।
Dhyānenā-tmani paśyanti kecid-ātmānam-ātmanā |
अन्ये सांख्येन योगेन कर्मयोगेन चापरे ।। (24)
Anye sāṅkhyena yogena karmayogena cāpare ||
अन्ये त्वेवमजानन्तः श्रुत्वान्येभ्य उपासते ।
Anye tve-vaṁ-ajānantaḥ śrutvā-nyebhya upāsate |
तेऽपि चातितरन्त्येव मृत्यं श्रुतिपरायणाः ।। (25)
Te-pi cā-titarnty-eva mṛtyuṁ śrutiparāyaṇāḥ ||
यावत्संजायते किंचित्सत्त्वं स्थावरजङगमम् ।
Yāvat-sañjāyate kiṁcit-sattvaṁ sthāvarajaṅgamaṁ |
क्षेत्रक्षेत्रज्ञसंयोगात्तद्विद्धि भरतर्षभ ।। (26)
Kṣetra-kṣetrajña-saṁyogāt-tad-viddhi bharatarṣabh ||
समं सर्वेषु भूतेषु तिष्टन्तं परमेश्वरम् ।
Samaṁ sarveṣu bhūteṣu tiṣṭantaṁ parameśvaraṁ |
विनश्यत्स्वविनश्यन्तं यः पश्यति स पश्यति ।। (27)
Vinaśyatsv-avinaśyantaṁ yaḥ paśyati sa paśyati ||
समं पश्यन्हि सर्वत्र समवस्थितमीश्वरम् ।
samaṁ paśyan-hi sarvatra samavasthitam-īśvaraṁ |

न हिनस्त्यात्मनात्मानं ततो याति परां गतिम् ।। (28)
Na hinasty-ātmanā-tmānaṁ tato yāti parāṁ gatiṁ ||
प्रकृत्यैव च कर्माणि क्रियमाणानि सर्वशः ।
Prakṛtyai-va ca karmāṇi kriyamāṇāni sarvaśaḥ |
यः पश्यति तथात्मानमकर्तारं स पश्यति ।। (29)
Yaḥ paśyati tathā-tmānam-akartāraṁ sa paśyati ||
यदा भूतपृथग्भावमेकस्थमनुपश्यति ।
Yadā bhūt-pṛthagbhāvam-ekasthaṁ-anupaśyati |
तत एव च विस्तारं ब्रह्म संपद्यते तदा ।। (30)
Tata eva ca vistāraṁ brahma saṁpadyate tadā ||
अनादित्वान्निर्गुणत्वात्परमात्मायमव्ययः ।
Anāditvān-nirguṇatvāt-paramātmā-yaṁ-avyayaḥ |
शरीरस्थोऽपि कौन्तेय न करोति न लिप्यते ।। (31)
Śarīrastho-'pi kaunteya na karoti na lipyate ||
यथा सर्वगतं सौक्ष्म्यादाकाशं नोपलिप्यते ।
Yathā sarvagataṁ saukṣmyād-ākāśaṁ no-palipyate |
सर्वत्रावस्थितो देहे तथात्मा नोपलिप्यते ।। (32)
Sarvatrā-vasthito dehe tathā-tmā no-palipyate |
यथा प्रकाशयत्येकः कृत्स्नं लोकमिमं रविः ।
Yathā prakāśayaty-ekaḥ kṛtsnaṁ lokam-imaṁ raviḥ
क्षेत्र क्षेत्री तथा कृतस्नं प्रकाशयति भारत ।। (33)
Kṣetraṁ kṣetrī tathā kṛtsnaṁprakāśayati bhārata ||
क्षेत्रक्षेत्रज्ञयोरेवमन्तरं ज्ञानचक्षुषा ।
Kṣetra-kṣetrajñayor-evaṁ-antaraṁ jñāna-cakṣuṣā |
भूतप्रकृतिमोक्षं च ये विदुर्यान्ति ते परम् ।। (34)
Bhūta-prakṛti-mokṣaṁ ca ye vidur-yānti te paraṁ ||
इति श्रीमद्भगवद्गीता.......क्षेत्रक्षेत्रज्ञयोगो नाम त्रयोदशोऽध्यायः ।।
Iti Śrīmadbhagavadgītā .... Kṣetra-kṣetrajña -yogo nāmatrayodaśo-'dhyāyaḥ ||

CHAPTER XIV

श्रीभगवानुवाच / *Sribhagavān-uvāca*

परं भूयः प्रवक्ष्यामि ज्ञानानां ज्ञानमुत्तमम् ।

Paraṁ bhūyaḥ pravakṣyāmi jñānānāṁ Jñānaṁ-uttamaṁ

यज्ज्ञात्वा मुनयः सर्वे परां सिद्धिमितो गताः ।। (1)

Yaj-jñātvā munayaḥ sarve parāṁ siddhiṁ-ito gatāḥ ||

इदं ज्ञानमुपाश्रित्य मम साधर्म्यमागताः ।

Idaṁ jñānaṁ-upāśritya mama sādharmyaṁ-āgatāḥ |

सर्गेऽपि नोपजायन्ते प्रलये न व्यथन्ति च ।। (2)

Sarge-pi no-'pajāyante pralaye na Vyathanti ca ||

मम योनिर्महद्ब्रह्म तस्मिन्गर्भं दधाम्यहम् ।

Mama yonir-mahad-brahma tasmin-garbhaṁ dadhāmyahaṁ|

संभवः सर्वभूतानां ततो भवति भारत ।। (3)

Saṁbhavaḥ sarvabhūtānāṁ tato bhavati bhārata ||

सर्वयोनिषु कौन्तेय मुर्तयः सम्भवन्ति याः ।

Sarvayoniṣu kaunteya mūrtayaḥ sambhavanti yāḥ |

तासां ब्रह्म महद्योनिरहं बीजप्रदः पिता ।। (4)

Tāsāṁ brahma mahad-yonir-ahaṁ bījapradaḥ pitā ||

सत्त्वं रजस्तम इति गुणाः प्रकुतिसंभवाः ।

Sattvaṁ rajas-tama iti guṇāḥ prakṛtisambhavāḥ |

निबध्नन्ति महाबाहो देहे देहिनमव्ययम् ।। (5)

Nibadhnati mahābāho dehe dehinam-avyayaṁ ||

तत्र सत्वं निर्मलत्वात्प्रकाशकमनामयम् ।

Tatra satvaṁ nirmalatvāt-prakāśakam-anāmayaṁ |

सुखसङ्गेन बध्नाति ज्ञानसङ्गेन चानघ ।। (6)

Sukhasaṅgena badhnāti jñānasaṅgena cā-nagha ||

रजो रागात्मकं विद्धि तृष्णासङ्गसमुद्भवम् ।
Rajo rāgātmakaṁ viddhi tr̥ṣṇāsaṅga-samudbhavaṁ |
तन्निबध्नाति कौन्तेय कर्मसङ्गेन देहिनम् ।। (7)
Tan-nibadhnāti kaunteya karmasaṅgena dehinaṁ ||
तमस्त्वज्ञानजं विद्धि मोहनं सर्वदेहिनाम् ।
Tamas-tv-ajñānajaṁ viddhi mohanaṁ sarvadehināṁ |
प्रमादालस्यनिद्राभिस्तन्निबध्नाति भारत ।। (8)
Pramādā-lasya-nidrābhis-tan-nibadhnāti bhārata |
सत्त्वं सुखे सञ्जयति रजः कर्मणि भारत ।
Sattvaṁ sukhe sañjayati rajaḥ karmaṇi bhārata |
ज्ञानमावृत्य तु तमः प्रमादे सञ्जयत्युत ।। (9)
Jñānam-āvr̥tya tu tamaḥ pramāde sañjayaty-uta ||
रजस्तमश्चाभिभूय सत्त्वं भवति भारत ।
Rajas-tamaś-cā-bhibhūya sattvaṁ bhavati Bhārata |
रजः सत्त्वं तमश्चैव तमः सत्त्वं रजस्तथा ।। (10)
Rajaḥ sattvaṁ tamaś-cai-va tamaḥ sattvaṁ rajas-tathā ||
सर्वद्वारेषु देहेऽस्मिन्प्रकाश उपजायते ।
Sarvadvāreṣu dehe-'smin-prakāśa upajāyate |
ज्ञानं यदा तदा विद्याद्विवृद्धिं सत्त्वमित्युत ।। (11)
Jñānaṁ yada tadā vidyād-vivr̥ddhim sattvam-ity-uta ||
लोभः प्रवृत्तिरारम्भः कर्मणामशमः स्पृहा ।
lobhaḥ pravr̥ttir-ārambhaḥ karmaṇām-aśamaḥ spr̥hā
रजस्येतानि जायन्ते विवृद्धे भरतर्षभ ।। (12)
Rajasy-etāni jāyante vivr̥ddhaṁ bharatarṣabha ||
अप्रकाशोऽप्रवृत्तिश्च प्रमादो मोह एव च ।
Aprakāśo-pravr̥ttiś-ca pramādo moha eva ca |
तमस्येतानि जायन्ते विवृद्धे कुरूनन्दन ।। (13)
Tamasy-etāni jāyante vivr̥ddhe kurunandana ||
यदा सत्त्वे प्रवृद्धे तु प्रलयं याति देहभृत ।
Yadā sattve pravr̥ddhe tu pralayam yāti dehabhr̥t |

तदोत्तमविदां लोकानमलान्प्रतिपद्यते ।। (14)
Tado-ttamavidām lokān-amalān-pratipadyate ||

रजसि प्रलयं गत्वा कर्मसङ्गिषु जायते ।
Rajasi pralayaṁ gatvā karmasaṅgiṣu jāyate |
तथा प्रलीनस्तमसि मूढयोनिषु जायते ।। (15)
Tathā pralinas-tamasi mūḍhayoniṣu jāyate||

कर्मणः सुकृतस्याहुः सात्विकं निर्मलं फलम् ।
Karmaṇaḥ sukṛtasyāhuḥ sātvikaṁ nirmalaṁ phalaṁ |
रजसस्तु फलं दुःखमज्ञानं तमसः फलम् ।। (16)
Rajasas-tu phalaṁ duḥkham-ajñānaṁ tamasaḥ phalaṁ |

सत्त्वात्संजायते ज्ञानं रजसो लोभ एव च ।
Sattvāt-saṁjāyate jñānaṁ rajaso lobha eva ca |
प्रमादमोहौ तमसो भवतोऽज्ञानमेव च ।। (17)
Pramādamohau tamaso bhavato'jñānam-eva-ca ||

ऊर्ध्वं गच्छन्ति सत्त्वस्था मध्ये तिष्ठन्ति राजसाः ।
Ūrdhvaṁ gacchanti sattvasthā madhye tiṣṭhanti rājasāḥ |
जघन्यगुणवृत्तिस्था अधो गच्छन्ति तामसाः ।। (18)
Jaghanya-guṇavṛttisthā adho gacchanti tāmasāḥ ||

नान्यं गुणेभ्यः कर्तारं यदा द्रष्टानुपश्यति ।
Nānyaṁ guṇebhyaḥ kartāraṁ yadā draṣṭānupaśyati |
गुणेभ्यश्च परं वेत्ति मद्भावं सोऽधिगच्छति ।। (19)
Guṇebhyaś-ca paraṁ vetti mad-bhāvaṁ so-'dhigacchati ||

गुणनेतानतीत्य त्रीन्देही देहसम्रद्भवान् ।
Guṇān-etān-atītya trīn-dehī dehasamudbhavān
जन्ममृत्युजरादुःखैर्विमुक्तोऽमुतमश्नुते ।। (20)
Janma-mṛtyu-jarā-duḥkhair-vimukto-'mṛtaṁ-aśnute ||

अर्जुन उवाच /*Arjuna Uvāca*

कैलिङ्गैस्त्रीन्गुणानेतानतीतो भवति प्रभो ।
Kair-lingais-trīṅ-guṇān-etān-atīto bhavati prabho |

किमाचारः कथं चैतांस्त्रीन् गुणनतिवर्तते ।। (21)
Kimā-cāraḥ kathaṁ cai-tāṁs-trīṅ guṇān-ativartate |

श्रीभगवानुवाच /*Sribhagavān-uvāca*

प्रकाशं च प्रवृतिं च मोहमेव च पाण्डव ।
Prakāśaṁ ca pravṛttiṁ ca mohameva ca Pāṇḍava |
न द्वेष्टि सप्रवृत्तानि न निवृत्तानि काङ्क्षति ।। (22)
Na dveṣṭi saṁpravṛttāni na nivṛttāni kāṅkṣati ||
उदासीनवदासीनो गुणैर्यो न विचाल्यते ।
Udāsinavad-āsino guṇair yo na vicālyate |
गुणा वर्तन्त इत्येव योऽवतिष्ठति नेङ्गते ।। (23)
Guṇā vartanta ity-eva yo'vatiṣhati ne-ṅgate ||
समदुःखसुखः स्वस्थः समलोष्टाश्मकाऽचनः ।
Śamaduḥkhasukhaḥ svasthaḥ samaloṣṭā-śma-kāñcanaḥ
तुल्यप्रियाप्रियो धीरस्तुल्यनिन्दात्मसंस्तुतिः ।। (24)
Tulya-priyā-priyo dhīras-tulya-nindā-tmasaṁstutiḥ ||
मानापमानयोस्तुल्यस्तुल्यो मित्रारिपक्षयोः ।
Mānāpamānayos-tulyas-tulyo mitrāripakṣayoḥ |
सर्वारम्भपरित्यागी गुणातीतः स उच्यते ।। (25)
Sarvārambha-parityāgī guṇātītaḥ sa ucyate ||
मां च योऽव्यभिचारेण भक्तियोगेन सेवते ।
Māṁ ca yo'vyabhicāreṇa bhaktīyogena sevate |
स गुणान्समतीत्यैतान्ब्रह्मभूयाय कल्पते ।। (26)
Śa guṇān-samatītyai-tān brahmabhūyāya kalpate ||
ब्रह्मणो हि प्रतिष्ठाहममृतस्याव्यय च ।
Brahmaṇo hi pratiṣṭhā-ham-amṛtasyā-vyayasya ca |
शाश्वतस्य च धर्मस्य सुखस्यैकान्तिकस्य च ।। (27)
Śāśatasya ca dharmasya sukhasyai-kāntikasya ca |
इति श्रीमद्भगवद्गीता....... गुणत्रयविभागयोगो नाम चतुर्दशोऽयायः।।
Iti Śrīmadbhagavadgītā .... gunatraya vibhāgayogo nāma caturdaśo'dhyāyaḥ ||

CHAPTER XV

श्रीभगवानुवाच / *Śribhagavān-uvāca*

ऊर्ध्वमूलमधःशाखमश्वत्थं प्राहुरव्ययम् ।
Ūrdhvamūlam-adhaḥśākhaṁ-aśvatthaṁ prāhur avyayam
छन्दांसि यस्य पर्णानि यस्तं वेद स वेदवित् ।। (1)
Chandāṁsi yasya parṇāni yas-taṁ veda sa vedavit ||

अधश्चोर्ध्व प्रसृतास्तस्य शाखा गुणप्रवृद्धा विषयप्रवालाः ।
Adhaś-co-rdhvaṁ prasṛtās-tasya śākhā Guṇapravṛddhā viṣayapravālāḥ |
अधश्च मूलान्यनुसंततानि कर्मानुबन्धीनि मनुष्यलोके ।। (2)
Adhaśca mūlāny-anusantatāni Kaṛmānubandhīni manuṣyaloke||

न रूपमस्येह तथोपलभ्यते नान्तो न चादिर्न च संप्रतिष्ठा ।
Na rūpam-asye-ha tatho-palabhayate Nā-nto na cā-dir-na ca saṁpratiṣṭha |
अश्वत्थमेनं सुविरूढमूलम् असङ्गशस्त्रेण दृढेन छित्वा ।। (3)
aśvattham-enaṁ suvirūḍhamūlam-aṣaṅgaśastreṇa dṛḍhena chitvā||

ततः पदं तत्परिमार्गितव्यं यस्मिन्गाता न निवर्तन्ति भूयः ।
Tataḥ padaṁ tat-parimārgitavyaṁ Yasmin-gatā na nivartanti bhūyaḥ |
तमेव चाद्यं पुरूषं प्रपद्ये यतंः प्रवृतिः प्रसृता पुराणी ।। (4)
Tam-eva cā-dyaṁ purūṣaṁ prapadye Yataḥ pravṛttiḥ praṣṛtā purāṇī ||

निर्मानमोहा जितसङ्गदोषा अध्यात्मनित्या विनिवृत्तकामाः ।
Nirmānamohā jitasaṅgadoṣā Adhyātmanityā vinivṛttakāmāḥ||
द्वन्द्वविमुक्ताः सुखदुःखसंज्ञैर-गच्छन्त्यमूढाः पदमव्ययं तत् ।। (5)
Dvandvair-vimuktāḥ sukhaduhkhasaṁjñair- gacchanty-amūḍhaḥ padam-avyayaṁ tat ||

न तद्भासयते सूर्यो न शशाङ्को न पावकः ।
Na tad-bhāsayate sūryo no śasāṅko na pāvakaḥ |
यद्गत्वा न निवर्तन्ते तद्धाम परमं मम ।। (6)
Yad-gatvā na nivartante tad-dhāma paramaṁ mama ||
ममैवांशो जीवलोके जीवभूतः सनातनः ।
Mamai-vā-ṁśo jīvaloke jīvabhūtaḥ sanātanaḥ |
मनःषष्टानीन्द्रियाणि प्रकृतिस्थानि कर्षति ।। (7)
Manaḥṣaṣṭānī-ndriyāṇī prakṛtisthāni karṣati ||
शरीरं यदवाप्नोति यच्चाप्युत्क्रामतीश्वरः ।
Śarīraṁ yad-avāpnoti yac-cā-pyutkrāmatī-śvaraḥ
गृहीत्वैतानि संयाति वायुर्गन्धानिवाशयात् ।। (8)
Gṛhītvai-tāni saṁyāti vāyur-gandhān-ivā-śayāt ||
श्रोत्रं चक्षुः स्पर्शनं च रसनं घ्राणमेव च ।
Śrotraṁ cakṣuḥ sparśanaṁ ca rasanaṁ ghrāṇaṁ-eva ca |
अधिष्ठाय मनश्चायं विषयानुपसेवते ।। (9)
Adhiṣṭhāya manaś-cā-yaṁ viṣayān-upasevate ||
उत्क्रामन्तं स्थितं वापि भुञ्जानं वा गुणान्वितम् ।
Utkrāmantaṁ sthitaṁ vā-pi bhuñjānaṁ vā guṇānvitaṁ |
विमूढा नानुपश्यन्ति पश्यन्ति ज्ञानचक्षुषः ।। (10)
Vimūḍhā nā-nupasyanti paśyanti jñānacakṣuṣaḥ ||
यतन्तो योगिनश्चैनं पश्यन्त्यात्मन्यवस्थितम् ।
Yatanto yoginas-cai-naṁ paśyanty-ātmany-avasthitaṁ |
यतन्तोऽप्यकृतात्मानो नैनं पश्यन्त्यचेतसः ।। (11)
Yatanto'py-akṛtātmāno nai-naṁ pasyanty-acetasaḥ ||
यदादित्यगतं तेजो जगद्भासयतेऽखिलम् ।
Yad-ādityagataṁ tejo Jagad-bhāsayate'khilaṁ |
यच्चन्द्रमसि यच्चाग्नौ तत्तेजो विद्धि मामकम् ।। (12)
Yac-candramasi yas-cā-gnau tat-tejo viddhi māmakaṁ |
गामाविश्य च भूतानि धारयाम्यहमोजसा ।
Gām-āviśya ca bhūtāni dhārayāmyaham-ojasā |

पुष्णामि चौषधीः सर्वाः सोमो भूत्वा रसात्मकः ।। (13)
Puṣṇāmi cauṣadhiḥ sarvāḥ somo bhūtvā rasātmakaḥ ||
अहं वैश्वानरो भूत्वा प्राणिनां देहमाश्रितः ।
Ahaṁ vaiśvānaro bhūtvā prāṇinām dehaṁ-āśritaḥ |
प्राणापानसमायुक्तः पचाम्यन्नं चतुर्विधम् ।। (14)
Prāṇāpānasamāyuktaḥ pacāmy-annaṁ caturvidham
सर्वस्य चाहं हृदि सन्निविष्टो मत्तः स्मृतिर्ज्ञानमपोहनं च ।
Sarvasya cā-haṁ hṛdi sanniviṣṭo Mattaḥ smṛtir-jñānam-apōhanaṁ ca
वेदैश्च सर्वैरहमेव वेद्यो वेदान्तकृद्वेदविदेव चाहम् ।। (15)
vedaiś-ca sarvair-aham-eva vedyo Vedāntakṛd-vedavid-eva cā-haṁ||
द्वाविमौ पुरूषौ लोके क्षरश्चाक्षर एव च ।
Dvāvi-mau puruṣau loke kṣaraś-cā-kṣara-eva ca |
क्षरः सर्वाणि भूतानि कूटस्थोऽक्षर उच्यते ।। (16)
Kṣaraḥ sarvāṇi bhūtāni kūṭastho'kṣara ucyate ||
उत्तमः पुरूषस्त्वन्यः परमात्मेत्युदाहृतः ।
Uttamaḥ purūṣas-tv-anyaḥ paramātme-ty-udāhṛtaḥ |
यो लोकत्रयमाविश्य बिभर्त्यव्यय ईश्वरः ।। (17)
Yo lokatrayam-āviśya bibharty-avyaya īśvaraḥ ||
यस्मात्क्षरमतीतोऽहमक्षरादपि चोत्तमः ।
Yasmāt-kṣaram-atīto'haṁ-akṣarād-api-co-ttamaḥ |
अतोऽस्मि लोके वेदे च प्रथितः पुरूषोत्तमः ।। (18)
Ato-smi loke Vede ca prathitaḥ puruṣottamaḥ
यो मामेवमसंमूढो जानाति पुरूषोत्तमम् ।
Yo mām-evam-asaṁmūḍho jānāti puruṣottamaṁ |
स सर्वविद्भजति मां सर्वभावेन भारत ।। (19)
Sa sarvavid-bhajati māṁ sarvabhāvena bhārata ||
इति गृह्यतमं शास्त्रमिदमुक्तं मयानघ ।
Iti guhyatamaṁ śāstram-idaṁ-uktaṁ mayā-nagha |

एवद्बुद्ध्वा बुद्धिमान्स्यात्कृतकृत्यश्च भारत ।। (20)
Etad-buddhvā buddhimān-syāt-kṛta-kṛtyas-ca bhārata ||

इति श्रीमद्भगवद्गीता......पुरूषोत्तमयोगो नाम पंचदशोऽध्याय: ।।
Iti Śrīmadbhagavadgītā ...... Puruṣottamayogo nāma pañcadaśo'adhyāyaḥ|

CHAPTER XVI

श्रीभगवानुवाच / *Śribhagavān-uvāca*

अभयं सत्त्वसंशुद्धिर्ज्ञानयोगव्यवस्थितिः ।
Abhayaṁsattvasṁśuddhir-jñānayoga-vyavasthitiḥ |
दानं दमश्च यज्ञश्च स्वाध्यायस्तप आर्जवम् ।। (1)
Dānaṁ damaś-cā yajñaś-ca svādhyāyas-tapa ārjavaṁ ||

अहिंसा सत्यमक्रोधस्त्यागः शान्तिरपैशुनम् ।
Ahiṁsā satyam-akrodhas-tyāgaḥ-śāntir-apaiśunaṁ |
दया भूतेष्वलोलुप्त्वं मार्दवं ह्रीरचापलम् ।। (2)
Dayā bhūteṣv-aloluptvaṁ mārdavaṁ hrīr-acāpalaṁ ||

तेजः क्षमा धृतिः शौचमद्रोहो नातिमानिता ।
Tejaḥ kṣamā dhṛtiḥ śaucam-adroho nā-timānitā |
भवन्ति संपदं दैवीमभिजातस्य भारत ।। (3)
Bhavanti sampadaṁ daivīm-abhijātasya bhārata ||

दम्भो दर्पोऽभिमानश्च क्रोधः पारूष्यमेव च ।
Dambho darpo'bhimānaś-ca krodhaḥ pāruṣyaṁ eva ca |
अज्ञानं चाभिजातस्य पार्थ संपदमासुरीम् ।। (4)
Ajñānaṁ cā-bhijātasya pārtha saṁpadaṁ-āsuriṁ ||

दैवी संपद्विमोक्षाय निबन्धायासुरी मता ।
Daivī saṁpad-vimokṣāya nibandhāyā-surī matā |
मा शुचः संपदं दैवीमभिजातोऽसि पाण्डव ।। (5)
Mā śucaḥ saṁpadaṁ daivīm-abhijāto-'si pāṇḍava ||

द्वौ भूतसर्गौ लोकेऽस्मिन्दैव आसुर एव च ।
Dvau bhūtasargau loke-'smin-daiva āsura eva ca |
दैवो विस्तरशः प्रोक्त आसुरं पार्थ मे शृणु ।। (6)
Daivo vistaraśaḥ prokta āsuraṁ pārtha me sṛṇu ||

प्रवृतिं च निवृत्तिं च जना न विदुरासुराः ।
Pravṛttiṁ ca nivṛttiṁ ca janā na vidur-āsurāḥ |

न शौचं नापि चाचारो न सत्यं तेषु विद्यते ।। (7)

Na śaucaṁ nā-pi cā-cāro na satyaṁ teṣu vidyate ||

असत्यमप्रतिष्टं ते जगदाहुरनीश्वरम् ।

Asatyam-apratiṣṭaṁ te jagad-āhur-anīśvaraṁ |

अपरस्परसंभूतं किमन्यत्कामहैतुकम् ।। (8)

Aparasparasambhūtaṁ kim-anyat-kāmahaitukaṁ ||

एतां दृष्टिमवष्टभ्य नष्टात्मानोऽल्पबुद्धयः ।

Etāṁ dṛṣṭm-avaṣṭabhya naṣṭātmāno'lpabuddhayaḥ |

प्रभवन्त्युग्रकर्माणः क्षयाय जगतोऽहिताः ।। (9)

Prabhavanty-ugrakarmāṇaḥ kṣayāya jagato-'hitāḥ ||

काममाश्रित्य दुष्पूरं दम्भमानमदान्विताः ।

Kāmam-āśritya duṣpūraṁ dambhamāna-madānvitāḥ |

मोहाद्गृहीत्वासद्ग्राहान्प्रवर्तन्तेऽशुचिव्रताः ।। (10)

Mohād-gṛhītvā'-sadgrāhān-pravartante'śucivrataḥ ||

चिन्तामपरिमेयां च प्रलयान्तामुपाश्रिताः ।

Cintām-aparimeyāṁ ca pralayāntām-upāśritāḥ |

कामोपभोगपरमा एतावदिति निश्चिताः ।। (11)

Kāmopabhogaparamā etāvad-iti niścitāḥ ||

आशापाशशतैर्बद्धाः कामक्रोधपरायणाः ।

Āśāpāśaṣatair-baddhāḥ kāmakrodhaparāyaṇāḥ |

ईहन्ते कामभोगार्थमन्यायेनार्थसंचयान् ।। (12)

Īhante-kāmabhogārtham-anyāyenā-rthasaṁcayān ||

इदमद्य मया लब्धमिमंप्राप्स्ये मनोरथम् ।

Idam-adya mayā labdham-imaṁ-prāpsye manorathaṁ |

इदमस्तीदमपि मे भविष्यति पुनर्धनम् ।। (13)

Imaṁ-astī-dam-api me bhaviṣyati punar-dhanaṁ ||

असौ मया हतः शत्रुर्हनिष्ये चापरानपि ।

Asau mayā hatah śatrur-haniṣye cā-parān-api |

ईश्वरोऽहमहं भोगी सिद्धोऽहं बलवान्सुखी ।। (14)

Iśvaro-'ham-ahaṁ bhogī siddho-'haṁ balavānsukhī ||

आद्योऽभिजनवानस्मि कोऽन्योऽस्ति सदृशो मया ।
Āḍhyo-'bhijanavānasmi ko-'nyo-'sti sadṛśo mayā |
यक्ष्ये दास्यामि मोदिष्य इत्यज्ञानविमोहिताः ।। (15)
Yakṣye dāsyāmi modiṣya ity-ajñānavimohitāḥ ||
अनेकचित्तविभ्रान्ता मोहजाल समावृताः ।
Anekacittavibharāntā mohajāla samāvṛtāḥ |
प्रसक्ताः कामभोगेषु पतन्ति नरकेऽशुचौ ।। (16)
Prasaktāḥ kāmabhogeṣu patanti narake-'śucau ||
आत्मसंभाविताः स्तब्धा धनमानमदान्विताः ।
Ātmasambhāvitāḥ stabdhā dhana-māna-madānvitāḥ |
यजन्ते नाम यज्ञैस्ते दम्भनाविधिपूर्वकम् ।। (17)
Yajante nāma yajñais-te dambhenā-vidhipūrvakaṁ ||
अहंकारं बलं दर्पं कामं क्रोधं च संश्रिताः ।
Ahaṁkāraṁ balaṁ darpaṁ kāmaṁ krodhaṁ ca saṁśritāḥ
मामात्मपरदेहेषु प्रद्विषन्तोऽभ्यसूयकाः ।। (18)
Māmātmaparadeheṣu pradviṣanto'bhyasūyakāḥ |
तानहं द्विषतः क्रूरान्संसारेषु नराधमान् ।
Tān-ahaṁ dviṣatah krūrān-saṁsāreṣu narādhamān |
क्षिपाम्यजस्रमशुभानासुरीष्वेव योनिषु ।। (19)
Kṣipāmy-ajasram-aśubhān-āsurīṣ-veva yoniṣu ||
आसुरीं योनिमापन्ना मूढा जन्मनि जन्मनि ।
Āsurīṁ yonim-āpannā mūḍhā janmani-janmani |
मामप्रप्यैव कौन्तेय ततो यान्त्यधमां गतिम् ।। (20)
Mām-aprāpyai-va kaunteya tato yānty-adhamāṁ gatiṁ ||
त्रिविधं नरकस्येदं द्वारं नाशनमात्मनः ।
Trividhaṁ narakasye-daṁ dvāraṁ nāśanam-ātmanaḥ |
कामः क्रोधस्तथा लोभस्तस्मादेतत्त्रयं त्यजेत् ।। (21)
Kāmaḥ krodhas-tathā lobhas-tasmād-etat-trayaṁ tyajet ||
एतैर्विमुक्तः कौन्तेय तमोद्वारैस्त्रिभिर्नरः ।
Etair-vimuktaḥ kaunteya tamodvārais-tribhir-naraḥ |

आचरन्त्यात्मन श्रेयस्ततो याति परां गतिम् ।। (22)
Acaranty-atmanaḥ śreyas-tato yāti parāṁ gatiṁ ||
यः शास्त्रविधिमुत्सृज्य वर्तते कामकारतः ।
Yaḥ śāstravidhim-utsṛjya vartate kāmakārataḥ |
न स सिद्धिमवाप्नोति न सुखं न परां गतिम् ।। (23)
Na sa siddhim-avāpnoti na sukhaṁ na parāṁ gatiṁ ||
तस्माच्छास्त्रं प्रमाणं ते कार्याकार्यव्यवस्थितौ ।
Tasmāc-chāstraṁ pramāṇaṁ te kāryā-kārya-vyavasthitau
ज्ञात्वा शास्त्रविधानोक्तं कर्म कर्तुमिहार्हसि ।। (24)
Jñātvā śāstravidhānoktaṁ karma kartum-ihā-rhasi ||

इति श्रीमद्भगवद्गीता....... दैवासुरसम्पद् विभागयोगो नाम षोडशोऽध्यायः।।

Iti Śrīmadbhagavadgītā .... Daivāsura-sampad vibhāgayogo nāma ṣoḍaśo-'dhyāyaḥ ||

CHAPTER XVII

अर्जुन उवाच / *Arjuna-uvāca*

ये शास्त्रविधिमुत्सृज्य यजन्ते श्रद्धयान्विताः ।
Ye śāstravidhiṁ-utsṛjya yajante śraddhayā-nvitāḥ |
तेषां निष्ठा तु का कृष्ण सत्त्वमाहो रजस्तमः ।। (1)
Teṣāṁ niṣthā-tu kā krṣṇa satvam-āho rajas-tamaḥ ||

श्रीभगवानुवाच / *Śribhagavān-uvāca*

त्रिविधा भवति श्रद्धा देहिनां सा स्वभावजा ।
Trividhā bhavati śraddhā dehināṁ sā svabhāvajā
सात्त्विकी राजसी चैव तामसी चेति तां शृणु ।। (2)
sātviki rājasī-cai-va tāmasī ce-ti tāṁ śṛṇu ||
सत्त्वानुरूपा सर्वस्य श्रद्धा भवति भारत ।
Sattvānurūpā sarvasya śraddhā bhavati bhārata |
श्रद्धामयोऽयं पुरूषो यो यच्छ्रद्धः स एव सः ।। (3)
Śraddhāmayo-gaṁ puruṣo yo yac-chraddhaḥ sa eva saḥ ||
यजन्ते सात्त्विका देवान्यक्षरक्षांसि राजसाः ।
Yajante sātvikā devān-yakṣa-rakṣāṁsi rājasāḥ |
प्रेतान्भूतगणांश्चान्य यजन्ते तामसा जनाः ।। (4)
Pretān-bhūtagaṇāmś-cā-nye yajante tāmasā janāḥ ||
अशास्त्रविहितं घोरं तप्यन्ते ये तपो जनाः ।
Aśāstravihitaṁ ghoraṁ tapyante ye tapo janāḥ |
दम्भाहंकारसंयुक्ताः कामरागबलान्विताः ।। (5)
Dambhāhaṁkārasaṁyuktāḥ kāmarāgabalānvitāḥ ||
कर्षयन्तः शरीरस्थं भूतग्राममचेतसः ।
Karṣayantaḥ śarīrasthaṁ bhūtagrāmaṁ-acetasaḥ |
मां चैवान्तःशरीरस्थं तान्विद्ध्यासुरनिश्चयान् ।। (6)
Māṁ cai-vā-ntaḥśarīrasthaṁ tān-viddhy-āsura-niścayān ||

आहारस्त्वपि सर्वस्य त्रिविधो भवति प्रियः ।
Ahāras-tv-api sarvasya trividho bhavati priyaḥ |
यज्ञस्तपस्तथा दानं तेषां भेदमिमं शृणु ।। (7)
Yajñas-tapas-tathā dānaṁ teṣāṁ bhedam-imaṁ śṛṇu ||
आयुः सत्त्वबलारोग्यसुखप्रीतिविवर्धनाः ।
Āyuḥ sattva-balārogya-sukha-prīti-vivardhanāḥ |
रस्याः स्निग्धाः स्थिरा हृद्या आहाराः सात्त्विकप्रियाः ।। (8)
Rasyāḥ snigdhāḥ sthirā hṛdyā āhārāḥ sātvikapriyāḥ ||
कट्वम्ललवणात्युष्णतीक्ष्यरूक्षविदाहिनः ।
Kaṭvamla-lavaṇā-tyuṣṇa-tīkṣṇarūkṣavidāhinaḥ |
आहारा राजसस्येष्टा दुःखशोकामयप्रदाः ।। (9)
Āhārā rājasasye-ṣṭā duḥkha-śokāmayapradāḥ |
यातयामं गतरसं पूति पर्युषितं च यत् ।
Yātayāmaṁ gatarasaṁ pūti paryuṣitaṁ ca yat |
उच्छिष्टमपि चामेध्यं भोजनं तामसप्रियम् ।। (10)
Ucchiṣṭam-api cā-medhyaṁ bhojanaṁ tāmasapriyaṁ ||
अफलाकाङ्क्षिभिर्यज्ञो विधिदृष्टो य इज्यते ।
Aphalākāṅkṣibhir-yajño vidhidṛṣṭo ya ijyate |
यष्टव्यमेवेति मनः समाधाय स सात्विकः ।। (11)
Yaṣṭavyam-eve-ti manaḥ samādhāya sa sātvikaḥ ||
अभिसंधाय तु फलं दम्भार्थमपि चैव यत् ।
Abhisandhāya tu phalaṁ dambhārthaṁ-api cai-va-yat |
इज्यते भरतश्रेष्ठ तं यज्ञं विद्धि राजसम् ।। (12)
Ijyate bharataśreṣṭha taṁ yajñaṁ viddhi rājasaṁ ||
विधिहीनमसृष्टान्नं मन्त्रहीनमदक्षिणम् ।
Vidhihīnam-asṛṣṭānnaṁ mantrahīnam-adakṣiṇaṁ |
श्रद्धाविरहितं यज्ञं तामसं परिचक्षते ।। (13)
Śraddhāvirahitaṁ yajñaṁ tāmasaṁ paricakṣate ||
देवद्विजगुरूप्राज्ञपूजनं शौचमार्जवम ।
Devadvija-guru-prājñapūjanaṁ śaucam-ārjavaṁ |

ब्रह्मचर्यमहिंसा च शारीरं तप उच्यते ।। (14)
Brahmacaryam-ahimsā ca śārīraṁ tapa ucyate ||
अनुद्वेगकरं वाक्यं सत्यं प्रियहितं च यत् ।
Anudvegakaraṁ vākyaṁ satyaṁ priyahitaṁ ca yat |
स्वाध्यायाभ्यसनं चैव वाङ्मयं तप उच्यते ।। (15)
Svādhyāyābhyasanaṁ cai-va vāṅmayaṁ tapa ucyate||
मनः प्रसादः सौम्यत्वं मौनमात्मविनिग्रहः ।
Manaḥ prasādaḥ saumyatvaṁ maunam-ātmavinigrahaḥ
भावसंशुद्धिरित्येतत्तपो मानसमुच्यते ।। (16)
Bhāvasaṁśuddhir-ity-etat-tapo mānasaṁ-ucyate ||
श्रद्धया परया तप्तं तपस्तत्त्रिविधं नरैः ।
Śraddhayā parayā taptaṁ tapas-tat-trividhaṁ naraiḥ |
अफलाकाङ्क्षिभिर्युक्तैः सात्विकं परिचक्षते ।। (17)
Aphalākāṅkṣibhir-yuktaiḥ sātvikaṁ paricakṣate ||
सत्कारमानपूजार्थं तपो दम्भेन चैव यत् ।
Satkāramānapūjārthaṁ tapo dambhena cai-va yat |
क्रियते तदिह प्रोक्तं राजसं चलमध्रुवम् ।। (18)
Kriyate tadiha proktaṁ rājasaṁ calam-adhruvaṁ ||
मूढग्राहेणात्मनो यत्पीडया क्रियते तपः ।
Mūḍhagrāheṇā-tmano yat-pīḍayā kriyate tapaḥ |
परस्योत्सादनार्थं वा तत्तामसमुदाहृतम् ।। (19)
Parasyo-tsādanārthaṁ vā tat-tāmasaṁ-udāhṛtaṁ ||
दातव्यमिति यद्दानं दीयतेऽनुपकारिणे ।
Dātavyam-iti yad-dānaṁ dīyate-'nupakāriṇe |
देशे काले च पात्रे च तद्दानं सात्विकं स्मृतम् ।। (20)
Deśe kāle ca pātre ca tad-dānaṁ sātvikaṁ smṛtaṁ ||
यत्तु प्रत्युपकारार्थं फलमुद्दिश्य वा पुनः ।
Yat-tu pratyupakārārthaṁ phalam-uddiśya vā punaḥ
दीयते च परिक्लिष्टं तद्दानं राजसं स्मृतम् ।। (21)
Dīyate ca parikliṣṭaṁ tad-dānaṁ rājasaṁ smṛtaṁ ||
अदेशकाले यद्दानमपात्रेभ्यश्च दीयते ।

Adeśakāle yad-dānam-apātrebhyaś-ca dīyate |
असत्कृतमवज्ञातं तत्तामसमुदाहृतम् ।। (22)
Asatkṛtam-avajñātaṁ tat-tāmasam-udāhṛtaṁ ||
ओं तत्सदिति निर्देशो ब्रह्मणस्त्रिविधः स्मृतः ।
Oṁ tatsad-iti nirdeśo brahmaṇas-trividhaḥ smṛtaḥ |
ब्राह्मणास्तेन वेदाश्च यज्ञाश्च विहिताः पुरा ।। (23)
Brāhmaṇās-tena vedāś-ca yajñāś-ca vihitāḥ purāḥ ||
तस्मादोमित्युदाहृत्य यज्ञदान तपः क्रियाः ।
Tasmād-aum-ity udāhṛtya yajña-dāna-tapaḥ-kriyāḥ |
प्रवर्तन्ते विधानोक्ताः सततं ब्रह्मवादिनाम् ।। (24)
Pravartante vidhānoktāḥ satataṁ brahmavādināṁ ||
तदित्यनभिसन्धाय फलं यज्ञतपः क्रियाः ।
Tad-ity-anabhisandhāya phalaṁ yajñatapaḥ kriyā |
दानक्रियाश्च विविधाः क्रियन्ते मोक्षकाङ्क्षिभिः ।। (25)
Dānakriyāś-ca vividhāḥ kriyante mokṣakāṅkṣibhiḥ|
सद्भावे साधुभावे च सदित्येतत्प्रयुज्यते ।
Sadbhāve sādhubhāve ca sad-ity-etat-prayujyate |
प्रशस्ते कर्मणि तथा सच्छदः पार्थ युज्यते ।। (26)
Praśaste karmaṇi tathā sacchabdaḥ Pārtha yujyate ||
यज्ञे तपसि दाने च स्थितिः सदिति चोच्यते ।
Yajñe tapasi dāne ca sthitiḥ sad-iti co-cyate |
कर्म चैव तदर्थीयं सदित्येवाभिधीयते ।। (27)
Karma cai-va tadarthīyaṁ sad-ity-evā-bhidhīyate ||
अश्रद्धया हुतं दत्तं तपस्तप्तं कृतं च यत् ।
Aśraddhayā hutaṁ dattaṁ tapas-taptaṁ kṛtaṁ ca yat |
असदित्युच्यते पार्थ न च तत्प्रेत्य नो इह ।। (28)
Asad-ity-ucyate Pārtha na ca tat-pretya no iha ||
इति श्रीमद्भगवद्गीता....... श्रद्धात्रयविभागयोगो नाम सप्तदशोऽध्यायः।।
Iti Śrīmadbhagavadgītā ....Śraddhātraya-vibhāgayogo nāma saptadaśo 'dhyāyaḥ ||

CHAPTER XVIII

अर्जुन उवाच / *Arjuna Uvāca*

संन्यासस्य महाबाहो तत्त्वमिच्छामि वेदितुम् ।
Saṁnyāsasya mahābāho tattvam-icchāmi veditum |
त्यागस्य च हृषीकेश पृथक्केशिनिषूदन ।। (1)
Tyāgasya ca hṛṣikeśa pṛthak-keśiniṣūdana

श्री भगवानुवाच / *Śribhagavān-uvāca*

काम्यानां कर्मणां न्यासं सन्यासं कवयो विदुः ।
Kāmyānāṁ karmaṇāṁ nyāsaṁ samnyāsaṁ kavayo viduḥ |
सर्वकर्मफलत्यागं प्राहुस्त्यागं विचक्षणाः ।। (2)
Sarvakarmaphalatyāgaṁ prāhus-tyāgam vicakṣaṇāḥ ||
त्याज्यं दोषवदित्येके कर्म प्राहुर्मनीषिणः ।
Tyājyam doṣavad-ity-eke karma prāhur-manīṣiṇaḥ |
यज्ञदानतपःकर्म न त्याज्यमिति चापरे ।। (3)
Yajñadānatapaḥkarma na tyājyam-iti-cā-pare ||
निश्चयं शृणु मे तत्र त्यागे भरतसत्तम ।
Niścayaṁ śṛṇu me tatra tyāge bharatasattama|
त्यागो हि पुरूषव्याघ्र त्रिविधः संप्रकीर्तितः ।। (4)
Tyāgo hi puruṣavyāghra trividhaḥ samprakirtitaḥ ||
यज्ञदानतपःकर्म न त्याज्यं कार्यमेव तत् ।
Yajña-dānatapaḥ karma na tyājyaṁ kāryameva tat |
यज्ञो दानं तपश्चैव पावनानि मनीषिणाम् ।। (5)
Yajño dānaṁ tapaś-cai-va pāvanāni-manīṣiṇāṁ ||
एतान्यपि तु कर्माणि सङ्गं त्यक्त्वा फलानि च ।
Etāny-api tu karmāṇi saṅgam tyaktvā phalāni ca |
कर्तव्यानीति मे पार्थ निश्चितं मतमुत्तमम् ।। (6)
Kartavyāni-ti me pārtha niścitaṁ mataṁ-uttamaṁ ||

नियतस्य तु संन्यासः कर्मणो नोपपद्यते ।
Niyatasya tu saṁnyāsaḥ karmaṇo no-papadyate |
मोहात्तस्य परित्यागस्तामसः परिकीर्तितः ।। (7)
Mohāt-tasya parityāgas-tāmasaḥ parikīrtitaḥ ||
दुःखमित्येव यत्कर्म कायक्लेशभयात्त्यजेत् ।
Duḥkhaṁ-ity-eva yat-karma kāyakleśa bhayāt-tyajet |
स कृत्वा राजसं त्यागं नैव त्यागफलं लभेत् ।। (8)
Sa kṛtvā rājasaṁ tyāgaṁ nai-va tyāgaphalaṁ labhet
कार्यमित्येव यत्कर्म नियतं कुरूतेऽर्जुन ।
Kāryam-ity-eva yat-karma niyataṁ kurute-rjuna |
सङ्गं त्यक्त्वा फलं चैव स त्यागः सात्त्विको मतः ।। (9)
Sangaṁ tyaktvā phalaṁ cai-va sa tyāgaḥ sātviko mataḥ ||
न द्वेष्ट्यकुशलं कर्म कुशले नानुषज्जते ।
Na dveṣṭy-akuśalaṁ karma kuśale nā-nuṣajjate |
त्यागी सत्त्वसमाविष्टो मेधावी छिन्नसंशयः ।। (10)
Tyāgi-sattvasamāviṣṭo medhāvī chinnasamśayaḥ ||
न हि देहभृता शक्यं त्यक्तुं कर्माण्यशेषतः ।
Na hi dehabhṛtā śakyaṁ tyaktuṁ karmaṇy-aśeṣataḥ |
यस्तु कर्मफलत्यागी स त्यागीत्यभिधीयते ।। (11)
Yas-tu karmaphalatyāgī sa tyāgī-tyabhidhīyate ||
अनिष्टमिष्टं मिश्रं च त्रिविधं कर्मणः फलम् ।
Aniṣṭam-iṣṭaṁ miśraṁ ca trividhaṁ karmaṇaḥ phalaṁ |
भवत्यत्यागिनां प्रेत्य न तु संन्यासिनां क्वचित् ।। (12)
Bhavaty-atyāgināṁ pretya na tu samnyāsināṁ kvacit ||
पञ्चैतानि महाबाहो कारणानि निबोध मे ।
Pañcai-tāni mahābāho kāraṇāni nibodha me |
सांख्ये कृतान्ते प्रोक्तानि सिद्धये सर्वकर्मणाम् ।। (13)
Sāṁkhye kṛtānte proktāni siddhaye sarvkar-maṇāṁ ||
अधिष्ठानं तथा कर्ता करणं च पृथग्विधम् ।
Adhiṣṭānaṁ tathā kartā karaṇaṁ ca pṛthagvidhaṁ |

विविधाश्च पृथक्चेष्टा दैवं चैवात्र पञ्चमम् ।। (14)
Vividhāś-ca pṛthakceṣṭā daivaṁ cai-vā-tra pañcamam |

शरीरवाङ्मनोभिर्यत्कर्म प्रारभते नरः ।
Śarīravaṅmanobhir-yatkarma prārabhate naraḥ |

न्याय्यं वा विपरीतं वा पञ्चैते तस्य हेतवः ।। (15)
Nyāyyaṁ vā viparītaṁ vā pañcai-te tasya hetavaḥ ||

तत्रैवं सति कर्तारमात्मानं केवलं तु यः ।
Tatrai-vaṁ sati kartāram-ātmānaṁ kevalaṁ tu yaḥ |

पश्यत्यकृतबुद्धित्वान्न स पश्यति दुर्मतिः ।। (16)
Pasyaty-akṛtabuddhitvān-na sa paśyati durmatiḥ ||

यस्य नाहंकृतो भावो बुद्धिर्यस्य न लिप्यते ।
Yasya nāhaṁkṛto bhāvo buddhir-yasya na lipyate |

हत्वापि स इमांल्लोकान्न हन्ति न निबध्यते ।। (17)
Hatvāpi sa imāṁl-lokān-na hanti na nibadhyate ||

ज्ञानं ज्ञेयं परिज्ञाता त्रिविधा कर्मचोदना ।
Jñānaṁ jñeyaṁ parijñatā trividhā karmacodanā |

करणं कर्म कर्तेति त्रिविधः कर्मसंग्रहः ।। (18)
Karaṇaṁ karma karte-ti trividhaḥ karma-saṁgrahaḥ ||

ज्ञानं कर्म च कर्ता च त्रिधैव गुणभेदतः ।
Jñānaṁ karma ca kartā ca tridhai-va guṇa bhedataḥ|

प्रोच्यते गुणसंख्याने यथावच्छृणु तान्यपि ।। (19)
Procyate guṇasaṁkhyāne yathāvac-chṛṇu tāny-api ||

सर्वभूतेषु येनैकं भावमव्ययमीक्षते ।
Sarvabhūteṣu, yenai-kam bhāvam-avyayam-īkṣate |

अविभक्तं विभक्तेषु तज्ज्ञानं विद्धि सात्विकम् ।। (20)
Avibhaktaṁ vibhakteṣu taj-jñānam viddhi sātvikaṁ ||

पृथक्त्वेन तु यज्ज्ञानं नानाभावान्पृथग्विधान् ।
Pṛthaktvena tu yaj-jñānaṁ nānābhāvān-pṛthagvidhān |

वेत्ति सर्वेषु भूतेषु तज्ज्ञानं विद्धि राजसम् ।। (21)
Vetti sarveṣu bhūteṣu taj-jñanaṁ viddhi rājasam.

यत्तु कृत्सनवदेकस्मिन्कार्ये सक्तमहैतुकम् ।
Yat tu kṛtsnavad-ekasmin-kārye saktam-ahaitukaṁ |
अतत्त्वार्थवदल्पं च तत्तामसमुदाहृतम् ।। (22)
Atattvārthavad-alpaṁ ca tat-tāmasam-udāhṛtam ||
नियतं सङ्गरहितमरागद्वेषतः कृतम् ।
Niyataṁ saṅgarahitam-arāgadveṣataḥ kṛtaṁ |
अफलप्रेप्सुना कर्म यत्तत्सात्विकमुच्यते ।। (23)
Aphalaprepsunā karma yat-tat-sātvikam-ucyate ||
यत्तु कामेप्सुना कर्म साहंकारेण वा पुनः ।
Yat-tu kāmepsunā karma sāhaṁkāreṇa vā punaḥ |
क्रियते बहुलायासं तद्राजसमुदाहृतम् ।। (24)
Kriyate bahulāyāsaṁ tad-rājasaṁ-udāhṛtaṁ ||
अनुबन्धं क्षयं हिंसामनपेक्ष्य च पौरूषम् ।
Anubandhaṁ kṣayaṁ hiṁsāṁ-anapekṣya ca pauruṣaṁ
मोहादारभ्यते कर्म तत्तामसमुदाहृतम् ।। (25)
Mohād-ārabhyate karma tat-tāmasaṁ-udāhṛtaṁ ||
मुक्तसङ्गोऽनहंवादी धृत्युत्साहसमन्वितः ।
Mukt'saṅgo-nahaṁvādī dhṛtyutsāhasamanvitaḥ |
सिद्ध्यसिद्ध्योर्निर्विकारः कर्ता सात्विक उच्यते ।। (26)
Siddhyasidhyor-nirvikāraḥ kartā sāttvika ucyate ||
रागी कर्मफलप्रेप्सुर्लुब्धो हिसात्मकोऽशुचिः ।
Rāgī karmaphalaprepsur-lubdho hiṁsātmako-suciḥ|
हर्षशोकान्वितः कर्ता राजसः परिकीर्तितः ।। (27)
Harṣaśokānvitaḥ kartā rājasaḥ parikīrtitaḥ ||
अयुक्तः प्राकृतः स्तब्ध शठो नैष्कृतिकोऽलसः ।
Ayuktaḥ prākṛtaḥ stabdhaḥ saṭho naiṣkṛtiko-'lasaḥ |
विषादी दीर्घसूत्री च कर्ता तामस उच्यते ।। (28)
Viṣādī dīrghasūtrī ca kartā tāmasa ucyate ||
बुद्धेर्भेदं धृतेश्चैव गुणतस्त्रिविधं शृणु ।
Buddher-bhedaṁ dhṛteś-cai-va guṇatas-trividhaṁ sṛṇu |

प्रोच्यमानमशेषेण पृथक्त्वेन धनंजय ।। (29)
Procyamānam-aśeṣeṇa pṛthaktvena dhanañjaya ||
प्रवृतिं च निवृत्तिं च कार्याकार्ये भयाभये ।
Pravṛttiṁ ca nivṛttiṁ ca kāryākārye bhayābhaye
बन्धं मोक्षं च या वेत्ति बुद्धिः सा पार्थ सात्त्विकी ।। (30)
Bandhaṁ mokṣaṁ ca yā vetti buddhiḥ sā Pārtha sātviki ||
यया धर्ममधर्म च कार्य चाकार्यमेव च ।
Yayā dharmaṁ-adharmaṁ ca kāryam-cā-kāryam-eva ca |
अयथावत्प्रजानाति बुद्धिः सा पार्थ राजसी ।। (31)
Ayathāvat-prajānāti buddhiḥ sā Pārtha rājasī||
अधर्मं धर्ममिति या मन्यते तम्रसावृता ।
Adharmaṁ dharmam-iti yā manyate tamasā-vṛtā
सर्वार्थान्विपरीतांश्च बुद्धिः सा पार्थ तामसी ।। (32)
Sarvarthān-viparītāṁś-ca-buddhiḥ sā Pārtha tāmasī ||
धृत्या यया धारयते मनः प्राणेन्द्रियक्रियाः ।
Dhṛtyā yayā dhārayate manaḥprāṇendriyakriyāḥ |
योगेनाव्यभिचारिण्या धृतिः सा पार्थ सात्त्विकी ।। (33)
Yogenāvyabhicāriṇyā dhṛtiḥ sā Pārtha sāttviki ||
यया तु धर्मकामार्थान्धृत्या धारयतेऽर्जुन ।
Yayā tu dharmakāmārthān-dhṛtyā dhārayate-'rjuna |
प्रसङ्गेन फलाकाङ्क्षी धृतिः सा पार्थ राजसी ।। (34)
Prasaṅgena phalākāṅkṣī dhṛtiḥ sā Pārtha rājasī ||
यया स्वप्नं भयं शोकं विषादं मदमेव च ।
Yayā svapnam bhayam sokamviṣādaṁ madam-eva ca |
न विमुञ्चति दुर्मेधा धृति सा पार्थ तामसी ।। (35)
na vimuncati dumedhā dhṛtiḥ sā Pārtha tāmasī ||
सुख त्विदानी त्रिविध श्रृणु मे भरतर्षभ ।
Sukham tv-idānīm trividham sṛṇu me bharatarṣabha|
अभ्यासाद्रमते यत्र दुःखान्त च निगच्छति ।। (36)
Abhyāsād-ramate yatra dukkhāntam ca nigacchati ||

यत्तदग्रे विषमिव परिणामेऽमृतोपमम् ।
Yat-tad-agre viṣam-iva pariṇāme-'mṛtopamaṁ |
तत्सुखं सात्विकं प्रोक्तमात्मबुद्धिप्रसादजम् ।। (37)
Tat-sukhaṁ sātvikaṁ proktaṁ-ātmabuddhiprasādajaṁ ||
विषयेन्द्रियसंयोगाद्यत्तदग्रेऽमृतोपमम् ।
Viṣayendriyasaṁyogād-yat-tad-agre-'mritopamam |
परिणामे विषमिव तत्सुखं राजसं स्मृतम् ।। (38)
Pariṇāme viṣame-iva tat-sukhaṁ rājasaṁ smṛtaṁ ||
यदग्रे चानुबन्धे च सुखं मोहनमात्मनः ।
Yad-agre cā-nubandhe ca sukhaṁ mohanaṁ-ātmanaḥ |
निद्रालस्य प्रमादोत्थं तत्तामसमुदाहतम् ।। (39)
Nidrālasyapramādotthaṁ tat-tāmasam-udāhṛtaṁ ||
न तदस्ति पृथिव्यां वा दिवि देवेषु वा पुनः ।
Na'tad-'asti pṛthivyāṁ vā divi deveṣu vā punaḥ ||
सत्त्वं प्रकृतिजैर्मुक्तं यदेभिः स्यात्त्रिभिर्गुणैः ।। (40)
Sattvaṁ prakṛtijair-muktaṁ yad-ebhiḥ yāt-tribhir guṇaiḥ ||
ब्राह्मणक्षत्रियविशां श्रूद्राणां च परन्तप ।
Brāhmaṇakṣatriyaviśām śūdrāṇām ca paramtapa ||
कर्माणि प्रविभक्तानि स्वभावप्रभवैर्गुणैः ।। (41)
Karmāṇi pravibhaktāni svabhāvaprabhavair guṇaiḥ ||
शमो दमस्तपः शौचं क्षन्तिरार्जवमेव च ।
Samo damas-tapaḥ śaucam kṣāntir-ārjavam eva ca |
ज्ञानं विज्ञानमास्तिक्यं ब्रह्मकर्म स्वभावजम् ।। (42)
Jñānaṁ vijñānam-āstikyaṁ brahmakarma Svabhāvajaṁ ||
शौर्य तेजो धृतिर्दाक्ष्यं युद्धे चाप्यपलायनम् ।
Śauryaṁ tejo dhṛtir-dākṣyaṁ yuddhe cā-pyapalāyanaṁ |
दानमीश्वरभावश्च क्षात्रं कर्म स्वभावजम् ।। (43)
Dānam-īśvarabhāvaś-ca kṣātraṁ karma svabhāvajaṁ ||
कृषिगोरक्ष्यवाणिज्यं वेश्यकर्म स्वभावजम् ।
Kṛṣi-gorakṣya-vāṇijyaṁ vaiśya-kama svabhāvajaṁ |

परिचर्यात्मकं कर्म शूद्रस्यापि स्वभावजम् ।। (44)
paricaryātmakaṁ karma śūdrasyā-pi svabhāvajaṁ ||
स्वे स्वे कर्मण्यभिरतः संसिद्धिं लभते नरः ।
Sve sve karmaṇy-abhirataḥ saṁsiddhiṁ labhate naraḥ
स्वकर्म निरतः सिद्धिं यथा विन्दन्ति तच्छृणु ।। (45)
Svakarma-nirataḥ siddhiṁ yathā vindati tac-chṛṇu ||
यतः प्रवृत्तिर्भूतानां येन सर्वमिदं ततम् ।
Yataḥ pravṛttir-bhūtānāṁ yena sarvaṁ-idaṁ tataṁ |
स्वकर्मणा तमभ्यर्च्य सिद्धिं विन्दति मानवः ।। (46)
Svakarmaṇā tam-abhyarcya siddhiṁ vindati mānavaḥ ||
श्रेयान्स्वधर्मो विगुणः परधर्मात्स्वनुष्ठितात् ।
Śreyān-svadharmo viguṇaḥ paradharmāt-svanuṣṭitāt |
स्वभावनियतं कर्म कुर्वन्नाप्नोति किल्बिषम् ।। (47)
Svabhāvaniyataṁ karma kurvan-nā-pnoti kilbiṣaṁ ||
सहजं कर्म कौन्तेय सदोषमपि न त्यजेत् ।
Sahajaṁ karma kaunteya sadoṣam-api na tyajet |
सर्वारम्भा हि दोषेण धूमेनाग्निरिवावृताः ।। (48)
Sarvārambhā hi doṣeṇa dhūmenā-gnir-ivā-vṛtāḥ ||
असक्त बुद्धिः सर्वत्र जितात्मा विगतस्पृहः ।
Asakta-buddhiḥ sarvatra jitatmā vigataspṛhaḥ |
नैष्कर्म्यसिद्धिं परमां संन्यासेनाधि गच्छति ।। (49)
Naiṣkarmyasiddhiṁ paramāṁ samnyāsenā-dhi gacchati ||
सिद्धि प्राप्तो यथाब्रह्म तथाप्नोति निबोध मे ।
Siddhiṁ prāpto yathā-brahma tathā-pnoti nibodha me |
समासेनैव कौन्तेय निष्ठा ज्ञानस्य या परा ।। (50)
Samāse-naiva Kaunteya niṣṭhā jñānasya yā parā ||
बुद्ध्या विशुद्धया युक्तो धृत्यात्मानं नियम्य च ।
Buddhyā viśuddhayā yukto, dhṛtyā-tmmnaṁ niyamya ca |
शब्दादीन्विषयांस्त्यक्त्वा रागद्वेषौ व्युदस्य च ।। (51)
Sabdādīn-viṣayāṁś-tyaktvā rāga-dveṣau-vyudasya ca |

विविक्तसेवी लघ्वासी यतवाक्कायमानसः ।
Viviktasevī laghvāśī yatavākkāyamānasaḥ |
ध्यानयोगपरो नित्यं वैराग्यं समुपाश्रितः ।। (52)
Dhyānayogaparo nityaṁ vairāgyaṁ samupāśritaḥ ||
अहंकारं बलं दर्प कामं क्रोधं परिग्रहम् ।
Ahaṁkāraṁ balaṁ darpaṁ kāmaṁ krodhaṁ parigrahaṁ
विमुच्य निर्ममः शान्तो ब्रह्म भूयाय कल्पते ।। (53)
Vimucya nirmamaḥ śānto brahma bhūyāya kalpate ||
ब्रह्मभूतः प्रसन्नात्मा न शोचति न काङ्क्षति ।
Brahmabhūtaḥ prasannātmā na śocati na kāṇkṣati |
समः सर्वेषु भूतेषु मद्भक्तिं लभते पराम् ।। (54)
Samaḥ sarveṣu bhūteṣu madbhaktiṁ labhate parāṁ |
भक्त्या मामभिजानाति यावान्यश्चास्मि तत्त्वतः ।
Bhaktyā mām-abhijānāti yāvān-yaś-cā-smi tattvataḥ |
ततो मां तत्त्वतो ज्ञात्वा विशते तदनन्तरम् ।। (55)
Tato māṁ tattvato jñātvā viśate tadanantaraṁ ||
सर्वकर्माण्यपि सदा कुर्वाणो मद्व्यपाश्रयः ।
Sarvakarmāṇy-api sadā kurvāṇo madvyapāśrayaḥ
मत्प्रसादादवाप्नोति शाश्वतं पदमव्ययम् ।। (56)
Matprasādād-avāpnoti śāśvataṁ padam-avyayaṁ ||
चेतसा सर्वकर्माणि मयि संन्यस्य मत्परः ।
Cetasā sarvakarmāṇi mayi saṁnyasya matparaḥ |
बुद्धियोगमुपाश्रित्य मच्चित्तः सततं भव ।। (57)
Buddhiyogaṁ-upāśritya mac-cittaḥ satataṁ bhava ||
मच्चितः सर्वदुर्गाणि मत्प्रसादात्तरिष्यसि ।
Maccitaḥ Sarvadurgāṇi matprasādāt-tariṣyasi |
अय चेत्त्वमहंकारान्न श्रोष्यसि विनक्ष्यसि ।। (58)
Atha cet-tvam-ahaṁkārān-na śroṣyasi vinakṣyasi ||
यदहंकारमाश्रित्य न योत्स्य इति मन्यसे ।
Yad-ahaṁkāram-āśritya na yotsya iti manyase |

मिथ्यैष व्यवसायस्ते प्रकृतिस्त्वां नियोक्ष्यति ।। (59)
Mithyai-ṣa vyavasāyas-te prakṛtis-tvāṁ niyokṣyati ||
स्वभावजेन कौन्तेय निबद्धः स्वेन कर्मणा।
Svabhāvajena kaunteya nibaddhaḥ svena karmaṇā |
कर्तुं नेच्छसि यन्मोहात्करिष्यस्यवशोऽपि तत् ।। (60)
Kartuṁ ne-cchasi yan-mohātkariṣyasy-avaśo- 'pi tat ||
ईश्वरः सर्वभूतानां हृद्देशेऽर्जुन तिष्टति ।
Īśvaraḥ sarvabhūtānāṁ hṛddeśe-'rjuna tiṣṭati |
भ्रामयन्सर्वभूतानि यन्त्रारूढानि मायया ।। (61)
Bhrāmayan-sarvabhūtāni yantrārūḍhāni māyayā ||
तमेव शरणं गच्छ सर्वभावेन भारत ।
Tam-eva śaraṇaṁ gaccha sarvabhavena bhārata
तत्प्रसादात्परां शान्तिं स्थानं प्राप्स्यसि शाश्वतम् ।। (62)
Tatprasādāt-parāṁ śāntim sthānaṁ prāpsyasi śāśvataṁ ||
इति ते ज्ञानमाख्यात गृह्याद्‌गुह्यतरं मया ।
Iti te jñānam-ākhyātaṁ guhyād-guhyataraṁ mayā |
विमृश्यैतदशेषेण यथेच्छसि तथा कुरू ।। (63)
Vimṛśyai-tad-aseṣeṇa yathe-cchasi tathā kuru ||
सर्वगुह्यतमं भूयः श्रृणु मे परमं वचः ।
Sarvaguhyatamaṁ bhūyaḥ śṛṇu me paramaṁ vacaḥ
इष्टोऽसि मे दृढमिति ततो वक्ष्यामि ते हितम् ।। (64)
Iṣṭo-'si me dṛḍham-iti tato vakṣyāmi te hitaṁ ||
मन्मना भव मद्‌भक्तो मद्याजी मां नमस्कुरू ।
Manmanā bhava madbhakto madyājī māṁ namaskuru
मामेवैष्यसि सत्यं ते प्रतिजाने प्रियोऽसि मे ।। (65)
Mām-evai-ṣyasi satyaṁ te pratijāne priyo-si me ||
सर्वधर्मान्परित्यज्य मामेकं शरणं व्रज ।
Sarvadharmān-parityajya mām-ekaṁ śaraṇaṁ vraja |
अहं त्वा सर्वपापेभ्यो मोक्षयिष्यामि मा शुचः ।। (66)
Ahaṁ tvā sarvapāpebhyo mokṣayiṣyāmi mā śucaḥ ||

इदं ते नातपस्काय नाभक्ताय कदाचन ।
Idam te nātapaskāya nābhaktāya kadācana |
न चाशुश्रूषवे वाच्यं न च मां योऽभ्यसूयति ।। (67)
Na cāśuśrūṣave vācyaṁ na ca māṁ yo-'bhyasūyati ||
य इदं परमं गुह्यं मद्भक्तेष्वभिधास्यति ।
Ya idaṁ paramaṁ guhyaṁ madbhakteṣv-abhidhāsyati |
भक्ति मयि परां कृत्वा ममेवैष्यत्यसंशय: ।। (68)
Bhaktiṁ mayi parāṁ kṛtvā Mām-evai-ṣyaty-asaṁśayaḥ |
न च तस्मान्मनुष्येषु कश्चिन्मे प्रियकृत्तम: ।
Na ca tasmān-manuṣyeṣu kaścin me priyakṛttamaḥ |
भविता न च मे तस्मादन्य: प्रियतरो भुवि ।। (69)
Bhavitā na ca me tasmād-anyaḥ priyataro bhuvi |
अध्येष्यते च य इमं धर्म्यं संवादमावयो: ।
Adhyeṣyate ya imaṁ dharmyaṁ saṁvādam-āvayoḥ |
ज्ञानयज्ञेन तेनाहमिष्ठ: स्यामिति मे मति: ।। (70)
Jñānayajñena tenā-ham-iṣṭaḥ syām-iti me matiḥ ||
श्रद्धावाननसूयश्च श्रृणुयादपि यो नर: ।
Śraddhāvān-anasūyaś-ca śṛṇuyād-api yo naraḥ
सोऽपि मुक्त: शुभाँल्लोकान्प्राप्नुयात् पुण्यकर्मणाम् ।। (71)
So-'pi muktaḥ śubhāṁl-lokān-prāpnuyāt puṇyakarmaṇām |
कच्चिदेतच्छ्रुतं पार्थ त्वयैकाग्रेण चेतसा ।
Kaccid-etac-chrutaṁ pārtha tvayai-kāgreṇa cetasā |
कच्चिदज्ञानसंमोह: प्रनष्टस्ते धनंजय ।। (72)
Kaccid-ajñānasaṁmohaḥ praṇaṣṭaste dhanaṁjaya |

अर्जुन उवाच / *Arjuna Uvāca*

नष्टो मोह: स्मृतिर्लब्धा.त्वत्प्रसादान्मयाच्युत ।
Naṣṭmohaḥsmṛtir-labdhā tvat-prasādān-mayā-'Cyuta
स्थितोऽस्मि गतसंदेह: करिष्यं वचनं तव ।। (73)
Sthito-'smi gatasaṁdehaḥ kariṣye vacanaṁ tava ||

संजय उवाच / *Sañjaya Uvāca*

इत्यहं वासुदेवस्य पार्थस्य च महात्मनः ।
Ity-ahaṁ vāsudevasya pārthasya ca mahātmanaḥ |
संवादमिममश्रौषमद्भुतं रोमहर्षणम् ।। (74)
Saṁvādaṁ-imam-aśrauṣaṁ-adbhutaṁ romaharṣaṇaṁ ||

व्यासप्रसादाच्छ्रुतवानेतद्गुह्यमहं परम् ।
Vyāsaprasādāc-chrutavān-etad-guhyaṁ-ahaṁ paraṁ |
योगं योगेश्वरात्कृष्णात्साक्षात्कथयतः स्वयम् ।। (75)
Yogaṁ yogeśvarāt-kṛṣṇāt-sākṣāt-kathayataḥ svayaṁ ||

राजन्संस्मृत्य संस्मृत्य संवादमिममद्भुतम् ।
Rājan-saṁsmṛtya saṁsmṛtya saṁvādam-imaṁ-adbhutaṁ |
केशवार्जुनयोः पुण्यं हृष्यामि च मुहुर्मुहुः ।। (76)
Keśavārjunayoḥ puṇyaṁ hṛṣyāmi ca muhur-muhuḥ |

तच्च संस्मृत्य संस्मृत्य रूपमत्यद्भुत हरेः ।
Tac-ca saṁsmṛtya saṁsmṛtya rūpam-atyadbhutaṁ hareḥ |
विस्मयो मे महान् राजन्हृष्यामि च पुनः पुनः ।। (77)
Vismayo me mahān rājan-hṛṣyāmi ca punaḥ punaḥ |

यत्र योगेश्वरः कृष्णो यत्र पार्थो धनुर्धरः ।
Yatra yogeśvaraḥ kṛṣṇo yatra pārtho dhanurdharaḥ
तत्र श्रीर्विजयो भूतिर्धुवा नीतिर्मतिर्मम ।। (78)
Tatra srīr-vijayo bhūtir-dhruvā nītir matir mama ||

इति श्रीमद्भगवद्गीतासूपनिषत्सु ब्रह्मविद्यायां योगशास्त्रे श्रीकृष्णार्जुनसंवादे संन्यासयोगो नामाष्टादशोऽध्यायः ।।

Iti Śrīmad-bhagavadgītāsū-paniṣatsu Brahmavidyāyāṁ yogaśāstre śrīkṣṛṇārjunasaṁvāde Saṁnyāsayogo-nāmā-ṣṭādaśo-'dhyāyaḥ |

APPENDIX -I

Vyãsa : *The Author of Mahãbhãrata*

The great sage Bhagwãn Vyãsa endowed with extraordinary intellect, genius and knowledge wrote Mahabharata, 18 puranas that consist the ocean of Indian mythology, compiled the spiritual aphorisms of ***Vedic*** sages called ***Brahma sutra*** and arranged ***Vedas*** properly dividing them.

He is called Krishna because he was black, and called ***Dvaipayana*** since he was born in an island. He is called Vyãsa because he divided ***Vedas***. In high reverence he is addressed as ***Maharshi***, the great sage or ***Bhagwãn***, the Lord. His genius encompassed all the subjects in the world so it is said ***'Vyasoschistam Jagatsarvam***, the whole world is touched by Vyãsa. His Maha-bhãrata and 18 puranas, the mythological works, have immensely contributed in building up Indian culture, hence Vyãsa is rightly described as the 'great soul of India.'

He brought renaissance to long-forgotten Indian arts, literature, scriptures and spiritual learning. The Himãlayan task fulfilled by him is almost of miraculous nature. He is a great teacher of the entire human race. He always upheld morality and high ethical standards based on eternal principles of spirituality.

Vyãsa was a son of sage Parãshara and Satyavati who was a daughter of king Uparichar Vasu but was brought up by a fisherman Dãsraj living on the bank of Yamuna river. Satyavati used to help her father in his profession of a boatman who carried the people to cross the river Yamunã . Once when she was crossing the river carrying sage Parãshara in her boat the sage felt attracted towards her beauty and expressed his desire to mate with her. Changing the fish-smell of her body into pleasing fragrance Parashara fulfilled his desire by mating with her. In due course Vyãsa was born on a solitary island. On reaching his youth he married to Vatikã, the daughter of Jabali and begot from her a son by name Shuka who became famous as a illuminated soul of equal vision unsurpassed by anybody.

The western scholars have doubted the historical reality of Vyãsa. However the Indian scholars have accepted him as a historical person on the strength of the references in historical documents and ***Vedic*** literature establishing the lineage of Vasishtha, Parãshar, Vyãsa, Suka in succession. Based on history and tradition Indian scholars accept Vyasa as a historical person.

APPENDIX -II

Marga : *The Path*

The paths or the methods adopted by the spiritual aspirants to seek experience of God differ from individual to individual depending on his natural tendency and inborn or acquired ability. This path-concept in Hindu spiritual world has no parallel elsewhere. It is unique and original concept that carries extraordinary importance in India. God is one but the paths to realize Him are many. Gitã declares: "In whatever way men surrender unto me I accept them in that way. Whatever path they travel, it is my path. It leads to me alone". This all-embracing principle, "that there is only one Reality, ***Brahman*** but manifests Itself in many" accepts all religions as its manifestations having equal potential to realise it.

Dnyana, Karma, ***Yoga*** and ***Bhakti*** are four means by which the Absolute ***Brahman*** can be realised. The spiritual aspirants have full freedom to follow any of the four. All these paths have long traditions in India and their advocates have strongly debated not only the superiority but exclusive use of the path of their choice. Thus ***Dnyana, Karma, Yoga*** and ***Bhakti*** have respectively Shankarachãrya, Mimãnsakas, Patanjali and Shãndilya as their leaders. The word ***Yoga*** means to be in union with the ***Brahman***. So whatever path that leads to unitive experience of God is ***Yoga***.

Karma-mãrga : The path of Action

The ***Karma-mãrga*** originally propounded by the ***Mimãnsakas*** considers ***Moksha***- the liberation as eternal and imperishable since it does not depend on any cause. Whatever has a cause is invariably perishable. If the cause of the rebirth is destroyed by destroying the ***Karma,*** the action, liberation is attained. Opposed to liberation is the cycle of birth and death. The actions bind the soul to this cycle. Therefore one has to discard forbidden actions as well as actions caused by desiring fruits and faithfully carry out only those regular and occasional ones prescribed by the scriptures. Once the fruits of previous life, acquired by one's fate in this life are finished by living, there remains no cause for rebirth and the soul gets liberated.

Bhagavad-Gitã develops this ***Karma-theory*** into full-fledged ***Karma-Yoga*** defining it as the skill of performing action without inviting bondage. All actions except forbidden ones can be performed in this way. Action itself is not binding. When the action is performed discarding one's ego and without expecting any fruits, it becomes inaction. But when it is accompanied by the sense of ego and desires to enjoy fruits it creates bondage. Those who are outwardly inactive but full of desires within, also have no escape from this bondage.

Bhagavad-Gitã does not consider the path of detached action merely an instrument to liberation but as an independent way of life to be continued even after the enlightenment is attained. As opposed to the path of renunciation through knowledge Gitã strongly pleads for the active worldly life and discusses various philosophical and practical aspects of ***Karma*** in detail. In this ***Karmayoga*** the actions are either performed as the wish of God or worship offered to God, Pleased by such purified action God favours the aspirant by lifting his soul from the worldly affairs and the aspirant finally attains enlightenment.

Dnyana mãrga : The path of knowledge

The great religious leader of Hinduism Shri Ãdya Shankarãchãrya is the outstandingly excellent exponent of this path. Ignorance about the true nature of universe is the main cause of bondage and true knowledge only can liberate the soul from this bondage. The body and the mind are considered as the impediments in the way of liberation, so their assistance is not sought. Only instrument is the intellect. Deeper philosophic reasoning coupled with strong resolve makes the seeker of ***Brahman*** to renounce everything considering as unreal and temporary. The worldly surrounding is nothing but All ***Brahman***. The seeker wants to get rid of the material world by the force of his intellectual conviction. In his search of Reality he goes on negating every thing saying "not this, not this, ***'Neti-Neti'***. Action, sacrifice, austerity, pilgrimage, even study of ***Vedas*** are of no importance to him. Spiritual knowledge is the only source of liberation.

He uses his discrimination to know what is eternal and what is transitory in nature. The great ***Upanishadic*** statements called ***Mahãvãkyas*** provide him guiding light in studying various aspects of spiritual knowledge. So knowledge as an instrument in the preparatory stage and its culmination in the direct unitive knowledge of ***Brahman*** are two aspects of knowledge in this path.

Here the search of truth is by his analytical reasoning, first in the external work where he fails and then diverts his thoughts to his self within and then he finds realisation in self-knowledge. This is the unique state where Existence, Knowledge and Bliss are at once realised as unitive experience.

Participating in worldly actions is considered as the most unwanted thing that brings bondage and therefore all types of activities are renounced. Hence this path is known as path of renunciation through knowledge. In Gitã this path is referred to as ***Sãnkhya*** meaning thereby the knowledge that discriminates between real and unreal. The great sage Kapila's ***Sãnkhya Philosophy*** stresses the need of the self called ***Purusha*** realising his separate and independent existence from nature called ***Prakriti*** to attain liberation called ***Kaivalya***. Dr. S. Radhakrishnan describes the knowledge-based path as the path of the introvert and action-based path as the path of the extravert.

Bhakti-mãrga : The path of Devotion

The great sage Shãndilya, the proponent of this path defines devotion as intense love to God. *सा परानुरक्ति ईश्वरे ।* Divine sage Narada also called it as the intense love to God' *सा तु अस्मिन् परमप्रेमरूपा ।*

According to Shãndilya God is not All-knowledge but All-love. When unmanifest ***Brahman*** appears in a manifest form called ***Ishvara*** devotion becomes possible. All-mighty, All-knowing and All-merciful are the attributes of God and they inspire confidence in the devotee to seek His help in his misery. According to Swãmi Vivekãnanda the real and genuine search of God, beginning, continuing, and ending in love is devotion (***Bhakti***). God manifests everywhere in everything. Therefore there is no place for hatred nor the earthly benefits can be its goal.

Bhakti is the easiest and the most natural way to reach God. It is not supposed to degenerate into hatred of others who seek Him differently. No hatred, no material gains are the expressions of true devotion. A true devotee renounces all other little loves for the sake of All-Merciful God.

At the preparatory stage ***Bhakti*** is called ***Gauni*** *(गौणी)*, the secondary one and when fully absorbed into unity of God as ***Para*** *(परा)* the supreme. In its ideal state, knowledge, love and ***Yoga*** are harmoniously fused.

In the preparatory stage forms and ceremonies including rituals are used just to strengthen the devotee's resolve to seek God. Therefore many concrete helps are provided by the mythology and the symbology that add poetry, beauty and sublimity to devotee's life. Some consider devotional worship merely as instrument and not the goal, whereas some think it as both since it terminates into love and knowledge getting fused. Perfect knowledge is inseparable from perfect love. Bhagavad-Gitã supports this view.

The God worshipped in His personal form is not separate and different from the unmanifest ***Brahman***. All is ***Brahman***, the one without the second. Only the ***Brahman*** is too much an abstraction to be loved or worshipped. So the devotees choose the relative aspect of ***Brahman*** manifesting as ***Ishvara***, the supreme Ruler. ***Ishvara*** is the highest possible reading of Absolute ***Brahman*** conceived by the human mind.

Yoga-mãrga : The Path of Yogic Practice

In this path realization is attained through physical and mental control by scientifically following the discipline of ***Yoga*** that consists of eight stages called limbs. The mind being the main instrument of experiencing the world is brought under total control. If the mind stops functioning the whole world disappears.

Every moment the mind breaks into waves and constantly plays with all sorts of desires. It is always in love of objects of pleasures and hates everything that bring sorrows. To hold this mind steady in total calmness by stopping all external and internal causes by the power of will, a great science called ***Yogashãstra*** was developed in India by the great sage Patanjali.

Originally it was meant to reach thoughtless state of mind but in course of time the aspect of meditation upon God became the supreme goal of this ***Yoga***. The seer merges into his pure state of God realisation.

The eight steps elaborately prescribed in this science of ***Yoga***, are to be rigorously practised so that the state of transcendental joy called ***Samadhi*** is attained by the adherent.

Since it results into divine spiritual experience it is also called '***RajYoga***'.

The aim of the ***Yoga*** discipline is to confer trance, divine power and divine knowledge mainly through the control of the mind, breath and body. This necessitates observing morality of high order. One-pointed concentration upon God results into obtaining his grace and enlightenment. Therefore controlling passions is a prime necessity in ***Yoga***.

Yogashãstra while stressing the need of conquering the mind squarely deals with human psychology in all its depth. It has become a grand and priceless collection of psychological principles of eternal value. It does not preach for the suppression of passions but instead enables the adherent to purify them by spiritual austerity.

Bhagvad-Gitã recognizes the importance of this ***Yoga*** and prescribes its application for freeing the mind from the onslaught of passions, anger and fear.

In the sixth ***Adhyãya*** the spiritual discipline of Pãtanjal ***Yogashastra*** with its salient features has been briefly explained as means of concentration of the mind that results into making one's intellect steady.

APPENDIX -III

Some Important References from First Adhyaya

Verses

1. Dharmakshetre Kurukshetre : The place named after Kuru, the ancient king, the ancestor of Kauravas and pãndavas. He first ploughed this land when king of gods Indra blessed, 'one who dies here performing penance or fighting battle would go to heaven.' Since then regarded as holy. The great Bharat war took place here on this extensive plain which situated near Delhi then known as Hastinapura. The field of battle is referred to as the field of religion to suggest the conflict between the good and the evil. Many battles were fought on this battlefield in medieval period. Presently Kurukshetra is a railway station 100 miles north of Delhi. Still it is a famous pilgrim place.

2. Duryodhana : The eldest son of the blind Dhritarashtra who had one hundred sons known as Kauravas. He was wicked by nature and used crooked means to destroy Pãndavas who were his cousins. He tried to harm them even when they were too young. After the division of the kingdom he managed to win the Pãndava's kingdom by deceitfully winning the game of dice. As a condition he sent them to the forest to stay in exile for twelve years and to live incognito in the thirteenth year. After completing thirteen years' long ordeal when Pãndavas returned and asked for their kingdom, Duryodhana rudely refused their rightful claim. As a consequence the great Bhãrat war was declared which continued for eighteen days, killing almost all the warriors on both the sides. In the end Duryodhana hid in water but was chased and compelled to come out. In a single combat with Bhima he was killed mercilessly. He was expert in club fighting and exhibited his skill even if he died in the combat. At the commencement of the war after inspecting the army alignment, he is seen talking to his teacher-warrior Drona .

3. (a) Pãnduputra (Pandavas) : Five sons of king Pandu known as Pãndavas. Pandu ascended the throne of Hastinãpura after his father Vichitravirya. The elder brother Dhritarashtra being born blind Pandu became the king. Pandu secured five sons from two wives Kunti and Madri. Kunti is the mother of Yudhistira also known as Dharma, Bhima and Arjuna. Madri is the mother of Nakula and Sahadeva.

(b) Achãrya Drona : The great teacher who taught military science to Kauravas as well as Pãndavas. A warrior of extraordinary calibre, was a master of archery. He is a son of Bharadwaja and a disciple of Parashurãm who taught him secret mantras of archery. He remained loyal to his king Duryodhana and became the general of Kauravas's army after Bhishma's death. He was a school friend of Drupada, the king of Panchal. Being offended by Drupada, Drona got him captured by Pandavas but afterwards released him. Dhrishtadyumna, the son of Drupad avenged Drona by treacherously killing him in the great Bharat war.

(c) Drupadputra (Dhrishtadyumna) : Son of Drupad, a Panchal king and the father of Draupadi. He was born through the sacrificial fire. He was appointed the commander in chief of Pandavas' army. He killed Drona treacherously and was subsequently butchered in retaliation by Drona's son Ashwatthãmã, when he was asleep.

4. (a) Bhima : The second of five Pãndavas. He was born of Kunti by the favour of wind god Vãyu. He had enormous strength. He was expert in wrestling and club-fighting which he learnt from Balarãm, the elder brother of ShriKrishna. He killed many wicked demons like Bakasura and Hidimbã. He also killed Jarãsandha, Kichaka and all the hundred Kauravas. He avenged Draupadi's humiliation by breaking open the chest of Dusshasana who had dragged her in the royal court and had tried to strip her. In the end he killed Duryodhana, the villain of the war in a fierceful club-fighting by mercilessly smashing his thigh. He is referred here as the chief of Pandavas' army.

(b) Arjuna : The third of the Pandavas. Kunti begot him by the grace of Indra. He was unrivalled in archery and had won Draupadi by hitting the eye of the rotating fish. The most favourite student of Drona and the close friend and disciple of Shrikrishna. His despondency at the commencement of the great war motivated Lord Krishna to teach him and the world's great spiritual science got enshrined in Gita.

(c) Virãt : The King of Matsya Desha. The Pãndavas stayed incognito in his palace in their thirteenth year of exile. His daughter, Uttara was married to Abhimanyu, the son of Arjuna and Subhadrã who was Krishna's sister

(d) Saubhadra (Abhimanyu) : Son of Arjuna and Subhadrã. Though very young, he was famous for his bravery and valour. He actively participated in the great Bharata war and had exhibited extraordinary military skill by killing renowned warriors of Kaurava army. On the thirteenth day of the war he drove his chariot into the Chakravyuha and performed unequalled valour but at last was overpowered and killed by six warriors. His wife Uttarã was pregnant.. At the end of the war Drona's son Ashwatthamã blinded by his revengeful madness hurled his dreadful mystic weapon called Brahmãstra to kill Uttara's child in her womb. But Lord Krishna used his divine disc to nullify the weapon and protected the child, which was the only survivor of the Pandava`s race, known as Parikshita. He was later crowned by Yudhishtira when Pandavas decided to retire to the forest after war. He died of snake-bite and his son Janamejaya, the great grand son of Arjuna performed a serpent sacrifice in order to destroy the whole serpent-race. All the serpents were burnt except Takshaka, who was saved by the intervention of a sage Astika at whose request the sacrifice was closed.

8. (a) Bhishma (Devavrata) : Son of Shantanu and Gangã hence also known as Gangeya. To fulfil his father's desire to marry Matsyagandha (Satyavati) he accepted on oath her condition not to accept the kingdom and not to get himself married. Being happy with his son's sacrifice his father conferred on him a boon that death would not touch him unless he himself wished so. His real name was Devavrata but his terrible vow gave him this name 'Bhishma'. He was the grand uncle of the Pãndavas and Kauravas. He was appointed the commander in chief of Kaurava's army and fought valiantly for ten long days. He fell down on the bed of arrows on the tenth day. He laid on the bed till the sun had crossed the vernal equinox and then breathed his last.

Bhishma was known for his statesmanship and valour. He was considered to be the royal councillor and was responsible for bringing up Dhritarashtra and Pandu and their children too. Arjuna could defeat Bhisma by taking shelter behind Shikhandi against whom Bhisma did not fight since he had avowed so. Otherwise he was not conquerable.

(b) Karna : First son of Kunti born in her virginity through the favour of the Sun. He was thrown into river by Kunti but the charioteer by name Adhiratha found him. He was brought up by his wife Rãdhã who became his foster mother. As he was known for his bravery so also for his charity. He had gifted his life-saving protective armour to Indra on his deceitful demand fully knowing the consequence of the act. He was favourite of Duryodhana who made him the king of Angadesha. He was killed by Arjuna when he was lifting the wheel of his chariot. Except Kunti and Krishna, the secret of his birth was not known to anybody. One day before his death Kunti disclosed this secret to Karna to save Pãndava's lives.

(c) Ashwatthãmã (see 3(b) (c) and 5(a).

16. (a) Yudhishthira (Dharma) : Eldest of the Pandavas born through the favour of Yama, the god of death. He was a magnanimous personality, kind-hearted, just, humane and truthful man of wisdom never lost the peace of his mind. He was as great to perform Rajsuya sacrifice. But also lost everything in a gambling match with Duryodhana. He was a man of sublime character who never lost his temper.

(b) Nakul-Sahadeva : Fourth and fifth son of Pandu born from Mãdri. Nakul was very handsome and skilled in horsemanship. Sahadeva worked as the principal cowherd in the kingdom of Virãt when Pandavas stayed there incognito.

APPENDIX -IV

Indian Deities : Myths and Truth

India, big enough to be called subcontinent has a known history of over seven thousand years. It consists of the population of heterogeneous character created by the intermixture of many races of local as well as foreign origin. It's name 'Bharat Varsha' is derived from the ancient rulers of the Bharat clan. The world 'Varsha' means the region that comes under the same rainfall zone. Originally this country had several small but independent republics which in course of time formed one big nation having the same cultural heritage which astonishingly combines their initial diversities. First the north India, from the Himalayas to the Vindhya mountains was unified and then through the great efforts of the sage Agastya and Parshurãm, its contact with south India was established. Finally the great Indian subcontinent from Himalayas to Kanyakumari culturally became one country. People of divergent races, lifestyles and languages have lived their life on this ancient land considering it as the holiest place on earth. Thousands of casts and communities, most of them tribals, with their colours, manners and cultures, harmoniously led their lives under one roof. With their own dialects, sects, deities, beliefs, customs and occupations they enjoyed their community - life freely. The Aryans of the North and the Dravids of the south mainly Telang, Kannada, Tamil etc. Were the major two subcultures that have contributed to the cultural growth of this country.

For many centuries Sanskrit remained the main language of the religion and literature which gradually paved way to the regional languages that flourished in full bloom in the medieval period. The oldest literature in the world known as

'***Vedas***' is in Sanskrit language. Oral tradition, steadfastly observed and traditionally followed without break retained the ***Vedic*** literature in its original form, the only literature and the method of its kind in the world. The way the ***Vedic*** hymns were recited thousand years back are still recited in the same way even today.

Any centralized political power never existed in India. Bharatas, Pandavas, Mauryas, Guptas and many others dynasties had their empires but they never ruled India as a whole. Even the regions where they ruled for years retained their distinct characters undisturbed. At times many kingdoms simultaneously survived with peaceful coexistence.

There never was established any centralized religious order, authority or system in India. Neither was there any prophet to establish any particular religion nor was any organization to force the spread of any particular cult. Religion remained a free expression for every individual. Many schools of religious thoughts freely flourished in India and the people silently followed the cults of their own choice. Though there exists one and the same God it was generously accepted that the same God can be approached through His various forms and names and by different paths. There was full freedom to all to accept and worship any God of his belief. There existed various God and Goddesses simultaneously but no God or Goddess was underestimated or insulted. Universal acceptance by tolerance was considered to be the great virtue of religion.

Many outside groups belonging to different races came to India but all were assimilated by absorbing their cultural contributions without any struggle. The mutual existence of various forms of worship, and religious sects remained the main characteristic of Indian's religious system.

Wherever there exists the divine glory or the divine strength that is considered as a deity by the Indian mind.

Imaginary and invisible world of deities of various kinds is a unique feature of Indian religion. These deities, it is believed fulfil the desires of their devotees if they are worshipped with intense love and devotion. Indra, Agni, Varuna, etc., of ***Vedic*** times and Shiva, Vishnu, Kali, Durga, Ganapati and others of the later period are the deities of this category.

The man in his uncivilized stage conceived the idea of God out of fear and worshipped any stone, tree or mountain as God. The ***Vedic*** sages in India were highly civilized and rational minded. Their idea of God was developed by thought process. First time in Rigveda they talk of deities that represent various natural as well as human powers experienced by them in day to day life. The wind God Maruta, Agni, the Fire, Sõma, the intoxicating herb, the Earth the supporter, the Sun the light giver, Prajapati and Shiva, the creators, the Brahmanaspati, the knowledge giver, Indra, the valorous were some of the deities worshipped by the ***Vedic*** sages. The stormy winds, the torrential rains, the floods, the earthquakes, the thundering, the lightening and many other natural phenomena were seen as divine powers. It was a mixed experience of fear, awe and usefulness. The ***Vedic*** sages bowed down to these powers and sang beautiful prayers. Magnificent, beautiful and sacred manifestations of the nature in different forms inspired the ***Vedic*** sages to sing and the orderliness, regularity and lawfulness observed in the natural activities motivated them to philosophise with remarkable rationality.

In the next stage they conceived the independent deities that control the natural phenomena by their powers. Varuna, Brihaspati, Prajapati, Aditi, Usha and others fall in this category. Still these deities were formless. But gradually the deities started getting human forms and there appeared four-armed Vishnu, eight-armed goddess Durga, three-eyed

Shiva, four-faced Brahma. Their superhuman divine powers were symbolized through their multiple hands, faces etc. Unlike earlier deities these deities were not harmful but full of compassion. The relation between the God and the man changed from fear to devotion and love. It became the inspiring force for the Indian people that established the grand tradition of devotional worship.

In the later stage these deities represented morality, truth, honesty and other virtues and were considered as the manifestations of one God alone. From this attitude evolved the great principle of 'Ekam sat' - one Reality behind everything. The idea of one supreme God was established in the later part of the ***Vedas***. In the Upanishadic periods the idea got further developed into Ishvara, Supreme Lord who illuminates the whole universe along with the lower deities of supernatural powers. Upanishadic search of one Absolute Brahman provided perennial inspiration to all the future philosophical works including the Bhagvadgita.

The total humanization of the other deities was predominant during the period of Brahman literature. The deities like human beings, had their families with relations of father, mother, son, daughter, brother, sister etc. They had likes, dislikes, they lost, they quarrelled, they erred, they failed. They were also shown as selfish, envious, jealous, proud etc. Men were advised to worship them but warned not to follow them.

The Upanishads, were the philosophical lettering of spontaneous revelations of the great sages. They spoke of the one Absolute Brahman and the centers of its glory existing in the universe and the man. Bhagavadgita in its 10th ***Adhyaya*** enumerated some selected centers of glory of the Lord. They include some deities mentioned in the Rigveda by their ancient names which are in fact the powerful natural phenomena. Gita tried to integrate the old concepts into new logical forms.

Organizing, illuminating and activating of the universe was controlled by different powers of the one Absolute Brahman who has created this universe and remained eminent in it. Everything in the universe is a divine manifestation of the Absolute Brahman. This was the culminating point of the concept of God in the Indian philosophical system. Here the sages freely talked about the process of cosmic creation. With the strong motivation to search for the superior God amongst all the Gods conceived earlier Upanishads arrived at the concept of one supreme Absolute Brahman for the first time in human history. The great sages realized the lofty truth of oneness through their mystic experience and gave spontaneous expressions to their revelations in fearless mood but in powerful words.

Soon the great mythological era of the Indian history began and the world of Indian deities which had already set the trend of humanization underwent a drastic change. That change influenced the Indian masses in such a way that the lofty and profound spiritual principles established by the Upanishads were pushed back to learned few and the supernatural and imaginary ideas of gods and goddesses took the hold of the common people. Upanishadic approach to God was intellectually rational and mystical at the same time. But this intellectual and spiritual approach was beyond the grasp of the common man. Whereas the use of the supernatural element, world of wonders, and miracles, the exaggeration and the flights of imagination helped the mythological works called Puranas to spread their sway like a wild fire. Almost all the ***Vedic*** deities lost their importance and were pushed to the lower position as mere protectors of the space. The Puranas changed the characters of some deities from good to bad and some from bad to good. The deity of death, Yama became the lord of the hell and divided the fate of the dead according to his merits or sins acquired during lifetime. The Ganesh who initially was the god of the obstacles became the remover of obstacles. The Purana's efforts were to harmonise the different schools of thoughts, deities, forms of worship and divergent ideas into one larger unity. Their emphasis was on strengthening the religious faiths rather than recording the history. They achieved this goal by hundreds of mythological stories they created through their vast imagination and untiring zeal. The idea of incarnations was further developed and strengthened by expanding and restricting the number to ten important incarnations as Matsya-the fish, Kurma,-the tortoise, Varãha-the boar, Narsimha-the lion-man combination, Vãmana-the dwarf, Parashurãma, Rãma, Krishna, Buddha and Kalki. Interestingly some researchers have tried to interpret these incarnations as the theory of evolution of man.

Bhagavdtgitã has rationalized this concept of incarnation by expanding it to as many births of the Godhead as necessary to establish virtue by destroying evil whenever virtue subsides and wickedness prevails. The worship through devotion remained the pivotal point of all the Puranas and that resulted in replacing the ritualistic as well as intellectual approaches in the realm of God-worship.

The struggles between gods and demons, immensely used in these mythological stories had its origin in the Rig-*Vedas* as the symbolic and imaginary fights between light and darkness or good and bad mentioned as deva and asura. But the Puranas presented these struggles as true historical facts. The demons who overpowered heavenly gods like Indra and troubled human beings by power acquired from Lord Shiva's worship and hard penances. The demons were killed by Vishnu and other gods when intensely prayed for protection. The Puranas are full of such stories wherein Indra killed Vritra and Andhaka; the goddess Durgã killed Mahisha, Kumbha-Nikumbh; Rudra killed Tripura; Ganapati killed Sindhura and Vighna, Vishnu killed Madhu and Kaitabha, Rãma killed Rãvana, Krishna killed Dhenuka, Naraka, Agha, etc….. so on and so forth. The symbolism and imagination were totally converted into realism.

In due course, the trinity gods Brahma, Vishnu and Mahesha, representing respectively creation, preservation and dissolution of the universe received extraordinary importance and barring Brahma, became the prominent Gods to be worshipped for personal favours. This led to the formation of two popular cult of worship known as Vaishnava and Shaiva which in history, at times, created serious quarrels over the superiority issue. The Puranas usually propagated unity among all the three gods.

Bhagavadgitã accepted the trinity principle as symbolic representation and discarding the personalized forms elevated the idea to three functions of the Absolute Brahman-they are the three major stages through which all sentient and non sentient beings pass through. Even the universe has to pass through these stages. The eleventh ***Adhyaya*** of the Gita wherein the Lord Krishna revealed his cosmic form to Arjuna covers these three aspects in visual form by integrating them in the body of the supreme God, Ishvara.

As in mythology the Indian philosophy too, accepts the principle of God's appearance in human form, but not in super natural way. The fourth ***Adhyaya*** of Gita speaks of the Lord Krishna appearing in human forms as Incarnations at an appointed time to help the distressed and to kill the wicked. Strictly observing of human laws and not by miracles these incarnations fulfil the divine purpose of their descent on this earth. The Puranas did not follow this approach.

In addition to Vishnu and Shiva, Puranas included three more deities for worship, making the group of five popularly known as Panchayatan. These three are goddess Shakti, Ganapati and Surya, the Sun. Shiva and Vishnu retained their mythological importance by alternately enjoying the supreme position. Devi or shakti or Jagadamba or Durga or Kali are but the names of the same goddess with the feirceful form that destroyed the demoniac powers. Ganapati, the god with elephant head is the god of learning and also the remover of obstacles. Surya, the sun was already in worship in ***Vedic*** age but by the influence of Shaka Kushana races who came as invaders, the occult practice was added to sun-worship.

In the humanization process the Puranas had also thought of the gods with their wives in company. Mainly Saraswati, Laxmi and Pãrvati, the wives of Brahma, Vishnu and Mahesha respectively were given their distinct roles as the presiding deities of learning and art, divine strength, and the wealth and prosperity. They are independently worshipped; individually or collectively; daily or occasionally.

The imaginary world of Indian deities was created and enriched by the mythological stories of the Puranas to unify the divergent streams of thoughts and modes of worship existing in different regions and communities of India. The temples and temple arts; fairs and festivals flourished in India in such magnificent form that it has become the most colourful and joyful treasure of Indian culture. The role of super natural power in assisting human efforts is so deeply rooted in Indian soil that it has resulted into thousands of village gods, family gods, ancestral gods etc. Flourishing in every nook and corner of the country. The faith that they are the protectors and the wish-fulfillers provide divine cover to human strength and efforts. However this has also led to lot of superstitious ideas overpowering the minds of the weak.

Behind all these formulations of gods, goddesses and deities in various forms stands one eternally accepted truth that no man can really see God except through these human manifestations. Intellectually this may appear to be absurd. But without transcending human nature, it is very difficult to know God in his true nature. Till then man has to see Him in man as man. The Puranas contributed by creating humanized versions of God prepare the man to go higher and higher in his pursuit of Absolute Truth. The devotional worship in various forms that exist in India for centuries together has kept this big nation united and peaceful. The mythology and symbolism have become the integral part of all religions all over the world as a necessity to help the aspirant soul in his Godward march. India is exceptionally rich in producing the spiritual saints because of the exuberant growth of devotional cults that sprung up every where due to its mythology and ritualism.

Lord Krishna's declaration in Bhagavadgita about his incarnations in human forms is a matter of solace to humanity since all the major religions of the world have experienced this truth in one form or the other. The soul of Indian philosophy lies in its acceptance of all religions as equally true and their thoughts and paths are equally capable of reaching the final Truth. Bhagavadgita asserts this principle repeatedly.

The Puranas were also responsible for turning the religion from its ritualistic grandeur to simplified modes of worship. Emotional nobility of the mind and the physical involvement attained the key position in worship. To achieve this they converted the ***Yadnya*** institution into temple institution that revolutionized the whole socio-cultural life of India. It was the compulsion that they devised certain rituals and worship-systems because the ordinary people were not capable to understand the higher ideals of supreme devotion. At the preparatory stage of worship the inclusion of priest services, festivals, pilgrimages, fairs, story telling, singing, dancing, etc., were included in the temple activities to popularize the worship of the divine.

Since antiquity Indian people loved and enjoyed the surrounding nature where they saw beauty and divinity combined. - Indian nature is very rich in all respects. The flora and fauna of India were never treated as the material wealth for human consumption. The people saw in them the wonders and powers of divinity. Their love for nature was converted into worship of divinity. Their love for nature was converted in to worship of nature. Fish, turtle, crocodile, bore, cow, bullock, snake, eagle, peacock, elephant, lion, tiger, swan and many such creatures either became gods or the vehicles of their gods. Fish, tortoise and bore had the distinction of manifesting as incarnations. In the same way holy waters of rivers like Gangã, Yamunã, Saraswati, Krishnã, Godãvari, Narmadã, Kãveri etc. were given forms of goddesses. Seas and lakes too were not excluded. The heavenly bodies like earth, sun, moon, stars, planets etc. were offered the status of deities. Even in the world of vegetation certain plants and trees like baniyan tree, fig tree, tulsi etc became sacred beings for worship. Animal-form- gods like Hanuman, the divine monkey, Ganapati, the elephant headed and Narsimha, the man-lion combined incarnation received the highest veneration. Hanumãn and Ganapati are the most popular deities of Hindus that protect them from all evils. In tenth ***Adhyaya*** of Bhagavadgita Lord Krishna, while describing his divine glory has cited many of such examples as his manifestations.

The Image-worship is very popular in India and almost all deities and gods in innumerable number, appear in one form or the other not necessarily in human forms though human forms are very popular in majority. These idols are inseparably associated with the particular aspect of God. Most of them are the revealed forms experienced by the great sages in their deepest spiritual perception. They symbolise and express as nearly as possible, the particular view of God. In India different gods and goddesses representing different divine aspects are worshipped in hundreds of temples and festivals throughout the year.

All these gods and goddesses are worshipped as independent powers or the manifestations of the one and the same supreme Brahman, appearing in its Almighty, all knowing and all merciful form of Ishvara. Bhagavadgita has categorically stated that any gods or other beings when worshipped for themselves and for worldly gains, such worship is only a ritualistic ***Karma*** and it gives the worshipper that particular fruit which he desires from it. But when the same god or goddess or beings are looked upon as Brahman and worshipped, the result obtained is the same as by worshipping the supreme God. Bhagavadgita prefers the second approach as a preparatory instrument for a beginner until he goes beyond and sees the Absolute as Absolute. Narrow-minded and selfish worshippers according to Gita are of inferior nature.

Whatever outwardly appears to be contradictory or superstitious or fallacious in Indian religion has a deep philosophical foundation which if not understood in proper sense creates lot of misunderstanding. The truth lies hidden some where else and the myths are carried forward.

APPENDIX -V

(A) Names, Epithets and Adjectives Used for Calling or Addressing Krishna

Adhyaya-Verses	Initial Reference
1-14	माधव - Mãdhava-The husband of the goddess of fortune, Laxmi.
1-15	हृषीकेश - Hrisikesha - the controller of the senses.
1-21	अच्युत - Achyuta - infallable one, Name of Krishna.
1-28	केशण - Krishna
1-30	केशव - Keshava - one with beautiful hair.
1-32	गोविंद - Govinda - Name of Krishna a cowhard or imparter of knowledge.
1-34	मधुसूदन - Madhusudana - killer of the demon, madhu
1-35	जनार्दन - Janãrdana - liberator of men, and all living entities.
1-40	वार्ष्णेय - Varshneya - descendant of Vrishni
2-4	अरिसूदन - Arisudana - killer of the enemies.
10-14	पुरूषोत्तम - Purushottama - greatest of all persons.
10-15	भूतभावन - Bhutbhãvan - Origin of all beings
10-15	भूतेष - Bhutesha - lord of all creatures.
10-16	देवदेव - Deva-Deva - lord of all demigods
10-17	भगवन् Bhagvan - supreme.
11-3	परमेश्वर - Parameshvara - supreme lord.

11-4	योगेश्वर - Yogeshwara - lord of all mystic power.
11-9	हरि-Hari-The supreme personality of Godhead.
11-15	देव - Deva - Lord
11-16	विश्वेश्वर - Vishveshvara - Lord of the universe
11-16	विश्वरूप - Vishvarupa - in the form of the universe
11-20	महात्मन् - Mahãtman - great one.
11-23	माहाबाहो - Mahãbaho - O mighty armed one.
11-24	विष्णो - Vishno - O Lord Visnu.
11-25	देवेश - Devesha - Lord of all Lords.
11-31	देववर - Devavara - great one amongst the demigods.
11-37	जगन्निवास - Jagannivasa - refuge of the universe.
11-37	अनन्त - Ananta - unlimited.
11-38	अनन्तरूप - Anantarupa - of unlimited form.
11-43	अ प्र ति म प्र भा ा व -Apratimaprabhava immeasurable power.
11-46	सहस्त्रबाहो - Sahasrabãho-O thousand-handed one.
11-46	विश्वभूते Vishvabhute - O universal form.
11-50	वासुदेव - Vãsudeva - Krishna, son of Vãsudeva.
14-21	प्रभो - Prabho - O my Lord
18-1	केशिनिसूदन - Keshinishudan - killer of Keshi demon.

(B) Names, Epithets and Adjectives used for Calling or Addressing Arjuna

Adhyaya-Verses	Initial Reference
14	पाण्डव: - Pãndava - Arjuna (the son of Pandu).
1-20	कपिध्वज - Kapidhwaja - he whose flag was marked with Hanuman.
1-24	गुडाकेश - Gudakesha - Arjuna with thick hair.
1-26	पार्थ - Pãrtha - Arjuna son of Prutha (Kunti).
1-27	कौन्तेय - Kaunteya - the son of Kunti.
1-45	अर्जुन - Arjuna
2-3	परंतप - Parantapa - chastiser of the enemies.
2-10	भारत - Bhãrata - descendant of Bharata.
2-15	पुरूषर्षभ - Purusharshabha - best among men.
2-26	महाबाहो - Mahabaho - mighty armed one.
2-41	कुरूनन्दन - Kurunandana -beloved child of the Kuru.
2-48	धनंजय - Dhananjaya - Arjuna, conquerer of wealth.
3-3	अनघ - Anagha - O sinless one.
4-31	कुरूसत्तम - Kurusattama - best amongst the Kurus.
18-78	धनुर्धर - Dhanurdhara - Master of archery.
6-40	तात - Tãta - O Dear.
7-11	भरतर्षभ - Bharatarshabha - Lord of the Bharatas.
8-4	देहभृतांवर-Dehabhrutamvara - best of the embodied beings.
9-1	अनसूयवे - Anasuyave - the non envious.

10-19	कुरूश्रेष्ठ - Kurushreshtha - best of the Kurus.
11-33	सव्यसाचिन - Savyasãchin - Savyasãchi, name of Arjuna.
11-35	किरीटी - Kiriti - name of Arjuna.
11-48	करूप्रवीर - Kurupravir - Hero of the Kurus.
17-12	भरतश्रेष्ठ - Bharatashreshtha - the excellent of the Bharatas.
18-4	भरतसत्तम - Bharatasattama - The best among the Bharatas.
18-4	पुरूषव्याध्र - Purushavyãghra - tigre among men.